THE TROUBLE WITH NOWADAYS

For Rosemary Courtney

with the knowledge
she will read it in
order and not higgledy
piggledy —

Cleveland Amory

Memphis
October 23, 1979

Books by Cleveland Amory

The Trouble with Nowadays

NONFICTION

The Proper Bostonians
The Last Resorts
Who Killed Society?
Man Kind?
Animail

FICTION

Home Town

EDITOR

Celebrity Register
Vanity Fair Anthology

THE TROUBLE WITH NOWADAYS

A CURMUDGEON STRIKES BACK

BY

Cleveland Amory

ARBOR HOUSE  *New York*

Contents

Opening Statement

I DIDN'T want an introduction, but the damn publisher did, so we compromised, and now I'm doing this silly "Opening Statement." I detest compromises.

I don't like introductions either in books, or at dinner parties. I much prefer the English way of doing things. If you're there, it's because you know your host and hostess. If you're not, who are you?

And, speaking of that, I also detest the kinds of people who go around at parties with asinine smiles on their faces, saying "I'm so and so." Witter Hardee has a bully answer to that. "Well," he says, "I'm not."

The other thing I can't stand is this everlasting modern

"what do you do?" Nowadays, it's what do you do before how do you do. I'll tell any man what I do anytime, thank you very much, but I'll be damned if I'll tell him before he's had the decency to say how do you do. Frankly there's not much use in my telling him anyway, because after I've told him about being the youngest 50-year man in the Club, and having founded the Fortnightly and being Chairman of the Games Committee and all the rest of it, then I'm going to have to stand there and listen to a whole story about whatever his little job is. If there's one thing that makes my blood boil, it's people taking advantage. I'm a busy man, and I don't have a decent staff. Nowadays, nobody has a decent staff. That's one of your main troubles with nowadays—the entire world is over-populated and under-staffed.

Where was I? Oh, about not having an introduction. Today, your average introduction is done by one of these celebrity fellows, who tell you why the book you are about to read is a fine book. Well, you don't have it here. This book is a fine book because I say it's a fine book. And, if you know me, that should be enough for you. If you don't, I'm not at all sure I want you for a reader anyway.

Which reminds me, I don't want you skipping around. I've put a good deal of time into the organization of this book, and I'll thank you to do me the courtesy of reading it in that order, and not jumping the gun on me or reading higgledy-piggledy. You do your job. I've done mine. Thank you.

CHAPTER I

How This Book Came About

I WAS, as most of you know, '29.

Twenty-nine was a good year. It may not have been another Ought Nine—the old boys are always talking about their damned Ought Nine—but I say if '29 wasn't another Ought Nine, how many other Ought Nines were there? Ought—that's how many—*ought.*

We didn't have an undefeated season, all right. But we did win our share of games. And in The Game, you'll recall, Tubby kicked three field goals. Drop-kicked them too, of course—although I don't suppose the young people today would know a dropped kick from a dropped egg. They'd probably call them poached anyway. Honestly, when I think of all those *place* kicks today, it makes my blood boil. Any damn fool can have the ball put down and have someone hold it for him, and *then* kick it. Drop-kicking was an art.

But no matter. The point is that '29 was, when you come right down to it, the last good year. This is obvious on the face of it from the fact that after we came along and had a few decent months, bingo, the crash came and the whole shebang came apart at the seams. How could it have been otherwise? Because first there was the First Term and then there was the Second Term and then there was the Third Term and then there was the Fourth Term. I suppose there'll even be some young people around who won't remember there *was* a Fourth Term. But there was, boy, there was. And don't forget it. Look it up. And, remember, I *lived* through it.

I'll say one thing, though. No, I won't. What's the use? Anyway I'm not one of these fellows who blame That Man for everything. You can't blame just him—you've got to remember his wife and all those damned children.

In any case, everybody agrees now—hindsight, as I've always said, is the cheapest thing there is—but remember I said it then —the world went to hell in a hack and nothing, not even the hack, ever came back the way it was.

In its place came a whole new world. Now I'm not like some people I could mention, against everything in this damn new world just because it's new. I'm a very objective person, if I do say so. I even object objectively—and if there is something wrong with something besides the fact it's new, I go out of my way to find it. I have an open mind and I pride myself on keeping up to date, and if something is actually new and good, I'm the very first to say well and good. But George it better be good, and nowadays, when all is said and done, damn few

2

things are. And that, I might add, includes all these damn new people.

All right, I know what you're thinking, and the answer is yes, it's true. We do take some of these new fellows right into the Club. We have to. Others do it, we do it—although if I do say so, we naturally get a generally higher type.

But don't pretend for a moment it's the same thing. These new fellows are all very well, but facts are facts and the best of them are pretty small beer. They simply don't have the same interests. Or the same objectives. Or the same view of things. Or even—how shall I put it—the same backbone. Why should they? They come from entirely different backgrounds.

Now we of the Class of '29 were men of an entirely different stripe. We weren't picked for scholastic eminence or athletic eminence or extracurricular eminence or any other damn eminence. Come to think of it, we weren't picked at all. No school picked *us*, for Pete's sweet sake, *we* picked the school. We picked every single school or college we ever darkened the door of. And, if you ask me, that's the main trouble with your schools and colleges today. They do the picking. And, of course, they're not up to it. If any one of those Deans of Admission ever sat on the Admissions Committee of a first-rate Club *anywhere*—either here or on the Continent—I'll eat two hats.

It's been said that when we came along, they broke the mold. Well, that's not for us to say. But not to put too fine a point on it, there's a lot of truth in it. As for the class of '30 who could, I suppose, claim that they lived through some of the good old days, well, they did—but then they ran amok. Class of '30, class of '40—what difference does it make? It's splitting hairs, or, as Witter Hardee always says, "splitting heirs." Witter's English, you know, and a great believer in primogeniture.

Anyway, first it was '30 and then it was '32 and then it was '42 and '52 and heaven knows what else. The other day I heard some young whippersnapper who was a guest at the Common Table say he was in the class of '82! A legacy too. Direct. Son of a Member. If, I wanted to say, there *is* an '82. But I didn't. What's the use? Legacy or no legacy, he wouldn't have had the ghost of an idea what I was talking about. That's another of your very main troubles with nowadays—these new fellows just don't have any humor. Least of all about themselves. And of all the people who need it, it's those birds. You'd think they could get a start on it just by looking in the mirror.

No matter. Before I get off on '29 or Ought Nine or any other Ought perhaps I also ought to tell you that I've been doing the Fortnightly introductions for so long that only the other day Witter Hardee was saying that he hadn't even begun to think of who they'd get after I'd gone. Well, I told him, he'd better get started while I was still here to help. The idea of Witter and Fish Frobisher and Edgy Bull and Fog Horne and Tubby and the others looking around by themselves without me there to guide them would be enough to make me turn in my grave. But, as I also told them, you have to face facts. No one goes on forever—although to be frank, around here you'd never know it.

Speaking of that, look at this Oldest Living Member thing. Talk about Watergate. Watergate my foot. We didn't even have time to think about Watergate. We had our own Watergate right here in the *Club*. And cover-up too. Ask Fish Frobisher. In his opinion, it's high time we took a brand new look at the whole O.L.M. It just doesn't get the job done anymore. In the old days it had real distinction. Your Oldest Living Member

4

and the others in the running kept right on doing everything they had been doing right down to the wire. Today, right here and now, as I'm writing this, there are two O.L.M. candidates I could mention, but I won't—who just go around babying themselves. They live right here in the Club, mind you, and I tell you if its raining they won't go out of their damn rooms, let alone out of the Club. Never take any kind of a chance at all. I say it's just plain damn bad form. Not the way the game was played in the old days at all. I go beyond Fish. I say the next time I recognize an Oldest Living Member it will be over my dead body. All right, I'm perfectly prepared to admit that wherever you turn nowadays it's a world full of people on the make and corner cutters and shoddy workmanship. But when it all comes home to roost in the O.L.M. in a Club like this, it's worse than shoddy. It's shocking.

The O.L.M. thing was one of the reasons we formed Fortnightly. Not the only reason, mind you, one of the reasons. The other was that, frankly, we were just sick and tired of everybody and their brother getting into the Club and bringing their women in with them and talking in loud voices and making a Grand Central out of the place. The story was they did it for the out-of-city people and that that was also why they had these godawful Family Nights. Every time you turn around, there's one of these Family Nights. And they bring their children to them, too. That was the last straw. If there is one damn place where no damn children belong, it's a gentlemen's Club. The other day there was what they called a "Rock Brunch" at the Club. I am not exaggerating. A Rock Brunch put on by younger members, if you please, in the Club on Sunday morning. I tell you, you literally couldn't hear yourself think. Which of course was no problem for them.

5

Well, enough of that. People say the Fortnightly is a Club within a Club. There isn't one iota of truth in that statement. We haven't seceded, or anything like that. We're still Members of the Club. It's just that the other Members of the Club aren't necessarily Members of us. And why should they be? They aren't in the same class. That's a word you have to very careful about using nowadays, but the way we use it, there isn't a damn thing they can do about it. We're all Members, you see, as I told you, of the *class* of '29. Let's see—I am and Fog is and we really all are, except for Edgy Bull, who was '30, and Fish Frobisher, who was '27, and the Professor, who was '28, but he's M.A. '29, and Witter who was Oxford whatever he was, and the General, who really doesn't matter, because he was way back, and Tubby, who anyway isn't a member of any *other* class—Tubby never did graduate. So there isn't a damn thing the rest of the Club can do about it, and nobody's feelings are hurt—or at least they have no damn right to be. In the beginning we had in mind fourteen Members, but we settled on nine. We would still have nine too—two tables of bridge and a spare—if poor old Fairfield Field hadn't drunk himself to death. But Fair did drink and there you are. But he was '29 just the same.

They also say we blackball everybody. Blackball my eye. That's just a plain damn lie. No Member of the Fortnightly, to my certain knowledge, has ever in the last five years, put a single black ball in a single bowl anywhere in the Club. We used to do it, but it didn't work because, for one thing, Fog Horne lost the balls. For another, Fair Field was always asking for a black ball no matter who he was voting for. Actually, he had a perfectly good point from his point of view, because he thought even the Fortnightly was too big. But anyway we stopped. And now we do it just the way they do it at White's.

The English know how to do these things. The only true thing they say about Fortnightly is that it takes seven years to get in. My answer to that is that it takes seven years to get into White's and no one complains about that. So why should they pick on our little Fortnightly? We do it the same way exactly. You have your proposer and your seconders and then you post your man on the board and he stays there for seven years and you either put your name down under him as favoring him or you don't, as the case may be. And, if that is the case, you go quietly to a fellow on the Fortnightly Membership Committee, like Fish or myself, and tell him you don't like the man. And then we quietly take down the man's name. It really is the perfect system. It's all absolutely anonymous. And, as I say, nobody's feelings get hurt and you have those seven years to make up your mind. If there is anything you don't want a snap judgment about, it's making a man a Member of a Club.

There's one other thing I think I should mention in this regard. Some other Members of the Club, the young ones mostly, I'm glad to say—are always saying because we meet in the Club that they should be able to go to our dinners. My answer to this is that we used to let everybody and his brother in, and no questions asked. In fact, we even let them ask questions afterwards, but frankly they abused the privilege. So we simply had to put the kibosh on it. We now make it a hard and fast rule that they can come to the meeting but they can't come to the dinner beforehand or ask questions afterwards. The fact is that a lot of the other Members aren't broad-minded enough for us anyway. At our meetings we tackle head-on a lot of new things. And we have some very prominent guest speakers. And, afterwards, during the Question Period—well, that's the big difference between Fortnightly and our imitators—during *our*

Question Period the speaker asks *us* the questions and we give *him* the answers. Or at least that's the way it's supposed to work. After all, what's the use of having some bird from Washington who you and I are paying for with our tax money and having him go right back to Washington without having learned anything. And if we had every Tom, Dick and Harry at the dinner and during our Question Period, we wouldn't get a word in edgewise. We'd just have to sit around and listen to some prejudiced old fogey who didn't know the first thing about the subject.

Damn. I've lost my place again. Oh, I remember. The story of how this book came about. I promised it to you in the title of the chapter. Well, the idea came about from one of the younger Members of Club, albeit unwittingly, of course, whose name, he said, was Field. But he was no relation to Fair Field, or any Field you've ever heard of—they never are nowadays—so it is of no consequence. We had all gathered in the Card Room for our regular Dominoes Night, and we were playing away without a sound in the room, except for the clack of the dominoes, when all of a sudden Edgy Bull spoke up and said he had nobody opposite him. We looked up, and damned if Edgy wasn't right. Nobody was opposite him. Fog Horne had gone to sleep in the bar. Anyway Witter volunteered to go down to the Main Room, and see if there was anyone presentable enough to pass muster who could pinch hit. And in three shakes of a lamb's tail, he came back with this young Field fellow I was telling you about.

He wasn't, as it turned out, any great shakes as a dominoes player—he just didn't have the mind for it—but he was one of these non-stop talkers. And, during our regular break, he started telling us about some trip he had taken out West, to Pittsburgh or some place, where he had taken part in something he said was called a "Think Tank." If that isn't one of your typical modern expressions, I've never heard one. Anyway, the fellow was all full of a speech he had heard out there about the sum total of human knowledge—about how it had doubled for the first time around the time of the Renaissance or sometime and how it hadn't doubled again until 1900. And how now, as I understood him to say, the damned stuff was doubling every time you turned around.

I remember that, because just at that time Henry came around to take the drink orders and Edgy Bull—he is really getting very deaf and has the devil of a time with that hearing aid of his—anyway he told Henry to make his a double too. But you couldn't stop that young fellow with something like that. He went right on and told us he'd also heard another speech from some scientist fellow who said that 70 percent of all the scientists who ever lived were alive today. I remember he got very excited about that. "Think of it!" he repeated. *"Seventy percent of all the scientists who ever lived!"*

I remember that, because it was too much for Witter Hardee. He leaned over and told me he'd rather let them think about it—that they, of all people, should know about the pill. Even that didn't faze the young fellow. Because he then launched into a story about still another fellow he'd met out there. And this fellow, he said, told them the world had changed more from the time of his birth to now than it had from the death of Julius Caesar to his birth.

Well all Edgy Bull got out of that was that someone had a seizure, so of course he wanted to know who it was. Edgy tries his best to keep up, so then the fellow had to repeat it all over

9

again—that it was that bird's birth and that the world had changed as much from then to now as it had from Julius Caesar's death to that bird's birth.

Fish Frobisher wanted to know what class the fellow was in. Fish is always interested in what class someone is and he always wants to know, too, to whom he's related. You can't blame Fish —he just likes to get the facts. But by now the fellow was really exasperated. "How the hell do I know what class he was?" he said. "All he told us was that he was born in 1908."

Well, I want to tell you that when that young fellow said Ought Eight, it gave me a turn. George, I thought, *I* was born in Ought Eight.

At a time like that, at a moment of great crisis, at a turning point in one's life, a lot of people don't think at all. They run right out and marry some woman they wouldn't in their right mind have even thought of marrying or they sell some stock they shouldn't have even considered selling. On the other hand, a very few, at such a time, think very very clearly. I am, I am glad to say, one of your latter group. I think at that moment I thought as clearly as I've ever thought in my life. I remember distinctly thinking that if the world had changed all that much in just that little time—from the time of my birth to now—as it had in all that other time—from, you might say, time immemorial to me—then George it was high time to tell people about it. And not let any *more* damn time go by either.

Well, that's the whole story. And remember, it all happened because of that bird who couldn't play a decent game of dominoes. But that's what often happens with your great events in history. They occur over someone who couldn't of themselves be of less importance. Look at Archduke Ferdinand, who started the Great War. My father knew his share of Archdukes.

Even as Archdukes go, he used to say, Franz was pretty slim pickings. Actually, I remember looking up that young Field fellow in the Social Register, and he wasn't even in it. Imagine, the Social Register—I tell you it's the size of a telephone book today—and not even being in it. Well, it's a new world, and there you are.

CHAPTER II

Why Yours Truly Was the Only One to Carry the Spear

A T FIRST I didn't have the slightest idea that I would be writing this book. I didn't have the slightest idea that I would be writing this book. I repeat this, just so there will be no mistake. You have to repeat things nowadays, particularly for young people. In the first place, I am not a professional writer. I detest professional anythings but particularly professional writers. Most of them today are just garbage collectors. In the second place, even if I wanted to be one, I simply don't have the time for it. Being Chairman of the Games Committee, let alone my Fortnightly chores, leaves precious little time, I assure you, to pursue the Muses. In the third place, writing, in case you don't know it, is hard work—good writing, that is, like you're reading right now. In the fourth and final place, my old friend Somerset Maugham once said that a writer was someone who thought of what to say on the way home from the party. And that certainly let me out. I always think of what to say right at the party—particularly people's idea of a party nowadays. I don't even like the word "party"—in the old days you never used it, except for a children's party.

But even though I didn't think then I would be the one doing it, I knew someone had to do the book. After all, if there had been more changes in my lifetime than from Caesar's death to me, you weren't talking about any ordinary book. You were talking about the biggest book of your lifetime. And it had to be done, of course, by somebody who was born in Ought Eight, or otherwise your whole point went down the drain. So the first thing I did was go through the whole Club Book and look up every single soul who graduated in either '28, or '29, or '30, or who could have been born in Ought Eight. What I did was I got the Club Librarian to help me and we did a thorough research job on it—even telephoned some of them—to find out whether or not they were Ought Eight. And I want to tell you it gave me a turn. Do you know how many of us were left? Four, dammit, just four. That's these times for you—I tell you they are killers, these times. And, of course, attrition—the regular attrition you get in any times. But *four!* And it wasn't even really four. It was, if you didn't include me, three.

The worst of it was I only knew one of them—and I ruled him out right away. He was a lightweight in school and he's still a lightweight. He was no more up to a book like this than Adam's off ox. The other two I knew by sight—after all I know pretty nearly everybody in the Club by their damn sight—but their names meant nothing to me. So I put notes in their boxes and said I wanted to see them about something important. One of them, if you can believe it, never even answered. That's another thing about nowadays—manners. There ought to be a whole book about them. A whole book, that is, about the way they were in the old days—and then leave a half a page postscript for what's left of them today.

In any case, the other fellow finally did answer, although he took his own sweet time about it. And we made an appointment. I told him the whole story—I didn't pull any punches. I said I wanted the finished product a Bible—a Bible of all these damn changes—and while he was at it, he might as well have a look at the Bible too, because they had even changed that. I told him I wanted him to take it all the way from the date of our birth to today's damn younger generation, and then I asked him frankly if he thought he was man enough to take it on. I reminded him that he had to remember that we had allowed most of these damn changes to creep up on us when our backs were turned. The fellow had been a Morgan man back in the thirties, and I even quoted him one of good old Pierpont's adages: "You can't pick cherries with your back to the tree."

And do you know what? All the time I was talking to him, I noticed that he was often nodding when he should have been shaking his head, or else shaking his head when he should have been nodding. And then, when I got through, I realized he hadn't heard a single damn word. Deaf as a post, that's what he was. So I had to begin all over again, literally shouting at him. And this time, when I got to the part about the younger generation, do you know what he said? He said he didn't like the younger generation. I really blew up at that. I told him to pull up his socks, man, neither did I—that was the whole point.

But I also told him he was taking a very selfish attitude, particularly toward the younger generation, who would, after all, be the very ones who would profit most from the book. But I might as well have saved my breath. He had a closed mind. If there's anything that makes my blood boil, it's a closed mind.

Well, after that experience I went back to my room and did some long, hard thinking. I thought so long I was damn near late for Fortnightly bridge. But when I did think of that, it was lucky. Because then I had a brainstorm. A Fortnightly man, I suddenly thought, wouldn't necessarily have to be born exactly in Ought Eight. Any one of them could, if I, as their captain, called, have gone up on the line and put their shoulders to the wheel and done the job. That's the kind of men they are—that's why they are in Fortnightly to begin with. Princes. Salts of the earth.

However, even after I had my idea, I still had to be practical about it. I had to rule out some of my candidates, Fortnightly or no Fortnightly. Tubby was the first to go. I was sorry to lose Tubby, but honestly, the very idea of Tubby writing a book was a contradiction in terms. So far as I know, Tubby's never read one. He's just no reader. You give Tubby anything to read, even something short I myself have cut out of the paper—something he should know about, like Government spending, or a thing like that—and ten minutes later you look at him and he's dead to the world. Fast asleep. I gave him the first pages of this book—the very pages you're reading now—and damned if he didn't fall asleep over them. It just proves what I've always said—no man is a prophet in his own Club.

Just the same, whoever did the book would make a big mistake not to use Tubby—on a verbal basis. Tubby's a big talker, you know, on the subjects which interest him—sports, women,

16

your native problem, things like that. And Tubby's been all over the world, remember. India—before the end of the British Raj, of course—South Africa, White China—you name it, Tubby's been there. And not just to play polo either. Why Tubby made one trip to India just to bring back one servant. There is no question about it. If you wrote off Tubby altogether, you'd be hurting your book.

When it came to Edgy Bull, I had to rule him out on two scores. First, there's the matter of his deafness. He thinks his hearing aid is fine—he's very stubborn about it—but either it's not or he's a lot deafer than he'll admit. Anyway, it would make it virtually impossible for him to do the necessary research. Edgy is a good businessman and he knows a lot both about his own stocks and what's going on in the Club. But he's got a lot of blind spots, and when you've got a man who's both deaf and has blind spots, well he's got two strikes on him right there.

But the main reason I had to rule out Edgy is he's married. Now I have no objection to anyone being married—that's their own business. All of us have been married. Tubby's been married God knows how many times. Even the Professor was married once. I've been married myself, twice. But the point is, Edgy's *still* married—and to all that awful Betty Bull. Honestly, it's criminal seeing a Fortnightly man run around like a railroad. But that's what Betty does. And if Edgy took on a book, it would be only a matter of time before Betty got her hands on it—and then the whole thing would be out the window. I tell you, Betty has ideas that even the Government hasn't thought of. She's a very dangerous woman, you mark my words. I even think she's at the root of Edgy's deafness. I don't blame him —if I were married to Betty Bull and was in his position, I wouldn't even get a hearing aid. I'd just get a pair of first rate ear plugs. Those Bull children are just as bad—all brought up on this modern never-say-no thing. If Betty Bull got in one single idea of hers about raising children in a book like this, the only place the book would sell would be in Russia. Finally, if you think Betty and the children are bad, wait until you meet the grandchildren. I tell you they're poison. The last time Edgy brought them into the Club, they literally had the whole place under siege. The very idea of having Edgy doing a book on the trouble with nowadays when he has all the troubles of nowadays and then some, right in his own family, was just an absurdity. I'd have been just as well off with no book at all.

Last and I'm afraid least, I had to rule out the General and the Professor. But honestly there was so much trouble about both of them for a job like this that I scarcely knew where to begin. The main thing is that if you got either one of them, you'd have lost the other. They don't speak to each other. They haven't for years. I'm not going into the reasons now—I'll get to that later—and in one way I like it. We all do. It means there are still certain standards. In the old days, everybody had standards, and one of them was not speaking. If somebody did something you disapproved of, or said something about a friend of yours—say, made a remark about a lady friend—well, it was very simple, you just didn't speak to them again. And if you met them in the street, or somewhere, you cut them. But what's the use? Nowadays these young fellows wouldn't know what a cut is, and if they did, they wouldn't know how to deliver one if their life depended on it. My Uncle Bagnalls was a past master at it. Honestly, he was on non-speaking terms with half a hundred people before he died. And I tell you, you've never been cut until you were cut by my Uncle Bagnalls.

But, as I say, we all like the General and the Professor's

non-speaking in one way. And the way we handle it at Fortnightly is we make them observe the courtesy of speaking
through a third party. But my point is, for a book like this you'd
need them both—the General for the military, and the Professor for the students. And if you got one to write it, the other
wouldn't help at all. Just the same, let's pretend, for the sake
of argument, that they suddenly stopped their non-speaking.
Even then you wouldn't be out of the woods. Take the General
first. He's a good man for a Fortnightly talk, but he's no man
for a book. All right, he's sound as a nut militarily. His record
speaks for itself—Knickerbocker Greys, Seventh Regiment, all
the rest of it. In the Great War, he was the youngest officer
attached to the British Army in Southwest Africa. And he was
right there with Meinertzhagen against Lettow-Vorbeck. All in
all, you couldn't have a better man on foreign affairs than the
General. There'd be no hobnobbing with the Hottentots if the
General were in charge—you can go to the bank on that. But
remember, foreign affairs is just one of your problems. The
point is the General just can't stand civilians. Basically he believes that if you've got a problem, shoot it. It's not that I
wholly disagree with him about this, it's just that I'm more
practical. Much as you might want to declare war on everyone
over there, you just can't say so in a book like this. And if you
did, sure as shooting those damn peacenik critics would be out
gunning for you.

Finally, take the Professor. The trouble with the Professor is
he taught whatever it was he taught for entirely too long. He's
didactic. He never learns anything. He doesn't know what good
conversation is. He won't listen—all he wants to do is talk
himself. I'm sick and tired of trying to tell him something and
having him stand there not listening but just twitching around

19

and waiting until he can talk. And I'm also sick of hearing him tell me what's wrong with the undergraduates today. Dammit all, he was the one there, not me. Why the devil didn't he stop it? After all, a very large part of what is wrong today is your undergraduates. It seems to me that if you have a Professor who was there and not doing a damn thing to stop it, you'd also be defeating your whole purpose right at the start.

There's another thing too about the Professor, although I don't like to bring it up in a family book. The man is a Democrat. Oh, I know he's denied it—he says he isn't a practicing one, and I believe him—but the point is, do you want an objective book or don't you? If you do, the last man you'd want to write it would be a Democrat.

It's not that I'm one of your dyed-in-the-wool Republicans. As a matter of actual fact, although I don't advertise it, I myself have voted Democratic on a number of occasions in the past. In local elections, of course. And nowadays I hold no brief for either party. As far as I'm concerned, the only difference between the Republicans and the Democrats is the Republicans are Socialists and the Democrats are Bolsheviks.

Anyway, with Tubby and Edgy and the Professor and the General gone, that left me with just three choices—Witter Hardee, Fish Frobisher and Fog Horne. All of them first rate, of course. Witter Hardee, my first choice, seemed a natural. For one thing, he's our best known writer. You could look from now to Doomsday—and after all, that's what we were talking about, Doomsday—and I doubt if you could find a writer anywhere who appeals to as broad a spectrum of the Club public as Witter does. I don't mean just in the Fortnightly, I mean throughout the Club. Why? Well, there's only one thing everyone in the Club reads—and I mean reads regularly. Never misses. And what is it? Why, it's the obituaries of course. The obituaries in the Club Bulletin. And who does the obituaries? Witter does them. All of them, and often under pressure. Witter is often on a short deadline with these obituaries. People don't die when you want them to, you know, they die any old damn time. But that Bulletin has to come out, come hell or high water, on Mondays. And if somebody's died Sunday night, the Members of the Club aren't going to think about that, they're going to want to read it Monday morning just the same.

Witter never complains—even when he's got no time at all, he does a bang-up job on those obituaries. That one on Fair Field, for example, was a classic. Never once mentioned Fair's drinking and yet even got in the story of that Memorial Day when Fair, bless his soul, never paid for a single drink and set the Club record at golf dice—two straight five sixes. And as I've already indicated, Witter can turn a phrase with any of us. If somebody's said something funny around here, the chances are it was either Witter or myself said it. Witter's certainly our No. 2 man in that department at any rate. Of course, with obituaries, Witter's under wraps from the humor point of view. But, when you got right down to the bare bones of the thing, an obituary was exactly what you wanted—an obituary of our way of life. So why not go out and get yourself a top obituary man?

Even when it seemed like such a good idea, though, there was one trouble with it. Witter is too damned English. His clothes, his manner, his reserve, his accent, his use of words, even his thinking is English. And there is no reason it shouldn't be. Witter is half English. His mother was English—his father was over there at the time. And Witter spent half his life in London. Now, gracious knows, I have nothing against the English. Your top Englishman—your White's man or your Boodles man, is top drawer anywhere. But, as I told Witter frankly, dammit, if you're going to save this country, one of the many things you had to save it from is what has happened to England. Having an Englishman do it would just open an unnecessary can of worms.

With Witter out, I next turned to Fish Frobisher. In so many ways it seemed the perfect match-up of job and man. For one thing Fish is a belonger—he belongs to just about every Society you can name, so you could count on a good sale for your book right there. He's a member of the Cincinnati, the St. Nicholas, Colonial Wars and so on and so on. He's been president of Founders and Patriots and I honestly believe that's the toughest Society in America to be a member of, let alone president of. After all, you must not only descend from a Founder—and that, mind you, is prior to 1700—you must also descend from a Patriot. That's the way they stop so many of these social climbers. What it really amounts to is that you must have actually personally have fought in Washington's Army. Lineally, I mean, and not through any damn female line. And speaking of Founders and Patriots, don't forget what Fish founded right here in the Club. He personally founded The Society to Put Things Back the Way They Were. Now every single Member of Fortnightly belongs to it, and practically everywhere you look in the Club, you're looking at one more example of Fish's good work.

With it all, Fish is a man with as little "side" to him as anybody we've got. Again certainly our No. 2 man in this regard. I don't suppose the young people today would know what "side" was if they fell over it, which they probably often do because, God knows, they have so much of it. But no matter.

To get back to Fish, most people don't know it, but he's not just Fish Frobisher. He's Fish Frobisher the Fourth—Fish Frobisher IV—which, of course, doesn't mean he's the son of a Junior, or anything like that. Really there ought to be a law against these things—people get them so wrong. Only the other day they took in a fellow in the Club as a II who wasn't any more of a II than I am. He was the son of a Junior, for God's sake, and he was just named wrong. I told him, and instead of being grateful that someone would take the time to stop him making a fool of himself, he took umbrage, if you please.

It's so simple, really. First there's you and then there's your son, who's Junior, and there's his son, who's III, but *his* son is not IV, of course, he's V. Odd numbers. The only way you can be II is if you have a brother of the original and you want to name your son after him. Then you do and *that* son is a II. And then his son is IV and his son is VI and so forth. *Even* numbers. But people get confused and for some damn reason whoever's in charge of things like that lets them get away with it. There's also a lot of confusion when they all move up. But that too is perfectly simple. You move up on the death of your father. Junior moves to the original, III to Junior, V to III and so on. Among the evens, it's the same thing—VI to IV, IV to II—except, and this is where all the confusion comes in—in the case of unusual distinction. In the case of unusual distinction, you stay the way you are. John Rockefeller, Jr., son of the original John, for example, stayed John Rockefeller, Jr. to the end of his life. Henry Ford never should have been II. The only way he could be II was if the original Henry had a brother and this Henry was *his* son. But I guess in Detroit it doesn't make any difference. Obviously, they just don't know any better. Fish's case, though, was a particularly interesting one. After all,

Fish Frobisher II was a very well-known man. He was Chairman of the Admissions Committee for twenty years. Just the same, I don't think there'd have been too much criticism if Fish had moved up. But it's typical of the man that he decided not to.

All in all, I realize I've made Fish Frobisher sound ideal for the book. But the fact is, with all that's to be said for him, there are very severe drawbacks to Fishy. For one thing, he is—and I just can't emphasize this enough—too damn busy. Honestly, he's the only man in the Club who's busier than I am. I know perfectly well the old adage "If you want to get something done, get a busy person to do it," but there are limits. And Fish goes well beyond them. For another thing—and I want to be equally frank about this—Fish is prejudiced. And by prejudice I don't mean just the natural prejudices we all have. Fish doesn't like anybody *but* Episcopalians. Now I'm an Episcopalian too. But at least I've got an open mind toward some of your lesser sects. Some of my best friends, for example, are Unitarians. And you really have to have that kind of open-mindedness in a book like this. People are so damn sensitive about prejudice nowadays. You just couldn't have Fish going around like he does saying he's the last of the downtrodden minorities—that he's a free white Christian Episcopalian. He loves to say that, but sure as shooting, somebody would pick it up and use it against him and hurt the book. I know you might be able to keep Fish in line and just get the nuggets— but the odds are against you. You've got to have a man who can keep his prejudices to himself.

My final candidate, the last man I had to pin my hopes on, was Fog Horne. Foggy is a much more versatile fellow than you'd think if you saw him sitting there alone on his stool at the bar. Of course he is, first and foremost, a constitutionalist. In fact, whenever I hear the words "Founding Fathers," I think of Foggy. And I also think of that Fortnightly talk he gave when he told us you could get a Ph.D. in political science today and never have taken a single course on the Constitution. That's all he talked about, but he said it over and over. And really it was very effective. It even sank in on some of those younger Members.

But there's a lot more to Fog than just that. Like Edgy Bull he's a bearcat on details around here. And he's not too big a man to take care of them himself. And Fog's no small potatoes as a writer, either. His "Concerned Members of the Club" letters—that's the way he always signs them—are famous. And he not only addresses them to the House Committee and the Admissions Committee, he also puts them right on the board addressed to "Whom It May Concern." Of course any of those are publishable. But besides them he's had more letters actually published in the newspaper then any other man in the Club —and not just on Roosevelt, either. He's had them published on Truman, and Kennedy, and Johnson, and Carter and all the rest of them.

The way I decided to handle Foggy was to barge right in on him there at the bar and tell him he was my first choice for the book. Actually, I didn't see any necessity of mentioning Witter or Fish Frobisher. What I did was I first complimented him on his letters and then I told him just tie in all those letters and hang them together on all these damn changes in the world. I really gave him the whole idea on a platter—and I know it appealed to him even though he was obviously thinking of something else when I got there. Fog is always either thinking or asleep.

The trouble is I was just too damn anxious. After all, Fog was my last hope—and the fact is I got him late in the evening. We all know you can't talk to Fog about anything except the Constitution late in the evening. I don't mean to imply that Fog is an alcoholic. He's not. Just put it this way—from five o'clock on, he's increasingly perilous. And, after nine, he's unreliable. The damn thing was it was well after nine when I talked to him. But I'll say one thing for Foggy—he heard me out all the way through. Never interrupted once. But then he really floored me. He told me he was already doing a book. I asked him what it was about, but he said it was a secret. Well, you know Fog and his secrets. It took me just about one more drink to get it out of him. It was a book, if you please, about Alexander Hamilton—he had detected a liberal streak in him.

I really couldn't believe it—Fog is always detecting a liberal streak in somebody. And to be fair, it usually turns out he's absolutely right. But Hamilton! I tried to reason with him. I told him even if it was true, to forget Hamilton. Hamilton was yesterday, I told him, this book was today. The barbarians were at the gate right now. I shouldn't have done it, of course. You tell Foggy to forget something after nine o'clock at night—and you've got yourself a hornet's nest. I lost Foggy right there.

Anyway, you can see I tried. I went right down the list, trying to find someone to do the job. I went, as Mother used to say, the second mile. I even considered the idea of letting some younger fellow take it on. He could, the way I thought of it, interview me and the Oughter Eighters, and the Members of the Fortnightly, and get the facts. Again, it sounded all right in theory. But in practice, the plain and simple fact of the matter was that there was nobody in the younger generation—and by that I mean anybody up to, say, sixty—who could do the job. They simply do not have the maturity, the experience, the judgment and the cool detachment necessary to bring the thing off. Great balls of fire, how could they? They would be working entirely secondhand, strictly from hearsay. No, there was no use beating about the bush. All in all, when all was said and done, yours truly was the only man to carry the spear.

Of course I realized I could do the job. Good writing, after all, is just good thinking. Orderly thinking. And that, if I do say so, I am known for. Fog Horne once said he always thought of me as the last of the truly great modest men. It was at our Twenty-fifth, and Fog was feeling no pain, and he may well have been exaggerating. I am sure there are others I don't know who are just as modest. And for all I do know, there are probably some others who are so darned modest that nobody has ever heard of them. In my case, I'm afraid that would hardly be practical—I am, after all, widely known throughout the Club. And I have never believed in carrying modesty to the point of hypocrisy.

Although as I told you I don't think of myself as a writer, I have always enjoyed writing good letters. And frankly, as a letter writer, I have had my share of compliments. Only the other day, Prudie Field told me that the finest letter of condolence she received when Fair Field died was mine. And it hadn't been an easy letter to write. After all, as I told you, Fair dropped dead at the bar. But I just sat down and wrote her what I thought Fair stood for, and where I thought he fell down. I'm a very frank person. And I've found that even women like the truth once in a while. Particularly nowadays when they get so little of it from the kind of men they marry.

But I'll tell you something I've already noticed. There's a big difference between writing a good letter and writing a good book. In a letter, you're thinking all the time of the person to whom you are writing. In a book like this, you haven't got the slightest idea who your reader is going to be. He could be a very intelligent person—my intellectual equal—or on the other hand he could be a plain damn dumb bunny. It gives you an eerie feeling—a kind of lack of historical focus.

And, speaking of history, before we go one step further, I want to speak to that right here and now. I'm told by the Professor that the young people today don't study history the way we did at all. Honestly he showed me a report by the Society of American Historians or some such group that said the teaching of American history was now—and I quote—"in crisis." In *crisis,* if you please. And why was it in *crisis?* Because the students "preferred"—and I quote again "presentism." That's right, "presentism"—as if there was any such word let alone any such damn thing. And how do they define this damn "presentism"? You're not going to believe this—but they define it, as I quote a third and I promise you the last time— "Current events, social studies and ethnocentric subjects." *Ethnocentric!* No, I am not making it up. And no, I won't say it. This is a family book. I'll keep calm. But one thing I will do. I'll quote Thomas Babington Macaulay, because one thing those students should do, if they do nothing else in their brief lives, is to remember that he was the one who said that those who don't study history will be condemned to repeat it.

Speaking of Macaulay, I was brought up on *Horatius at the Bridge,* which reminds me of something else the young people don't do anymore, and that's study Latin. And, make no mistake, in many ways that's just as important as not studying history. I ask you, where would I be today if it wasn't for my thorough grounding in Latin. Frankly, I very much doubt that if I had not been able to read my Roman history in the original

Latin, you would right now be having the pleasure of reading this book. And yet the young people—and again the Professor is my authority—simply don't study it. They think it's a dead language. A dead language! And I suppose *The Decline and Fall of the Roman Empire* is a dead book. Well, they're dead wrong is what they are, they're dead wrong. And that's exactly what they're going to be damned soon—both dead and wrong.

The Professor says they don't study Latin because they don't like it. And they don't think it's "relevant." Like it and relevant! Everything these days is like, like, like. It doesn't matter whether they like it. They're not meant to like it, they're meant to learn it. And as far as that damn word "relevant" goes, I suppose it's not relevant when I tell them that when I meet a man who, as we used to say, had "small Latin and less Greek" —well, he's less a man to me. In fact, I'll be frank and say he's only half a man. And I mean half a man. You don't believe me? Ask Tubby. Tubby was over there in Africa where the pygmies are, you know. The girls over there, he told us, reach puberty at seven, and often have babies at eight. Now I'm not saying this wouldn't happen if they studied Latin, but it certainly couldn't hurt.

Which reminds me of that Field fellow we were talking about —the one in the think tank. The whole point of what that bird was talking about was something that neither he nor his whole tankful would have thought of if their lives had depended on it. All they were thinking about, in their shortsighted little way, was the *number* of changes. The number doesn't matter, for Pete's sake. The only thing that matters is that not one single solitary iota of all the damn changes they're talking about has been for the *better*.

Oh, I know it can be argued that an invention here or a new development there could, conceivably, be put down on the plus side of the ledger. I personally, for example, like Scrabble. But if you really stop to think about it and keep the whole thing in balance, with your mind on the broad sweep of things, you'd have to be just a plain damn fool not to admit that for every little tiny unimportant exception there are hundreds and hundreds of big important things that are just plain worse. And the only people who won't admit it wouldn't know the good old days if they fell over them. Such as, for one example, why they were called good. Ask yourself sometime. Have you ever heard one civilized person whose opinion you respect, at anytime, anywhere, in any civilized country anywhere, say the good new days? Of course not. And the only people who would say such a thing don't know the first thing about the old days for the very simple reason they never lived in them. And now, if they don't study history, they won't *ever* know about them—except right here in this book.

Go back to your Gibbon and your decline and fall. I tell you I'll take anything about those days or any days over today. Even your barbarians. I tell you I'll take the barbarians of those days over the barbarians of today any time, any place, anywhere. I don't care who you name—the Goths, the Franks, the Lombards, the Angles, the Saxons, the Jutes, the Frisians, the Burgundians, the Thuringians—I'll take any of them over today's boys. All right they called the Vandals the Vandals—but we were the ones who gave them *our* name, Vandals. And the Saxons, after all, *were* us. Why the morals of those Saxons were so much better than the morals of our barbarians today that there's no comparison. In Saxony—and remember I'm talking about old Saxony—if a virgin in her father's house or a married woman under the protection of her husband—well, if she committed adultery, do you know what they did to her? They burned her—that's what they did—and hung her seducer over her grave.

Even the Mongols weren't as bad as these damn moderns would have you believe. You hear a lot about the "Mongol hordes"—well, let me tell you something about those Mongol hordes. All right, they were swarthy, but they didn't have beards. And do you know why? Because on the very day of their son's birth, they cut his cheeks with a sword. Before they even let him have a drink of his mother's milk. The idea was that he must learn to endure wounds before he took nourishment.

So much for that. Now then there is something else. And that is how this book actually went from idea to your hands, where it is now. And for that I can thank here and now Fish Frobisher's brother, Schermerhorn Frobisher. "Skimmy," as he's of course known, knows everybody who is anybody. And it was he who spoke to a publisher about my book. And the next thing I knew, I had a contract. I'd never happened to have had any dealings with these publishing fellows before—they're not themselves anymore, you know, they're all owned by somebody else. But just the same, everything went fine about the contract and all. And then one day they sent over this girl to the Club. They apparently don't know much at that publisher's, because they sent her over, if you please, in the middle of the morning. Of course she couldn't get in. But William took care of her and got her in through the back door. And by now she's learned where and where not, after five o'clock, of course, women can go. Anyway, to make a long story short, we met. Her name is Marjorie, and I was very much taken with her right away. She really is a cunning little thing. It's actually amazing how so many of these young girls nowadays are so much more presentable than the young men you see with them. You wonder what on earth they see in them. Actually if these young girls would spruce up a little and get out of those awful pants, they would be perfectly able to attract an older man—someone with at least a modicum of maturity.

But I'm dreaming again. Anyway, after Marjorie and I had observed the usual amenities, I asked her to take out her book. Well, she looked at me as if I had two heads. I had thought, of course, she was going to take the book down in shorthand, but it not only turned out she didn't take shorthand—nowadays nobody takes shorthand—she also wasn't even a secretary. She was, if you can believe it, one of their top editors. I mean it— she showed me a piece of stationery. I couldn't imagine why they put a woman, to begin with, on an important job like this, let alone one who looked like a child. But it doesn't really matter, I've become very fond of her. And she's not a child by the way, she's twenty-nine—which really isn't that young anymore than I, in my sixties, more or less, am that old. But the point is, we now have a firm understanding. Every Friday afternoon, she comes round and collects what I have written and I read it to her and she tells me how much she likes it, and then we have a cup of tea. After that she then takes the pages back to the publisher. She makes some changes, of course—she has to, I guess—but generally speaking I have found her, particularly for a person like that, top drawer. She told me they had no trouble down there reading my longhand, which I knew they wouldn't, because I write a good hand. Of course, it's just one more lost art today. In my day the schools taught two things, love of country and penmanship—now they don't teach either. And that's why all these young people write in squiggly scrawls that no one over their age can possibly read. I tell you the combination of trying to read young people's writing and this terrible print in the newspapers—honestly, they make it smaller and smaller every year—well, it'll be the death of me, that's what it will be.

Actually, many Members of the Club have expressed considerable interest in my *modus operandi.* And I presume those of you on the outside share this interest, even at a distance. Therefore, without further ado, I shall tell you. I do not, like some authors I know, write any old hour of the day or night. There is no earthly reason for this save poor planning. Indeed, I see no reason for allowing one's writing to interfere with one's other daily activities. Since I began this book I have never, for example, missed either my morning newspaper—the *Wall Street Journal,* of course, I detest the *Times*—my morning constitutional or, for that matter, my appearance in the Morning Room before lunch to see what's going on or if anybody's died. After all, I was the first one who suggested we spell the Room with a "u." Incidentally, I write only in the mornings. In the afternoon, with bridge, dominoes, tea, etc., etc., there's just no time for it. Nor, I wish to make clear, do I write only some mornings. I write every morning. I do not, in other words, write just when the spirit moves. I move the spirit. And I write for two hours whether or not I have anything to say.

I write in the Morning Room or here in the Club Library, where I am now and which I prefer since I am at least ostensibly protected by our "Silence" sign. I write on ordinary foolscap with, of course, an old-fashioned fountain pen. If there's one thing that makes my blood boil, it's these damn stupid modern ball-point pens. Ball point! A ball isn't a point, to begin with. And to end with, the damn things don't write. Edgy Bull was given one in a restaurant the other evening—he'd left his in another coat—and he tried to sign the check with it and the damn thing wouldn't even finish Edgerton. Edgy got so mad he threw it across the room. He shouldn't have, of course, in a public place, but I didn't blame him. I remember when the damn things first came in. Someone put them all over the Library, up by the inkwells, and took the old dip pens away as a test. Well, they failed the test is what they did. Tubby put one down on the floor and stamped on it and when Tubby stamps on something let me tell you it stays stamped on. I said right away they'd never last, and they haven't. Someone called Fish Frobisher and he brought it up at the Society to Put Things Back the Way They Were, and we had a unanimous vote on them. Today you couldn't find one in the Club if you tried.

Members of the Club have also asked me how I can do such a tremendous job without leaving the Club. My answer to that is simple. If Sir Walter Raleigh could write his *History of the World* while he was in prison in the Tower of London, then I guess yours truly can do this job from the Club. Of course I realize I'm taking on a much larger canvas than Sir Walter— after all, it was a far smaller world in those days and it had a damn sight less wrong with it. And then too I have an advantage over Walter—I have recourse to the Club Library. The Club has, I believe, at least one of every book ever written by a Member—and we also have quite a few volumes by outsiders. Had quite a few, I should say, because the STPTBTWTW has really been after them. Fish and his boys have honestly been bearcats about it and I agree with them. They feel, and so do the rest of us, that if you're going to put things back the way they were you've also got to get rid of the things that someone let in to take the place of the other things—and that includes an awful lot of this modern trash and junk. Fish is really on the rampage. He's out to get the Library down to what it should be—Members' books and classics—and not one other volume.

Actually, I find I use the Library surprisingly little. In the first place, I have a good memory. In the second place, if I don't remember some date or fact or something, I'd much rather ask Witter or Fish or Fog or Edgy or even Tubby than rely on some modern reference book. Most of them are edited either by halfwits or out-and-out Bolsheviks. I'll give you an example. I am, as most of you know, often called the Club curmudgeon. Well, just for the fun of it the other day I asked some Members of the Club—not Fortnightlies of course, but others—what a curmudgeon was. And I got some answers it's hard to believe. One Member said he wasn't *sure*—not sure, mind you—but he thought it was a weapon. I told him it was a weapon I'd certainly like to have on the streets of New York. Anyway, another fellow told me he thought it was a kind of fish. Well, you may be sure I told Fish Frobisher about that.

Actually I had just about given up, so I decided to refresh my own memory on the thing. And I went to one of these modern dictionaries and what do you think I found under the word? You won't believe it. "A gruff and irritable elderly man," it said. Gruff and irritable—well, I guess to some people I sometimes do seem gruff and once in a rare while I am inclined to be irritable. But *elderly*—bah. Mature, yes. Maturity is part and parcel of decent curmudgeonship. But "elderly"—it's just one more example of this everlasting kowtowing to youth. As if there were any virtue in being young. It's just something older people have to put up with when future older people are growing up. It's certainly nothing to be proud of, and there's absolutely nothing virtuous about it. Incidentally, about the cur-

35

mudgeon thing. It's interesting when you think of it that women cannot be curmudgeons. They can be irritating, of course—after all they are women—but they cannot be curmudgeons. My Aunt Lolla tried all her life to be a curmudgeon but she never succeeded. What she did was make my Uncle Bagnalls a curmudgeon.

Now to press on. First off, it's not easy to know where to begin because wherever you look the story is the same—actually, that's exactly what it is, a story of simple sordid sameness. Modern art, modern music, modern architecture. What are they, when you come right down to it, but an easy way to cover up sloppy thinking, slipshod workmanship and just plain lack of backbone and good horse sense?

Modern people often think, for example, because of some tommyrot they've read about the old days that we were all rich and had yachts and private trains and all sorts of things on that order. And that, therefore, is why we liked those days. Poppycock. A few people had those things, of course. Why shouldn't they have them, if they could afford them? The point is that every single one of these modern rabble-rousers misses the point entirely. In those days not just rich people but every Tom, Dick and Harry had hundreds and hundreds of simple pleasures every single solitary last one of which has nowadays been systematically exterminated.

What were these simple pleasures in the old days? Well, I must speak plainly here—one of them was women. I mean, of course, good, old-fashioned women. Ask yourself what has changed more than the good, old-fashioned girl of yesterday to what you get today. You can't think of a thing, can you? I knew you couldn't. It just proves what I'm saying. All right, there was a double standard—everybody nowadays is always squawking about the double standard of the old days. But they completely miss the point. The point is the double standard was at least *a* standard. And it was double or nothing, it seems, because nowadays you haven't got any standard. And what we're left with, where women are concerned, is just exactly that —nothing.

After women—well, there are so many things. There's the Government for one, the servant problem for another. But remember, I'm talking here about total misery as compared to the good old days. But all in all, after women, I think I would place children next. After that—I don't know. Foreign affairs? Yes, I think I would put them up there. So there you are— women, children and foreign affairs. The Big Three—the Harvard, Yale, and Princeton, if you will—of the trouble with nowadays.

Although I shall make these my major points, I have no intention of limiting myself to them. Take, for example, this everlasting modern worrying about whether you are happy or not. What the devil is being happy? It's a silly word anyway. It's for children, really. I've never worried a day in my life about whether I'm happy. Being happy, as far as I'm concerned, is not being bothered. It's not being bothered by your wife or your children or your servants or your Government or your religion or anything else. That is happiness for me.

Several members of the Club, in looking over my list of Chapter Titles, have asked me what about Labor? I can understand why they ask. But I've told them and I'll tell you I simply cannot bring myself to do a chapter on Labor. For one thing, I don't trust myself to do it objectively. For another thing, I just don't want to—they've had entirely too much publicity as it is, and I have no intention of giving them one whit more. For still

37

a third thing, the plain damn simple fact is that there isn't any such thing anymore. *Labor.* What does the word mean? It means to me, and I'm sure it means to you, not only work but hard work. Well, ask yourself. When, outside of you and me, did you last see anybody anywhere actually doing hard work for a reasonable period of time? They don't even have hard labor in prisons anymore. You sentence a man to hard labor, and the next thing you know they put him in the prison library where he's writing a book and competing with me. *Me,* mind you, only remember, I'm paying with my hard-earned tax dollar for him to do it. I tell you it makes my blood boil just thinking about that bird. There'll be plenty about Labor in this book, never fear, but a separate chapter? No sirree.

Remember, I have set myself an almost superhuman task—actually, a more difficult one than Sir Walter Raleigh or Gibbon ever had. And remember, Gibbon had 2,767 pages to work with. My publishers won't let me have anything like that. They say it's too expensive, and that nobody would read it. Which is just an excuse, of course, for the fact that they don't know how to do their job. And it's also a sad reflection on the calibre of your reader nowadays.

Nonetheless, I'll do my best. Go back through the centuries, from Caesar's death to my birth, and you'll find a lot of changes, yes. But you won't find anything in a single one of those centuries to compare with the assault on every single thing you can name that's been made in *my* century. In every one of those centuries you still had servants in their place, you still had Government in its place, you still had Labor in its place, you still had women in their place and you still had children in their place. You had different religions, again yes. But you didn't have anybody fooling around with the religion you had. And you didn't have people re-writing the rules for everything every two minutes. The rules for your sports, the rules for your stockmarket, the rules for your employees, the rules for your women and all the rest of it. I tell you I've seen in my century an assault on every single one of my citadels.

In your first century, you had Caligula and Nero and Boadicea . . . you remember, who massacred the Romans in Britain. There were troubles, all right, but your basic values, your servants and your Labor, your women and children, were still there. In your second century, you had your Great Plague. It lasted from 164 to 180, and devastated all Asia. But again it was only sixteen years. And I've had some kind of trouble every single year in my lifetime. In the third century, you had all the troubles with the Goths. The French always have been difficult. But I ask you—what's a few Goths compared to our miseries? In the fourth century, you had Constantine the Great and Theodosius the Great and many other Greats. Once more, ask yourself. When was anybody called Great in my lifetime?

In the fifth century, you had not just more Goths and Ostrogoths, you also had Vandals and Visigoths, even Attila the Hun. But I'll tell you something. I'll take Attila any day compared to the kind of steady undermining I see today. But keep going. In the sixth century, you had another plague—in 590. But that was one plague—I've had at least ten of them in my lifetime. In the seventh century, you had the Moslems, and in the eighth they invaded Spain and even reached France. Well, as I've already told you, there's a lot more miseries than just Moslems today. And I'm no Charles Martel.

In the ninth century, it was the Russians—the Northmen they called them then. And you had them again in the tenth. Well what do you think I've got today? I've got Russians coming out of my ears. In the eleventh century, you had the Norman Conquest and Pestilence and your People's Crusade. Well, I'll take conquest and pestilence and a people's crusade any day in the week compared to a women's crusade. In the twelfth century, you had Saladin capturing Jerusalem and the Latins capturing Byzantium. But you've got to put it in perspective. As I've told you, for every citadel they overthrew in those days, they've overthrown ten of mine today. In the thirteenth century, you had the Mongols, Genghis Khan and Kublai Khan and all the others. They were terrors, but at least they stood for some kind of law and order. You also had your Children's Crusade. But look at it this way—at least it got rid of some of the more militant ones. In the fourteenth century—you had the Great Plague and the Black Death. For misery that fourteenth is, probably, when you come right down to it, the closest to my century—as my fellow historian, Barbara Tuchman, has noted. But the fact is even then you still had your chivalry and your basic sense of values.

In the fifteenth century, you had the Turks. Well, I'll tell you something about the Turks. I'll take the Old Turks of those days anytime compared to the Young Turks of today. In the sixteenth century, you had Ivan the Terrible. He was terrible, I'll give you that. But what kind of heads of state do you think I've lived under? Again, for straight undermining, they make old Ivan look like Little Lord Fauntleroy. In the seventeenth century, you had the Thirty Years War. All right, thirty years is a long time. But at least it was out in the field. I've had wars right in my bedroom since the day I was born. Now we're up to the eighteenth. Well, in that century, you had all these revolutions, one after another, that's true enough. But at least they had the decency to come one at a time—not all together, as in my century. And finally, in the nineteenth, well, I'll give you just one example. The year 1830. They called it the Year of Disturbance. Can you imagine one year in that whole century being called the Year of Disturbance? In my century, every single damn year has been a Year of Disturbance.

So there you have it. A child could see there's really no comparison. There have been far greater changes in my life-time than from Caesar's death to my birth. Far greater.

CHAPTER III

The Servant Problem

I START with the servant problem because if you can't get anybody to do anything for you, you can't get anything done. Why should I, for example, who have to do the hard thinking for the masses—after a whole day of that, which after all is for their benefit—then come home and have to rustle around for my own dinner at night? Or lug my own laundry around like a coolie? And yet that's what we're coming to, you mark my words.

Your servant is your foundation, and if you haven't got a foundation, you haven't got a house. You can't make bricks without straw. All right, I want to change the world—who doesn't. But charity begins at home. Remember the old adage,

43

"Brighten the corner where you are." In the old days they even made a hymn out of it—for servants. And God knows these days they need it a lot more than they did then, even here in the Club. They never dust in those corners.

Speaking of the Club, I'll tell you—and I'd tell any servant right to his or her face—that you wouldn't be enjoying this book right now were it not for the fact that we still have a fair standard of service in the Club. At least, being a Club, we don't have this awful modern tipping thing. I'll tell you, your tipping today is a holy terror—it's a racket, is what it is. Of course once in a while you get one of these damn women Members they have now—wives of Members who have these idiotic privilege cards—and they will tip, the way women do. After all, it isn't their money. I saw one of them take out her purse right in the main dining room. Naturally I went right over. "This is a Club, madam," I said. "A gentlemen's Club. Or at least it used to be. And there is no tipping." She got the point. But we still do have trouble at Christmas with this damnable "Employees Contribution Fund" thing. And to think I always thought it was for them to contribute to. But it's not—it's for us, if you please. And then they find out exactly what you've given. I tell you, it's outrageous. And to my mind, not in the spirit of Christmas at all.

All right, we have a fair standard of service at the Club. A *fair,* mind you—not a good one and fifty ways to Sunday from what it used to be. Honestly, Sunday morning you could starve to death in here for all anyone would care. It's because, William says, these new employees don't speak English. What am I meant to do—learn *their* mother tongue? But no matter. The fact is we do have a standard of service here that at least allows a man to live and let live. If I lived outside the Club—in a house, say—what chance do you think I'd have to get this job done? "A man's house is his castle." Don't make me laugh. Today a man's house is his dungeon, that's what it is. You're a prisoner—you might as well be bound and gagged. Particularly gagged. I remember when we used to say, *"Pas devant les domestiques"*—we said it in French. I've forgotten what we used to say in front of French servants, but the idea was not to talk about money and days off and things like that. Today nobody uses the phrase anymore because you can't say a word in front of a servant or the next thing you know he or she will run out and write a book about you.

Speaking of books, I looked up "Servants" in the index in the Club Library, and do you know what? There wasn't a single book about them—or the problem. Imagine that—in the entire Club Library. Not a single book about the biggest single problem we've got. That index, if you please, went right from "Serpents" to "Services"—as if there were any of those anymore. I looked at them because I was curious, and it was all about the Army and the Navy and the Air Force—that sort of thing. Actually I even went back and looked under "Serpents." Nowadays, that would be the place to put them, but of course they weren't there either.

I have often wondered where the good, old-fashioned servants have gone. They must be somewhere, they couldn't have *all* died. I remember one little Irish girl we had—she was a pretty little thing, she wasn't any older than I am—I wonder where she is now, if she got married—if she married the decent sort—why couldn't she and her husband come back and be a good, old-fashioned couple? But I'm dreaming. Even in the old days it was devilishly hard to get a good couple. I remember Mrs. Frobisher II, Fish's mother, saying there was just no such

45

thing. You always got, she used to say, one jewel and one lemon, and the trouble was the lemon always corrupted the jewel. It was never the other way around.

But to go back to where all the servants have gone, *somebody* ought to be able to find out. And then just get the good ones and leave the others where they are. In the old days we used to have "intelligence" offices—I never could see why they were called that. Of course there was an irony here—your intelligence department in the Government is, after all, the spy office. And yet it seems only yesterday, during the war, when every other servant you had turned out to be either a German or a Japanese spy. And then after that, of course, you had your Russian spy problem. After all, if you had a top OGPU man, where better would you put him than as my butler? Everything I said during the soup course would be in Moscow by dessert.

Actually, even in the good old days, your servants' intelligence was never their long suit. It's because they have untrained minds. The workings of your untrained mind are always peculiar. In mental equipment, at best, I'd put your average servant at the level of a child of, say, ten. Or, to give the devil his due, twelve. "Bestow too many facts at once," Mother used to say, "and all you do is confuse." Cornelia, my first wife, was terrible with servants—and it was all because, as Mother frankly told her, she was too familiar. I can remember Mother specifically telling her what she should talk about with her servants, and what she shouldn't—an interest in the girl's family, a question or two as to whether she had any of her own people on this side of the water—that sort of thing. We had trouble with that Irish girl, for example, with what we used to call her "followers." Mother told Cornelia to watch out—that was the rock she told her on which so many households foundered. "The wise mistress," Mother said, "pursues the straightest course." The servant girl could have her followers, yes—but the young men should come at a suitable hour and go at a suitable hour and not hang around the kitchen. I also remember Mother saying that the responsibility of the mistress did not go so far as to make it necessary for her to inquire into the antecedents of the young men who visited her kitchen. After all, she used to tell Cornelia, they're not coming into your drawing room. Mother was a marvelous mistress.

Go back to your great civilizations. What did you have at the bottom? Good servants, that's what you had—or rather that's what you had before those civilizations went down. Everywhere you look—Mesopotamia, Egypt, Greece, Rome, the Middle Ages, England—even Tyre and Nineveh. You had servants who knew their job and had pride in their profession. I have pride in my profession and I expect other people to have pride in theirs, no matter how humble it is. What do all these modern servants want, anyway? To have servants themselves? It just doesn't make sense. If everybody had servants, then there wouldn't be any servants for anybody. There isn't enough of them to go around. Surely even a servant should be able to figure that out.

Of course many of those older civilizations had slaves. Now I know slavery is a ticklish question. Certainly I have no wish to offend my Southern readers. I know, for example, my old friend Albert Sidney Johnston down in Atlanta will be reading this. And Albert Sidney is of course a direct descendant of *the* Albert Sidney Johnston. But remember, Albert's family freed every single slave long before it became the thing to do. He and I have talked about it, and he is the first to admit there were abuses. But he and I also agree that the right kind of slavery, where each party respected the other's position, was certainly not what all this modern propaganda today would have you believe. Never mind that roots nonsense. Roots roots roots—that's all you hear these days. But what about *my* roots? I can't carry on my way of life if every Johnny-come-lately is trying to knock the props out from under it. Honestly, what is the use of a civilization raising up a, say, me—and not at the same time raising at least a couple of decent servants to look after me in my declining years? Because one of these days, as I told William, there won't be any more me's and then whom will the servants serve?

Speaking of William, William has been at the Club since the year One, and he's just as honest as the day is long, and yet he's Irish too. God knows how old William is—he says he never had a birth certificate—but to give you an example of what measure of man he is, he's been called William by everybody in the Club for fifty years, and yet his name isn't William. His name is John, but the head hall porter before him was named William and when that William died, well, the Members didn't like it—he died very unexpectedly—and so they just went on calling the new one William. It's typical of William that he never complained or even ever asked a single soul not to call him William. And on his Fiftieth—his fiftieth year of service, that is—we elected him a Member of the Club. Under the name of William, of course. There was some criticism of it at the time, that it set a dangerous precedent—which of course it did—but it went right through the Admissions Committee 5 to 4, with the stipulation that his sons wouldn't be legacies. And of course they haven't been.

In any case, right after William's election, I asked him to be our Speaker at Fortnightly, on the subject of "Servants." The Club was up in arms about the whole problem. Fog Horne had come in on New Year's morning at a perfectly reasonable time —seven o'clock, he'd been out all night—and couldn't find a soul to get him a cup of coffee. Fog wrote one of his "Concerned Members of the Club" letters, and then all hell broke loose. Everybody remembered some abuse. Well, I had a talk with William and told him I wanted him as a guest speaker. I told him I didn't want him embarrassed by it. I wanted him to do it as a Member of the Club, which he after all was, and not as a servant. I told him never mind the "sir," just give us a speech, as he would to his own Irish friends. I told him I didn't want a long speech anyway. What I wanted was something very short, and then for us all to have the opportunity to impress on him afterwards how important it was for him to do what we really wanted him to do—to set himself up as a Committee of One to find out what the devil had happened to all the good servants and if there was any way of getting them back. Anyway, William finally agreed, as I knew he would. After all, he was the one who got Henry. But Henry's getting very deaf, and the others—well, I told William I didn't know where on God's green earth he found them but green they certainly were. Honestly, I had one just last week who was so awful that in desperation I finally asked him where Henry was and he said it was Henry's day off. That's one of your basic troubles with nowadays—it's always somebody's day off. In the old days you had every other Sunday to cope with and Thursday night—maid's night out. But on those nights you went to your Club, of course. Now, if people in the Club start vamoosing off anytime they feel like it, what have you got? You've got anarchy, that's what you've got.

49

Where were we? Oh, slavery. Well, go back to Gibbon again. All right, Rome had slaves—in fact Beloch estimates that Rome in 30 B.C.—Caesar was killed in 44 B.C. so that's between Caesar's time and my time, the time we're talking about—well, Rome in that time had 400,000 slaves, nearly half the population. And don't go asking me who Beloch was. I don't know any more than you do, look it up if you want to know. The point I am making is that at that time Rome had so many slaves they had to require them to wear different kinds of dress—they were afraid if they all wore the same thing they'd realize their numerical strength. Which reminds me of all the fuss servants have always made about not wearing uniforms. I remember that even in the good days of servants the waitress or the upstairs maid of somebody was always acting up about wearing a cap. It was ridiculous. Does your nurse at your hospital make a fuss about having to wear a cap?

In any case, 400,000 slaves! Just think of it. Of course, not all of them were happy, and there had to be rules. If a slave killed his master, for example, the law required that all the other slaves of the same master be put to death—but anyone can see the point in that. It's also true that here and there there were abuses. A fellow named Vedius Pollio, for example—he was apparently a well-known gourmet of the day—well he used to raise huge fish for his banquets in his own tanks, and he made a practice of feeding them with unsatisfactory slaves. Now no one can condone that as a general thing. But compare it to what happens today when you get unsatisfactory service. You have absolutely no recourse, except to sit and take it. The whole thing has just gotten turned completely around—we've gone full cycle. I had a piece of fish in a restaurant the other day—I won't name the restaurant, but it was one you know—

and it was so terrible I had to call the waiter over. And he was so arrogant that I couldn't help thinking of old Vedius Pollio. But what can you do? Today your hands are tied.

I heard one of these broadcasters the other day talking about Rome—that was unusual enough, usually they don't talk about anything that happened before breakfast—and I turned the damn thing off. He had given it as his opinion that the reason Rome went down was because of slavery. Frankly, when I'm doing a book like this, I don't want anybody else's opinion. I want facts—or my opinion. And my opinion *and* the fact is that the reason Rome went down is just exactly the opposite— because it *didn't* have slavery anymore. What there was, plain and simple, was a decline and fall of your calibre of slave. Don't forget when you're talking about slavery in Rome—my *old* Rome—you're not just talking about domestic slaves or foreign slaves. Not by a long shot. Very few people today—I even got Edgy Bull on this, and Edgy knows his business history—very few people today realize that at the time I am talking about in Rome, eighty percent of your employees in industry and retail trade were slaves. Just imagine that—in industry and retail trade! When you walked into a store or a restaurant, you had an eighty percent chance of getting a slave. Those are good odds.

Compare that with what you've got today when you walk into a store and you can't get a single soul to take the slightest interest in you. The customer is always right! John Wanamaker must be turning in his grave. If you're a customer today, you're an intruder. Between those sales-girls' coffee breaks and coke breaks and water cooler breaks and lunches and clock-watching and their endless cackling about their boyfriends, the only chance you have to get any service is if you are their boyfriend

—a fate I wouldn't wish on my ex-stepson-in-law. And he's pure poison, believe me. Muffie, my second wife, was married before, you know—and afterwards, too, if you can believe that.

But back to your restaurant today. I used to say I didn't like to go into a restaurant where the waiters were citizens of a country which was actually at war with us at the time I entered. Nowadays it's no joke—they apparently all are. You walk in and sit down and that's it—you sit. There are plenty of waiters around—doing nothing of course—but if you ask one of them for anything, he'll say it isn't his station. What does he think I am—a train? For all he knows about the word, I might as well be. The point is, in the good old days, there was such a thing as a station in life, and people knew their station. And in the case of that particular waiter, his station, in case he didn't know it, was to serve me—and hop to it. Mother, incidentally, was a bearcat on that word "station." She believed in giving presents to servants—at Christmas, kerchiefs for the maid servants, handkerchiefs for the man servants, that sort of thing. "But never," she used to say, "give a gift that excites beyond the station."

Speaking of waiters, what do you think is the derivation of the word "waiter?" It's "wait here"—from the Dutch, I think. Anyway, it doesn't matter what it's from. What matters is when was the last time you ever saw a waiter wait anywhere, except in the kitchen when you want them and you've run out of something. Tubby told me they had a regular school for waiters. I told him frankly I didn't believe it. The only kind of school I believed they had is one where they're taught not to notice anything. Catch their eye! *My* eye. You couldn't catch those birds' eyes if you set your table on fire.

Just imagine what it must have been like in Rome to be

served by slaves! I've often thought I was born in the wrong age. I realize we are all put here for a purpose, and if my purpose is to set things straight, then I won't complain. But George, I can dream, can't I? And one of the things I dream about is—well, remember it wasn't just in the shops and the restaurants you had slaves in Rome. You also had your *servi publici*—public slaves. They were in the Government. mind you, the *Government!* Doesn't it make your mouth water? Instead of all these idiots who call themselves public servants— they're no more public servants than I'm a scarlet tanager—all they do is go around robbing us blind every living breathing moment of the day and then at night they rob us when we're asleep, and after we're dead they dig into our graves and rob us there. These damned inheritance taxes today kill more people than any disease. But back in your great days, in old Rome, your *servi publici* did all your manual and clerical work in your Government—all the damned bureaucracy—and it didn't cost you, the taxpayer, a single sou, or rather, a single denarius. And remember, they were *yours*—your slaves. If they talked back to you, or were unsatisfactory—well remember Vedius Pollio. I tell you you'd get a much better class of public servant today if there was at least the threat there of feeding them to the fish.

Take your domestic field in Rome on this slave thing. It was a much broader field than we, in our pathetic little way today, think of as domestic. Your domestic in those days wasn't just your cook and your scullery maid and your chambermaid and your upstairs maid and so forth—there were all those, yes. But the Romans also classified as domestic the whole gamut of all the non-service areas we get today. Your handyman, for example—he wasn't just a handyman, he was also a hand *craftsman.*

He could not only fix things, he could also make things—there's that pride in your profession thing again. In the big household they even had artists as slaves. So therefore you naturally didn't have any of this abstract nonsense. Gibbon also tells us they even had writers as slaves. Of course I'm sure Gibbon didn't mean all writers—real historians like he was then or I am now. He meant your little fellows—your novelists and critics, people like that. But besides writers—and this is just as important, you had doctors and lawyers as slaves. Honestly, the more you study the thing, the more like Utopia it is. Imagine these damn doctors today, who won't make a house call. They were household *slaves.* At your beck and call, night and day, whenever you got anything wrong, like the backache I've got right now. I'd just hold up my hand, and he'd come on the double. And your lawyers too. Slaves also, to a man. There to do what you told them and not to argue with you every damn minute, and then send you a ridiculous bill. Honestly in those days, there was something for everybody. Even your wife's hairdresser was a slave. Just picture what that alone would save you.

Of course it was all too good to last. What ruined it was, actually, two things. First there was a really terrible systematic effort to undermine the whole thing by coddling the slaves. Emperor after Emperor played a part in this. Even Nero. Nero, for example, allowed slaves with grievances—I loathe that word "grievances," it's always somebody's else's grievance, it's never my grievance—anyway, Nero allowed them to use his statue as an asylum, and even appointed a civil judge to hear complaints. Their complaints, of course, never their owners' complaints. So of course you got nothing but the troublemakers and the whiners that you always get everywhere. Finally under Hadrian, the right of an owner to kill a slave without magisterial approval was ended forever. And there went the ball game. You didn't *have* to kill them, of course, but you had to have the *right.* You have to be able to put your foot down. That's the key thing. It's just like capital punishment. You take it away and you've got crime in the streets.

In the end, Rome went totally berserk. It freed all the slaves. It probably sounded all right at the time, but they must not have been looking at history either. Because the minute you freed your slave, where do you think he went? To the free market? You're dreaming! Of course he didn't. He went right out and sat on his backside and went on the dole, and you and I paid for him, that's what we did. You had on the one hand the steady emancipation of the slaves, and, on the other, your low native birth rate and your high alien rate—you always get that. And in no time at all, you didn't have any more ethnic homogeneity. Old Emperor Augustus saw it all coming and to his everlasting credit he did what he could. What he said was if you owned two slaves, you could free one, and if you owned from three to ten you could free half of them. Now that doesn't make sense, does it? How do you free half of three anyway? In any case, if you owned from eleven to thirty, you could free one-third of them and if you owned from 31 to 100, you could free a fourth of them. From 100 to 300 you could free a fifth of them, but no one, no matter how many he had, could free more than 100 total. It was a great try and Augustus deserves great credit for it, but not even Augustus could hold his hand in the dike forever. And when he was gone, they released the floodgates and just freed too many of them and Rome went right down the drain.

But enough of Rome. Here we're talking about the changes between Caesar's time and my time and we're spending all the time in *Caesar's* time. What about *my* time? I tell you I'm going to be very blunt about what's happened to servants—in fact I'll go so far as to say they're just as big a problem today as women and children. Actually, since today you can't find a decent man servant anywhere for love of money, most of them are women. And I've already told you they have the mind of a child—so there you are. But I promised you the facts, and I'm going to stick to them. Women and children or servants—it's all the same to me. And if it gets me in Dutch with some of the more sensitive of you, so be it. I might as well be hung for a sheep as a lamb.

When I was a young man, my father sent me on one of those Grand Tours—as all of us took in those days. England, France, Italy and Germany if they weren't at war. People took different Grand Tours, of course. Tubby's Tour, for example, was a really Grand one—his family sent him to get over a really unsuitable girl—so he even went to Africa. On the other hand, Fish's tour was very curtailed. Mrs. Frobisher wouldn't allow him to set foot in France. "The French," she used to say, "are a low lot. Give them two more legs and a tail and there you are." Poor Fish—he missed all the mamselles.

As for my Grand Tour, the thing I remember best was my stay in England. I stayed with a friend of my father's, the Hon. Frederick George Wynn. I'll never forget Freddie Wynn's country house—we never called them "stately homes" or any of that nonsense. They were just country houses and that's what they were. You just called Freddie "Mister" too. That's all he was, Mr. Wynn, even though he was Lord Newborough's heir at Glunliven Park—which, as you know, is in Caernarvon-shire. The thing I remember about that country house is how beautifully it was run. Mr. Wynn, mind you, was a bachelor living alone—just my age today, now that I think of it—yet here's what he had in staff. Count them now—I'm telling you exactly what he had. There was first the butler, of course, then the underbutler, three footmen, the groom of the chambers, the stewards' room boy and the odd man. Those were just the men servants, mind you. And beside them, on the distaff side —that's where the word "distaff" comes from, of course— there were the female servants. You had the cook, five kitchen maids, as I recall, at least six housemaids—let's see, the up-stairs maid, the chambermaid, and downstairs, well I remem-ber there was one just for the drawing room and library. And then you had two stillroom maids, and six laundry maids. And mind you again, I'm not counting the outside staff—the gar-deners, the chauffeurs and all those people.

Why do you know that in a household like that your maids were up at six o'clock in the morning? They were cleaning. Quietly, of course, so as not to wake Mr. Wynn or me or any of the other guests. Dusting, scrubbing, changing linen, brush-ing rugs and carpets—Mr. Wynn always had them do it bare-foot. Otherwise, he said, there'd always be one noisy one, and she'd wake everyone. But the men worked too. That groom of the chambers really worked like a Trojan—dawn to dark. His job was the reception rooms and the library. The downstairs maid did the cleaning, but he had to take care of the writing tables and the magazines and the newspapers. Do you know what he did first thing in the morning? He toasted and ironed the newspapers! Think about that the next time you're reading your beaten up, wrinkled newspaper. I tell you I could even read the *New York Times* if it was toasted and ironed.

There were so many little things like that. You could leave money in your room and not a soul would touch it. Except, when you came back, your bills would have been ironed. Not toasted, but ironed just the same. Imagine, ironed money. Honestly I can hardly go on—just thinking about it. There was Mr. Wynn, only *yesterday* it seems exactly my age today, as I told you, in the prime of life—and here am I, with what? Here I am doing my best at a bigger job than any job Freddie ever had in his life, and just making do, as seems to be my lot in life. Sitting here in the Club Library on the librarian's day off, with not a single solitary soul I can call my own to help me. I tell you, I don't care what kind of changes occurred from the time of *Genesis* to Caesar—the changes that have occurred from my birth to now are so much greater there's no comparison.

One thing I've never forgotten about Mr. Wynn is he never spoke to his servants face to face—he always spoke to them with his back turned. I asked him about it one day and he said it promoted too much familiarity. Actually, I think the real reason was he was a very shy man. He didn't really like looking at anybody, and I think he particularly didn't like looking at servants. At the same time, when anything went definitely wrong with the service, he'd make a strange baying sound, sort of like a wolf howl. It was still done with his back turned, of course—but it was a weird, mournful sound.

On the other hand, when the chips were down, Mr. Wynn always rose to the occasion. I remember once when the second footman broke a candelabra he was cleaning. If a servant broke something in those days, it was deducted from his or her wages. And a candelabra like that—silver—well, it could have been a year of that man's wages. That young footman had sand, I'll say that for him. He came right into the drawing room, where Mr. Wynn and I were having tea, with the remains of the candelabra in his hands, Mr. Wynn, of course, immediately turned his back and listened absolutely impassively while the young man told the story of how the candelabra had fallen from his grasp. Mr. Wynn didn't interrupt him once, and remember, the young man was talking about a fortune for him and he didn't know if he was going to be docked a year's wages, or, worse still, be sacked. And yet on Mr. Wynn's side, I'm sure that candelabra has been in his family for generations. Anyway, finally the footman finished and both he and I were expecting, at the very least, that wolf howl. Instead Mr. Wynn just raised his hand, "Worse things happen at sea, my boy," he said—and that was that. I tell you Freddie Wynn knew how to handle servants.

Frankly, I very much doubt if there's ever been a servant in history like your best English servant. What do you think kept England going so long? Their kings and queens. Hardly, boy, hardly. With rare exceptions, a Coeur de Lion here, a Henry VIII there, they were a pretty average lot. Your Prime Ministers? An occasional exception, yes—a Disraeli, a Salisbury, a Bonar Law, a Churchill—but again, your average is not much higher than your American Presidents. No, what kept your British Empire going was your servant. Your gentleman's gentleman at home and your Gunga Din overseas. Tubby has particularly asked me to include a Din he had in India, Chukka Din, he called him—he looked after Tubby's polo ponies—and the General asked me to include a gun bearer he had who literally saved his life in the Great War. So now I've included them. But what do you think kept the Forsytes going? The Forsytes? Not likely—top drawer though they were. Their *servants*. Their servants were their real saga. And *Upstairs Down-*

stairs. I watched every episode of that, and of course the reason the program was so popular was, never mind your upstairs, it was that nostalgia we all had for the downstairs. "Gone With the Wind," Fog Horne said one night when we were watching it, "Wind, hell," I said. "It's gone with the hurricane."

Take your butler. How many American butlers can anyone name? Outside of William here at the Club, I'll bet you'd probably make mistakes. So I'll do the honors for you. First of all, from my father's generation, I'll have to name two of dear old Pierpont Morgan's—both Physick and Biles. Poor Pierpont was always peeved about their names—I know they sounded like diseases—but they were two true blue butlers, make no mistake. And it was typical of Pierpont that he refused to change their names. Another odd-named great one—and don't go confusing them now with your odd men—who had a recognized position on the staff that had nothing to do with butling —anyway it was old E. J. Berwind's Wildgoose. Old E. J. was teased about his name, too—who knows, maybe the butler earned it with some of the maids. Let's see—three others that come to mind are Marshall Field's Hider, Herbert Satterlee's Beany and Newbold Morris's Slattery. I take it you agree with my list. But I've got you now. Because not a single one of them was American—every man Jack of them was British to the bone.

But what's the use? I don't suppose anyone nowadays would know a good butler if he fell over one—and he certainly wouldn't know how to dress him. My father saw a butler once in the West—it was either in Albany or Buffalo or somewhere out there—and the man, if you can picture it, was in full livery. Just like a footman. I tell you it was rich. Any real butler, of course, would rather be shot than wear livery. A real butler

60

wore striped trousers and a swallowtail for lunch, and in the evening, he wore either a dress suit and a white tie, just like you or me—except that of course we wear a white waistcoat with a white tie, and he wore a black tie. Or else on Sunday night or some informal occasion, he wore an ordinary tux. Incidentally, that is, of course pronounced "tuck." It's spelled "tux"—from tuxedo, of course—it originated at Tuxedo Park—but it's never pronounced "tux," it's "tuck." Honestly, if there's one thing that makes my blood boil, it's to hear someone say "tux." I heard a young fellow, who had apparently just been elected to the Club, say that the other night, and I couldn't believe my ears. I was sitting at the common table with him—I like to do that once in a while—and I started to find out who in hell sponsored him, but I ran into a blank wall. Finally, I told the young man that if he ever said that again, he'd have to eat at another table. I don't believe anybody should wear anything he can't pronounce.

Hold on now—I got off the track again. Oh, butlers. Well, the English butler of yesterday was as different from any servant today as chalk is from cheese. Take the late Lady Astor's Lee. "Lord" Lee, they used to call him—honestly, he had more nobility than a roomful of noblemen, and there probably never was a better butler. I remember once Nancy telling me the story of the only time Lee ever contradicted her. It was during the thirties—you remember, footmen even then were beginning to be hard to get. Anyway, Nancy had told Lee he would just have to come up with someone. They were down to two, and at Cliveden you can be sure that was bare bones. Well, Lee came up with a man and so of course Nancy had to put her "seal of approval," as she called it, on Lee's choice—as if she ever needed to. It must have been an incredible scene. She saw

the man and promptly started in by telling him that her footmen always had to be prepared to turn a hand to anything.
Would he clean windows and do anything that needed doing?
"No, milady," the footman perfectly properly replied. "I am
only prepared to do the duties normally expected of a footman." At this Nancy immediately got on her high horse, and
told the man he was not hired. And so, on the way out the man
equally properly told Lee his mistress apparently did not want
a footman—she wanted an odd man. After that, Lee went right
to Nancy and politely explained to her that she had been wrong
—the man had been entirely within his rights. To Nancy's
credit she at once ordered Lee to call the man back. And that
—she told the story on herself—was the only time Lee ever
contradicted her. "No, milady," he said, "that I cannot do. You
have created a situation from which there is no retreat."

What a world it was—with their rights and our privileges!
And not, of course, as those words have been turned around
today. And, don't forget, it was a world with rules. I myself was
at Cliveden when Lee let go the best footman he told me he
ever had. His name was Gordon, but when Gordon for some
reason married the girl who, as I recall, had charge of
Cliveden's flowers, that was that. Gordon knew the rules. Footmen on their hours off had their own "pug's parlour," as it was
called, and their powder room—not today's awful powder
room, of course—where they were perfectly at liberty, as long
as their work was done, to have what they used to call "a slap
and a tickle" with an occasional housemaid. But nothing steady
and nothing serious—obviously that sort of thing would have
seriously disturbed the smooth running of the whole household. Well, as I say, Gordon knew the rules and he broke them
—and he was, of course, sacked. The trouble with nowadays is,

very simply, there are no rules so obviously your women and children run riot and your servants run amok. Gordon, I'm sure, found another post and learned from the experience. If I've said it once, I've said it a thousand times—you either have rules or you have anarchy—which is, of course, exactly what we have now.

I know I sound like a broken record on the subject of English servants—but what else is there? One of the few remaining places where you'll find old-fashioned service today is on the *Queen Elizabeth 2.* I've crossed on her several times and I can tell you that some of the older stewards are first rate. In first class, of course. People say there are no more classes. If there's one thing that makes my blood boil, it's people saying there are no more classes. There'll be classes as long as there are people— you mark my words. What have you got if you don't have classes. You have Russia, that's what you have—Bolshevik Russia. Even in China, my latest information has it, they are dying to start classes again. And, speaking of China, when was the last time you saw a good Chinese servant? They used to be everywhere, but once they got that Red thing and this everlasting equality bug—well, now you just can't find a good Chinese servant. And the awful thing is that they were once first rate. Quick, willing and quiet. Those are your three basic criteria for a good servant. I'll repeat that—quick, willing and quiet.

The Professor said the other day I was prejudiced about servants. Pish tush, I told him. I don't have a prejudiced bone in my body. I believe in the American ideal of servanthood. I don't care about their race, creed or country of origin—I'm even color-blind about them. All I want is for there to be some decent ones. Lord knows nowadays you can't be prejudiced about them. Beggars can't be choosers. Even Betty Bull told me the other day you don't interview them nowadays—they interview you. Of course there was nothing original in that—there never is with Betty. But what was amazing was that she admitted it. She's just plain pinko, you know.

Anyway, Professor or no Professor and Betty or no Betty, I shall here and now, based on a lifetime of experience, rate servants for you. I have compiled a list, in order, of the twelve best races of servants in history. But before I give it to you, I want to tell you I've put a good deal of time on this list—most of the morning, in fact—and I want you to read it carefully. As a matter of fact, it might be helpful to you to jot it down and carry it with you the next time you have occasion to try to get a decent servant. Good luck.

(1)	English
(2)	Old Chinese
(3)	Old Southern
(4)	Old African
(5)	Old Filipino
(6)	Old Japanese
(7)	Old East Indian
(8)	German
(9)	French
(10)	Italian
(11)	Irish
(12)	American

Remember, this is a general list, not an individual thing. Here and there you might find an Irishman, say, who belongs right up there with your Old Chinese, or even a French maid or an Indian *ayah*—they were excellent maids, you know—who does her job as well as a Filipino houseboy. But these are relatively unimportant matters. Don't bother me with them now. And what difference does it make, really? Because the plain fact of the matter is that as soon as one race got reasonably good at being servants, we immediately spoiled them, and the next generation started on the road to being rotten. Look at your Caribbeans. Some of them were fine at first—and they had charming accents. But now you don't even dare go down there, let alone have them come up here.

Look over that list again. It really makes you heartsick, doesn't it, to see our country at the very bottom? Heartsick and ashamed. To think we couldn't even raise one measly generation of servants before we ruined them. Not a servant worthy of the name. And the real irony is it didn't have to be this way. Never mind Gibbon—look at American history. We had what should have been perfectly good servants right from the start, back in Colonial times. In the first place, we had four distinct classes of servants—you had slaves, you had occasional Indian help—never very satisfactory—you had indentured servants and finally you had the so-called "free willers."

And what are we left with today? Not one of those four categories. In fact we're left with no such things as servants at all. Ironically, there is still a thing called "housework" or "housekeeping"—which is what maids and servants used to do, and then wives did it, and now husbands do. Honestly—and Fog Horne is my authority for this—there's one so-called housekeeper in a Manhattan brownstone who spends her entire time running around to other brownstones and apartments trying to organize a union. A *union,* if you can believe it. A *union* of *servants.* And do you know the only thing stopping this woman? The fact that the servants won't admit they are servants. And yet they can't join unless they do admit it. The latest thing they want to be called, I hear, is "in-house engineers."

But, to go back to those four classes I told you about, you might as well write off any hope of slaves or Indians or free willers. Your only hope lies in the idea of bringing back indentured servants. I don't know who thought of it, but whoever it was, they should put up a statue to him—it was a capital idea. And it was a very fair thing. Stripped of its cumbersome legal phraseology, your indentureship included three main points— the time of service, the nature of the service to be performed —looking after the house and you, obviously—and finally the compensation to be given. Remember, it wasn't by any means a one way street. The employer—that's you and me, don't forget—bore the entire burden of his servant's passage. And then after the time of service was up, during which, remember, you paid them their wages—five years, say, if they were be- tween twelve and twenty, seven years under twelve, whatever —and then after that, you had to outfit them, give them clothes and so on to start their own life. And in some cases, this was no mere pittance. I remember reading about one woman who had, all right, a long indenture—ten years as I recall—but after that she received—let's see, I wrote this down somewhere—oh, yes, here it is, "three barrels of corn, one suit of pennistons, one suit of good serge with one black hood, two shifts of dowlas and shoes and hose convenient." And don't ask me what a penniston or a dowlas is. If I tell you, you won't remem- ber. I've told you before—a word looked up is a word remem- bered.

The hard thing, of course, in the early days, was judging your servant's age. All the colonies found that you just couldn't take their word for it—you rarely can with servants even now. So in almost all cases, the court was to be the judge of their age. At one time the courts decided that the indenture be five years if the servant was above fifteen years old. And all under the age of sixteen served until they were twenty-four. It was a good idea except that, as was pointed out in one interesting case, if "a Servant be adjudged ever soe little under sixteene yeares, the master pays for that small tyme three yeares service, and if he be adjudged more, the master looseth the like." Finally, it was resolved that if the servant was adjudged nineteen or over, he or she should serve five years, and if under that age, then as many years as he should lack of being twenty-four.

A lot of nonsense has been written about grabbing people and shoving them on boats and that sort of thing. Actually, in England, for anyone found guilty of kidnapping adults or children and sending them to the New World, the penalty was death. Furthermore, it was death without benefit of clergy—which is, incidentally, a form of punishment we should definitely revive. It would kill two birds with one stone—you'd get the criminal and at the same time, by denying him a clergyman present, you'd have others not wanting to do anything that bad. You'd not only have a better class of criminal but you'd also be giving a real shot in the arm to religion, which certainly needs it these days.

In the same way, a lot of nonsense has been written about the hardships of service. There were, naturally, penalties for running away. In Pennsylvania, for example, every servant absenting himself without leave—an occupational hazard of the breed then and now—had to serve, at the expiration of his indenture, five days for each day's absence. In South Carolina it was seven days. It is true that in those days the servant had to work hard—but hard work never hurt anybody—and then, as ever since, apparently, your abuses were far more likely to lie with the servant than with your master or mistress. If you don't believe it, read the literature from a wide variety of traveling writers who almost invariably, after a visit here, counseled friends considering a similar visit on no condition to bring their servants with them. Why? For one simple reason—because they would be—and I'm quoting from one of them, I've forgotten which—"hopelessly spoiled by contact with the slothful American servant."

Anyway, if William and his Committee of One come up, as all of us at Fortnightly hope they will, with some idea of where the decent servants have gone, and some plan for getting them back, I also hope they'll come up with some foolproof method for stopping them from being spoiled. It would be really heart-rending to go through all that trouble all over again and end up in exactly the same servantless morass we're in today.

CHAPTER IV

Your Government

PLEASE note that I have called this chapter "Your" Government. For all I know—I don't know you from Adam—it isn't yours. You may feel exactly the same way about it that I do—in which case I apologize. But one thing I do know—and that is that it isn't my Government. It might just as well be a foreign Government. I don't see why they don't run a foreign flag up the flagpole and be done with it. And hang it at half staff—in memory of the Government we started with and for the fact that we're all operating, as far as servants are concerned, with a half a staff anyway.

You think I'm exaggerating? I don't want you arguing with me. If you are going to argue, define your terms before you start. Remember, this country started as a Republic. And a Republic is not a democracy, thank God. Republicans and Democrats today—bah! You can't tell them apart with a fine tooth comb—which you need for the young ones.

But once upon a time there was a difference. The Republic was your *res*—your thing—and your *publica*—your public. I'm sorry *publica* is the feminine of "public," but there it is. Your Democracy, on the other hand, what is it? *Demos,* your common people, and *cracy,* which, as far as I'm concerned, are your crazies. Democrats don't have leaders, they have demagogues —they're the ones who appeal to the emotions and prejudices of the common people—from your *demos* and your *agogos* or "leaders." Leaders, my foot.

People are always talking nowadays about civil liberties. If there's one thing that makes my blood boil, it's civil liberties. In the first place they are not civil, they're very uncivil—and in the second place, as Edmund Burke put it, "Men are qualified for civil liberty in exact proportion to their disposition to put moral chains on their own appetites." When was the last time you saw anyone put a moral chain on his appetite for anything? Before the Great War. Right.

"Get out the vote," I hear people say at election time. "We've got to get out the vote!" They even say it on television. They shouldn't allow a thing like that on television. Get out the vote! It's the very last thing anyone ought to talk about, let alone do. You get out the vote and who do you get? The riffraff, that's who you get—flotsam and jetsam. The *hoi polloi*—the Greeks knew what they were doing when they called them hoi polloi. Edgy Bull's wife told me how proud she was last election to drive people to the polls. I tell you, that Betty Bull is going to be the death of me as well as of Edgy. Can you picture it?

70

Driving people in her automobile, for Pete's sake, to the polls.
I asked her if she had any idea how they would vote when they
got there, and of course she'd never thought of that. That's the
thing about women—they never think things through. In my
observation of them, it's because they only think of one thing
at a time. Anyway, Betty herself told me she didn't have the
ghost of an idea how they'd vote. I told her she might just as
well send the bill for her gas to the Kremlin.

You even hear people say—and seriously mean it, mind you
—that people ought to be fined if they don't vote. The General
told me that they were even doing that in some of these Social-
ist countries like Sweden and Norway—and they're countries
that ought to know better, after all they have a good cold
climate. Well, I'm telling you that people ought to be fined *if*
they vote—or else pay them not to. If I had my way, I'd have
elections held some place way out in the country, a long hard
place to get to, and I'd hold them on Friday or Saturday night
or sometime when all the young riffraff is rocking and rolling
and whatever else they do in their discotheques. Anyway by the
time they got home it would be all over.

Go back to Adam Smith. Do you know what *laissez-faire*
means? It means "to leave to do," that's what it means. And
that means for the Government to leave me alone. Government power, Smith said, was limited to the protection of my
right to my life, my liberty and my property, and any Government which interfered with any of these rights was illegitimate.
Well your Government today not only doesn't protect my life,
it takes away my liberty and confiscates my property. And I say
that illegitimate is exactly what it is—born out of wedlock.
We've gotten just as bad as England. And the same thing is
going to happen to us, you mark my words. We're going to

have a "brain drain" right over here. We've got Witter here now—he's part of your brain drain—but he'll probably have to leave here too the way taxes are. But where can he go?

I spoke of Sweden a moment ago. Do you know they've got a Minister of Education and Cultural Affairs over there in Sweden who's really a dilly. He said he didn't like the fact that some authors earn more than other authors. Really that's what he said—he found it "morally objectionable." Imagine! Morally objectionable. So what he proposed is that the royalties of all authors be pooled and divided according to need. Can't you just picture a meeting of all us authors and all discussing our need! Actually, I wouldn't have the slightest objection to dividing up some of those ill-gotten gains by these modern garbage collectors, but what people forget about this kind of outright Bolshevism—because that's what it is—is that it cuts two ways. There's a fellow here in this Club, for example, who's always going around writing poetry. We had him to a Fortnightly—we finally had to, he made such a fuss about it. Anyway, he came there and went on and on, reading the most terrible poems I've ever heard in my life. Not only didn't they make any sense, they didn't even rhyme. I called him on it, and he said they weren't supposed to rhyme, they were free verse. I told him I could understand that, but if he ever expected to charge for them, be ought to learn to rhyme. Anyway, my point is if I had to divide a single red cent with that bird—and red is just what it would be—I tell you wild horses couldn't drag another line out of me as long as I live.

Talk to me about my birth and the death of Caesar. All right, I'll speak to that. Take out your Gibbon. What do you think was going on in Rome during Caesar's second quinquennium?

Well, I'll give you a hint. It was when Caesar's back was turned and he was off in Gaul. No, it makes me so mad I can't wait for you. I'll tell what was happening. Pompey and Crassus, the consuls, were bribing voters right and left—mostly left, of course. In those days, before Caesar took over, anyone who would vote as he was paid to do was admitted to the polls whether he was a citizen or not. So obviously, your lowest element in Italy was attracted to Rome, just the way your lowest element in this country today is attracted to New York. Meanwhile, what did your men of affairs, the men of means and substance, like you and me, do? They did the only thing they could do. They hired bands of gladiators to protect themselves. You have to do that when mobs take over. I tell you if a band of gladiators advertised their services tomorrow morning in the *Wall Street Journal,* they couldn't answer their phone. Everyone would want them. I'd want them for one. I could use a band every time I step out the Club door.

It's as plain as the nose on your face—for anyone who isn't in the pay of a foreign Government. What happened in Rome is exactly what's happening here today. When you get right down to it, Rome won every war but the class war. But the trouble is your class war is the biggest damn war there is. And if you don't win it, you go down the drain. Franklin Roosevelt started it, of course, and then went off and left you and me to reap the whirlwind. All right, in Rome there was a narrow aristocracy. I'm prepared to grant that. I'll even grant there were very few Roman aristocrats who would come up to our Witter Hardees and Fish Frobishers. But remember what your word means—*aristos,* "best"—Government of the best. And if anyone can tell me what's wrong with that I'll eat every page of this book right up to here. Certainly there were excesses, but by and large the old aristocracy—your aristocracy, that is, that has at least three generations of being *aristos,* or best, behind it is—well, frankly I don't know how else to put it—best. Actually, your excesses come, as they always do, from your damn *nouveaux*—your people who had too much money for their own good and hadn't got either the patience or the simple decency to sit down and wait a couple of generations until they get the rough edges off.

Rome in my day—I mean in the day I'm talking about, before all your decline and fall set in—was really a first-rate well-run Club. On top were your patricians—the *patricii,* they called them—your people derived from your *patres* or fathers. Your legacies really. There were just a handful of them—there's always just a handful of your best—the Manlii, the Valerii, the Aemilii, the Cornelii, the Fabii, the Herachii, the Claudii and the Julii—they were all undoubtedly members of whatever Club in those days corresponds to our Club today. These *patrii* would take in here and there an occcasional businessman—but only the right sort—the kind of fellow who had been willing to wait at least one generation. As a matter of fact, the whole *populi* in those days, the very word "people" mind you—only took in, the way it always should have, just the upper classes. They were the *vox populi* too—not your later thing. Only later too did the *populi* include the *plebs,* as they were called. And these *plebs* admired the *patricii* very much. They always did, until people stirred them up. They not only admired them, they even called anything pertaining to the *patricii* by the term "classical." It meant of the highest rank or class. That's the true meaning of the word "classical"—it hasn't got a damn thing to do with classic, the way people think it does. It means class—pure and simple class.

The whole structure of Government was a class thing, as it was always meant to be—if you care about being good, let alone best. In Rome's Centurial Assembly, as it was called, you had at the top eighteen whole "centuries" of patricians and businessmen. That's eighteen hundred, and I know it seems a lot, but Rome wasn't small, you know, and they probably had that many good men. Then under them you had eighty centuries, or eight thousand, so-called "first class" men. And they were, obviously, first class—they had to have a hundred thousand asses worth of property. I asked Fog Horne how much an ass was worth in those days. They don't come any better than Fog when you give him one thing like that to do. He does it. He figured it as of the 1942 dollar because, as he told me, the damn dollar today isn't worth the paper it's printed on. Anyway, he figured your ass at .6 of the dollar which meant the Roman rich man would have had somewhere in the neighborhood of $60,000, which is certainly not rich, but it's at least comfortable, and remember, they had the patricians above them to guide them.

Anyway, after the first class of citizens, there was the second class, who were citizens owning between 100,000 and 75,000 asses, a third class owning between 75,000 and 50,000, a fourth, 50,000 to 25,000, and a fifth, 25,000 to 11,000. More important even than this, though, all the citizens who possessed—not earned, mind you, possessed—*under* 11,000 asses —all of them together were formed into just one century. And this century had just one vote—that's the way it was—one vote per century. And don't forget those patricians, well, there were eighteen centuries of them and then you had those eighty centuries of first class men. They had one other wonderful safeguard, too. And that was that each century voted in order

75

of its financial rank, and its vote was announced as soon as it was taken. Just think if we'd do that today. The first and second groups had 98 votes. Add it up. It was announced first and it was obviously a majority. So the net result was that your lower classes seldom bothered to vote at all. And don't forget, when I'm talking about lower classes, I'm talking about anyone who had less than 100,000 asses. If you had 99,999 asses, you didn't vote period.

Now I realize that this kind of aristocracy will probably never come again. But the point is it's an ideal to shoot for, instead of this everlasting down down down thing we've got today. Tax and tax, spend and spend, elect and elect—that's what it is. In Rome, every time they'd get a spender like that, as consul or something—well, they knew exactly what to do with him. In 486, when Spurius Cassius just proposed giving captured lands to the poor—just *proposed,* mind you—the patricians accused him of trying to curry popular favor and make himself king— and they had him killed. Killed him dead. Made an example of him—the only way to do it. In 439—I'm talking B.C. here, of course, although sometimes I get the feeling in this comparison between Caesar and me, there ought to be something which indicates B.C., and B.ME—anyway, in 439, they did the same thing when Spurius Maelius gave away wheat. We probably get our word from his first name. Anyway, he gave away wheat during a famine. He was doling it out like there was no tomorrow, either free or at a ridiculously low price. Of course that sort of thing can ruin an economy, and the Senate just up and sent an emissary to his home who killed him on the spot. Bingo.

Even if you were a former hero it was no excuse. Old General

Marcus Manlius, who in 384 had literally stopped the Gauls at the gates of Rome—well, later he went berserk and cooked up this cockeyed scheme of giving away money to people who couldn't pay their debts. Actually, it was his own money and it was never even proved that he did it. But just the *idea* of giving away a fortune for such a stupid reason was enough. So they put him to death, too. Many's the time I thought of old Marcus Manlius during Eisenhower's Administration. Fog Horne actually wrote him a Concerned Members letter. Fog warned him about Manlius but of course it didn't do any good. And Eisenhower was an honorary Member, too. We always elect Republican Presidents honorary members.

Another important thing in Old Rome, before the decline and fall, was the office of tribune. There were fourteen military tribunes, to lead in war, and ten peaceful ones, to lead in peace. And these ten were *sacrosancti* fellows. Do you know what that meant? It meant it was a sacrilege, as well as a capital crime, to lay violent hands on them. And do you know what the sole function of these tribunes was? It was to protect the people *from* the Government. They did it by a word constantly misused today. They did by the word "veto." What it means is, "I forbid." But it was never meant to be used by some President —or Governor—it was meant to be used by *you* against your Government. The tribune would go to a meeting of the Senate as a silent observer and when the time came, he could just stand up and shout "Veto!" "I forbid!" Just think of it. God, I wish I could go to just one House Committee meeting right here in the Club and get up and shout "Veto." And then I'd move right on out of here and take the first Pullman down to Washington and do the same thing down at the Capitol. I can see myself now—up in the Gallery—if that's the only place I can get to. But on my two feet, bill after bill, "Veto!" "I forbid!" "Veto!" "I forbid."

How, you may well ask at this stage, did the Romans keep their aristocracy for five centuries when we haven't even been able to keep ours for two centuries? Well one way they did it was by electing tribunes who were men of wealth and substance. They didn't get the wrong kind of men of wealth and substance the way we get our Roosevelts and our Rockefellers and our Harrimans and our Stevensons and our Kennedys and all the rest of them, because they controlled the vote. How many of those birds do you think we'd get if our men of wealth and substance controlled our vote? I'll bet not one of those men I mentioned got as many votes in the Club here as you can count on the fingers of your hand. The second way the Romans kept their aristocracy was, of course, by dictatorship. You hear a lot today about how we can't support some fellow overseas because he's a dictator—I'll be discussing that further in my chapter on Foreign Affairs. The point is for every person who hollers about us doing business with a dictator—there isn't one in a hundred of them who even makes a distinction, let alone asks the question, "What kind of a dictator?" How long has it been since you heard the phrase "benevolent dictator?" Ask yourself now. Honestly, how long? Well, in my own lifetime, I was brought up on those words, "benevolent dictator," and I still happen to think that a benevolent dictator is just about the finest form of Government you can have for anything—be it in the United States of America or in the Fiji Islands.

In Rome they proved it. Whenever they had any kind of real trouble the Senate could declare an emergency and then either of the consuls could name a dictator. But of course the whole thing depended—and for five centuries it worked—on the fact that every last one but one of those dictators came from the upper classes. I don't happen to recall who the one that wasn't was. But I'll lay you ten to one right now he was one of the worst dictators they had. The Senate, you see, virtually insured the benevolence of the dictators, because the man could not, without the Senate's consent, so much as touch the public funds. You didn't find one of them, like Roosevelt, putting his fingers into the till and then sprinkling it around like confetti, and then when he ran out, just printing more. Also, and this is just as important, his term was limited depending on the emergency to six months or a year. And every dictator had to obey the "dictates" of that limitation. They did their job like Cincinnatus did his job, and they went back to their farms.

The more I think about that Cincinnatus, the more my mouth waters. But people often ask me who, after Cincinnatus, I would choose among your great benevolent dictators. I know this is going to surprise you, but I would name Caesar as one. Hold on now, I know what you're thinking—that he favored the poor, seduced women, bribed ward leaders and wrote books. But look at it this way, I've done some of those things in my time myself. Of course I've never favored the poor, but I am, after all, writing a book—so who am I to cast the first stone at Caesar? Caesar and I have our differences, as I've said. But before you go condemning the man, just look at what he did. All right, he was a leader of the poor, but he wasn't one of your rail-at-the-richers. He didn't have an ounce of demagoguery, or for that matter democratic blood in him. He never got on with certain, well, Clubmen, it is true—your landed aristocracy of that day. But then neither do I get along with certain Members of this Club. Gibbon tells us that it was because Caesar wasn't to the manner born. That's to the man*ner* born, by the way, not man*or*. If there's one thing that makes my blood boil, it's people who write to the manor born—I am very sensitive about it. I can even detect it in conversation. It's always a slur —as if we all lived in big castles or something. It's to the manner born, as in the case of manners.

Damn, I've lost my place again. Oh, about what Caesar did. Well, for one thing, in the field of jurisprudence, he very wisely restricted jury service to the two upper classes, and he himself reserved the right to try the most important cases. I'd do the same thing—there'd be no namby-pamby judges sitting on my bench worrying about whether some criminal did what he did because his mother didn't love him for which she obviously had excellent reason. Finally, even though Caesar had very little religion himself, he protected all other religions, even the ones where he couldn't understand what the hell they did believe in. People forget things like that about Caesar, and they shouldn't. All in all, I can't think of anyone, with the possible exception of Witter Hardee or Fish Frobisher or Fog Horne or myself, who could have done any better.

My second choice—a man who meets every criteria I have of a fine benevolent dictator—is Sulla the Happy. You just can't laugh that Sulla the Happy off just because of his name. He got that name, you know, because of his laugh. His laugh was known all over Rome, just as I suppose Fog Horne's laugh is known in the Club. All right, Sulla was born poor. But I don't hold that against any man—as long as he's got the brains not to take up for the damn poor later in life. And Sulla certainly didn't. He became one of your greatest defenders of aristocracy in history, bar none. His Cornelian Laws—I suppose for

these young people today I might as well be writing in Latin
—well, all I can say is if they don't know their Cornelian Laws
I give up. Particularly when you realize they could have been
the basis for Rome's having a permanent aristocratic constitution. Just think of that for a minute, and remember I've always
said that if Rome hadn't gone down, England wouldn't have
gone down and you and I wouldn't be going down.

It's hard to pick and choose among the many and wise re-
forms of Sulla the Happy. My favorite was his Corn Law. By this
he simply suspended the state distribution of corn, and that
overnight of course stopped the ridiculous flocking to Rome of
all the poor. The same thing could be done right now, if anyone in New York had the gumption to do it. Stop your givea-
ways and you stop your influx of your riffraff. Of course, one
of your problems with Rome—and people sometimes forget
this—is that Rome was, after all, in Italy, and therefore you had
your Italian problem to begin with.

And don't forget that Sulla the Happy was as just as the day
is long. When one of his enemies was defeated—I've forgotten
which one it was—but the point was he was a fellow who was
betrayed and killed by his own slave—well, when Sulla heard
about it, he first rewarded the slave for his service to him by
giving the man his freedom. And then he put the man to death
for his treachery to the other fellow. How we need more justice
like that today! You'd not only have less of a crime problem,
you'd also have a better calibre of servant. Sulla the Happy,
incidentally, was one of the few rulers of Rome who died in
bed. By the time the term of his dictatorship ran out he had
given up all his authority and he went back to his house as a
private citizen and retired. Of course one reason he was able
to die in bed was he had taken the precaution of killing anyone

he thought was likely to assassinate him. But you can't blame him for that. He wrote it all in his own epitaph. "No friend ever served me," he said, "and no enemy ever wronged me, whom I have not repaid in full." Would that I could say the same. But, anyway, this book is a start.

My third favorite benevolent dictator would have to be Augustus—indeed I often think of my era at the Fortnightly as the Fortnightly's Augustan Age. To me Augustus and I are blood brothers. True, he was of middle class origin, but I have nothing against the middle class—you have to have a middle class as a bulwark—a buffer state if you will between you and your lower class. Also Augustus was, after all, the grandson of a banker, so he wasn't entirely without family. And he named more businessmen to high administrative posts than any other ruler in history. On top of that he saw to it that the richest of them went right on into the Senate. Augustus and I see absolutely eye to eye on that. Your right sort of rich man in the Senate is the only one you can trust not to rob you—he doesn't need to. Actually, Fog Horne believes what started our Government on the road to ruin was the popular election of Senators, and I agree with him.

In any case, Augustus did something that I'll bet many of you out there have forgotten. He confined the meetings of the Senate to the first and fifteenth of each month—one day sessions. That's enough, and it would be an excellent thing not only for our Senate today but also for our House. I'd give them two days a month, and then I'd clear the place out.

I've already told you what Augustus did about that freeing of slaves and then their all going on the dole. Remember, nobody could free more than a hundred, no matter who he was, even Augustus or me. But the most important thing of all

Augustus did was to get down to brass tacks on the morality thing. He believed, as all of us do, that freedom is not anarchy and liberty is not license. Rome was going downhill morally just the way we are—on a damn toboggan. Oh, for an Augustus today. No children at public entertainments. No women at athletic events—*at,* mind you, not *in.* And one thing he did that would have helped me so much years ago, he limited women's expenditures—even in the matter of dress and jewels. George, how I could have used him with my second wife, Muffie. I tell you that Muffie just about took me to the poorhouse.

Rome had the same problem with homosexuals that we have today—you always have it in your declining civilizations. Anyway, Augustus handled it to a T—without stirring up a lot of unnecessary fuss. You could be a homosexual in private all you pleased, but the minute you went out, look out. No adult single person, male or female, could inherit money or attend public festivals or games. And don't think Augustus went whole hog for this everlasting marrying whom you pleased, either. He didn't. He was a bearcat on people using their heads about marriage. Men of the Senatorial class, for example, that's you or me—could not marry a freed woman, an actress or a prostitute. And by the same token an actor or freed man could not marry a Senator's daughter—anyone with a sense of the fitness of things can see the point of that. Just the same, sometimes when I get discouraged and see a crowd of young people today, I feel Augustus and I have been shouting into the wrong end of the tunnel.

There is one other benevolent dictator I must name, even though he came much later—Diocletian. I'll be frank with you about Diocletian. I wouldn't put him up there with Sulla and Augustus. He did a lot of things that I would never have done

—such as his price fixing of goods. But he was superb on labor. Under Diocletian, labor was literally frozen to its job. When anyone wanted to gallivant around to some other job, or even move somewhere—there's entirely too much moving today, people just don't have roots—well, when you did that under Diocletian, well, the fact is you didn't do it. You were just immediately reminded—on pain of death, mind you—that the barbarians had Rome in a state of siege and everyone must stay at his post. We're in exactly the same state of siege today, but nobody down there in Washington even thinks of trying something like that. Again, it's that no-knowledge-of-history thing.

Speaking of Washington, the very best thing Diocletian did was to abandon Rome as the capital. Now that's just a simple, practical thing that any damfool President could do today—just get out of Washington. Rome was corrupt—Diocletian got out. Washington is corrupt—get out. I don't mean you'd want to make New York the capital—certainly not with the United Nations here. I think somewhere in Maine would be good, or possibly New Hampshire or Vermont. Anywhere where you can get away from corruption and get some good, simple honest values.

Of course, even at the worst of things, Rome never had the problems we have today. And, speaking of all these dictators' retirement brings to mind my own eventual retirement. Up until very recently your damn modern business wanted everybody and his brother to retire at sixty-five. Sixty-*five*, mind you, all because some damn union youngster wants to get in and push you out. Thank God, it's now being challenged, and I want to speak to this challenge. Here am I born in Ought Eight. I'm sixty-nine as I write these lines now. I am *not* seventy, as the Professor tried to tell me I was the other day. I don't care what I am, of course—age means nothing to me as long as I'm able to do my job. But add it up. I did it on my fingers. In Ought Nine I was one, in ten I was two, in eleven I was three, and so forth. And in '79 I'll be seventy. I suppose I was *one* in Ought Eight! A fat chance I was one—I was ought, that's what I was in Ought Eight, ought. But what's the use. None of these professors can add. The point is I've started a whole new productive life, and I'm years older than your stupid retirement age. That's one place the Government should step in—they should step out of everything else and step in there. And they shouldn't do one of their everlasting cut and dried arbitrary things. They should have a broadminded approach to the whole retirement problem. Have eighty, say, for a fellow like me, and have seventy-five for the next top group and then go right down and retire professors and Democrats and people like that at fifty or even forty-five. What possible good would my retirement do anybody? Except that you out there would have to pay for me with this bloody Social Security. You don't get a thing that way. This way you go out and buy my book and at least you're getting something for your money.

But enough of me. Back to what I know you've been waiting for—my rating of my Presidents in my lifetime. I'm not speaking here of Presidents of the Club, I'm speaking of Presidents of the country. We've had, of course, good and bad—you're bound to with our crazy system of every Tom, Dick and Harry voting. But among the good ones, the Republicans of course, there are just two that I believe could hold a candle to Caesar or Sulla. These two are, obviously, Coolidge and Hoover. After all, they presided over the great era of all our lifetimes. Many of my older readers will, I know, will be thinking Taft—not

Robert Taft, of course, he unfortunately never did get to be President, and I've never forgiven Eisenhower for that—but his father, Will Taft. I didn't know him as President—he was a little before my time—but I knew him later, as Chief Justice in the twenties. I went down to Washington as a boy with my father and I saw him—all 300 pounds of him. I remember my father telling me about the time he gave old Elihu Root about riding twenty-five miles on horseback in the Philippines, and saying it felt fine and old Elihu telegraphing back, "How is the horse?" People in those days, I know, made fun of Will Taft's habit of falling asleep at public banquets and things like that. But I don't see anything wrong with it. I myself have fallen asleep at a Fortnightly when one of those speakers went on and on, and I don't think Fog Horne has ever gotten through one without falling asleep sometime. But wake Fog up, and right away he's as sharp as a tack—he wants to know exactly what's going on.

Fog, incidentally, draws the line among your early Presidents with John Quincy Adams. I don't. I draw it with Martin Van Buren. I've always had a sneaking fondness for Martin Van Buren. He wrote his autobiography, you know, and never once mentioned his wife. Now that's what I call a man's man. The General put Teddy Roosevelt up there with your great Presidents. But again I demur. T.R. was a bearcat when it came to foreign affairs but domestically he was very, very left. And don't forget he damn near ruined our language. He was the one who took the "u" out of all those words like "colour" and "humour" and "glamour" and "honour" and all the rest of it. Well, The Society to Put Things Back the Way They Were made short shrift of that. We put those "u's" right back in, Roosevelt or no Roosevelt.

Between Coolidge and Hoover it's awfully hard to choose. Edgy Bull put a lot of pressure on me to choose Coolidge, and there is, of course, a lot to be said for him. But I had to allow for the fact that Edgy has a personal axe to grind—he really has a terrible time with his hearing and anybody as silent as Cal Coolidge would naturally appeal to him. Fish Frobisher, I think I should tell you, wouldn't give an inch on the subject of Hoover. On the other hand, I put in my two cents worth for Harding. I know it's not easy between Harding, Coolidge and Hoover—there is no question but that Hoover had tremendous ability. But my point is you have to remember that Hoover was always doing things. I really don't like my Government doing anything. Harding and Coolidge didn't do a damn thing—you can't name a thing they did—and yet Harding had that scandal too. Outright vilification just like Nixon. Only he rose above it so much better than Nixon. I've always felt he's never been appreciated. To me, he was a brick.

Anyway, without further ado, here are my ratings. As you can see, I have separate categories for Domestic and Foreign Affairs.

PRESIDENT	DOMESTIC	FOREIGN
Roosevelt, T.	Poor	Excellent
Taft	Excellent	Excellent
Wilson	Rotten	Rotten
Harding	Excellent	Excellent
Coolidge	Excellent	Excellent
Hoover	Excellent	Excellent
Roosevelt, F.	Rotten	Rotten
Truman	Rotten	Fair
Eisenhower	Fair	Fair

Kennedy	Rotten	Rotten
Johnson	Rotten	Fair
Nixon	Excellent	Excellent
Carter	Rotten	Poor

Who do I think was the worst President? I know this is going to surprise you because I'm not going to pick your Wilsons or your Franklin Roosevelts or your Trumans or your Lyndon Johnsons or your Kennedys—terrible as they all were—and it's still too early to write my final assessment of this awful Carter. No, the man I am going to pick is one I'll bet you thought was a lead pipe cinch to be one of my favorites—Dwight Eisenhower. The General is always putting in his two cents worth—and that's exactly what his political opinions are worth—for Eisenhower. But you can't go to the bank on that. Those Generals stick together. The reason I picked Eisenhower as the worst is because he was the biggest personal disappointment to me. He had a chance to go in there and call a halt to our damn downward slide and as far as I'm concerned he just got right down in the mud with it. I'm sorry, I've got no use for him. He had everything going his way and he just didn't bet his cards. In his way he let us down just as much as Nixon did.

Wilson was an interesting case. People tend to forget that before he was President of the U.S., he was President of Princeton. People are always exaggerating Princeton. It's always been on the flashy side and in those days it didn't amount to a hill of beans. But one thing Princeton did, and you've got to give it credit for that—it was the place where Wilson showed his stripes. He went after the Clubs down there, you remember—tried to get rid of them because of some damn fool democratic idea. It didn't work, of course, but it should have been a tip-off of what a mess he'd make as President of the country.

Wilson had been a professor too, remember that, before he was President of Princeton. Not every professor's bad news—we've got ours right in the Fortnightly. And there are times when he makes very valuable contributions to our discussions. But as President? Come on now—the very idea is a contradiction in terms. Remember the old adage—"Those who can, do; those who can't, teach." Well, that still stands up, except that nowadays you have them there at your colleges and not even teaching. And your Government, that's you and me, are paying for it. The fact is the very kind of a person who chooses to spend his life with children is a long, long way from the kind of person we want for the highest office in our land.

When you come to Roosevelt, well, of course there you've reached rock bottom. Really, he was in a class by himself—which is just where he belongs after starting that class war thing. I know that pretty nearly everything's been said about him that can be said in a book which women are going to read but something you rarely see mentioned is that, like all people who should never have been chosen himself, he was also a terrible chooser of other people. I can't think of one single solitary appointment that he made that he should have made —and that includes Harry Hopkins and Harry Truman and Henry Wallace and every other Tom, Dick and Harry and Henry. Look, for example, at the trouble he caused by sending Joe Kennedy to the Court of St. James. You might just as well have sent the Kaiser. It was an insult to the British and furthermore it gave prominence to the Kennedys. We'll be paying for that for heaven knows how long.

And never mind all the awful things Roosevelt did, think of what he left us with. Truman! How would you like to have that on your conscience? I've heard people say—I never knew him, of course—that Truman was a kind man and that if you asked him for something he'd give you the shirt off his back. Well, I still remember those shirts he wore and if the only way to get them off his back was to ask him for something, then, dammit, everyone should have been asking him for something every damn day. Lyndon Johnson was just as bad. The only thing you can say for him was that at least he had a first name—he wasn't named Harry or Jimmy. But he was exactly the same type. There are men you put in charge and men you do not put in charge. You give them any sort of job, but you do not put them in charge. There ought to be some qualification that just doesn't allow people like that to get to be President—the way you have your qualification that you have to be born in this country. That's obviously to keep out foreigners. Well, they ought to have another qualification. Like, for example, that one that you had to have at least 100,000 asses. This way you don't have to have 100,000 anything—and that's why we get asses for President.

I tell you if I live to be Oldest Living Member, I'll never forget that Fortnightly we had on the Government. In the first place, the man we'd asked for it to be our guest was the Director of the Budget. And do you know who they sent us? Not the Director, not even the Assistant Director, but the Deputy Assistant Director. Of course it was just one more example of how they don't know anything down there in Washington. A Deputy Assistant Director to Fortnightly! In the second place, the moment I heard about it, I called them down there and do you know the farthest I got? To the *Assistant* of the Deputy Assistant Director. So of course I gave up. What can you do? In the third place, when he arrived, we all looked at him as if we couldn't believe it. He was a child! I know as you grow more mature you go through two stages. First the policemen look like children and then your undergraduates look like babies. But this was something different. When the people you are paying for with your money in Washington begin looking this way you realize it's not you, it's them. From the moment he entered the room, he looked just like a child who had been caught stealing from the cookie jar. And of course he had—only it was your and my cookies. Budget, I said to Witter. He wouldn't know a budget from a beagle. I remember when we used to say that Roosevelt had never met a payroll—well, this boy had never met a piggy bank. He was one of your nervous Nellies, too. He couldn't look you in the eye. He had a sickly grin—and a terrible suit. At dinner I had to ask him where he was from, of course, for my introduction. And he said Ypsilanti. I thought he was making a joke, but he wasn't. I know there are people who had to go to places like that, on business trips and so forth, but you never think of anyone as *coming* from there. Anyway, after dinner he gave his little speech, which was of course of no consequence.

Well, as I've told you, the whole idea of Fortnightly is that their speeches don't matter a damn—it's what we can tell them afterwards. And you can imagine this time it got pretty warm. Even Tubby got excited. Tubby tries to like everybody and he rarely gets excited. But this time what happened was Tubby asked the man where he'd been to school. And you know what the man said? He named his high school. That was the tip-off. Well, Tubby tried to make it simple for him. He first explained to the man that when someone asks you what school you went to, they mean what college. And then he told the man that what worried him about the Government spending money like it was was that it was just like what was going on at his college. Tubby told the man that he'd been back to his Twenty-fifth, and from what he'd seen with his own eyes, he wasn't going to give the school another penny. Tubby had entered his own son, you know, and what had happened is that his son hadn't gotten in. Imagine, ten unbroken generations of Tubbys—broken, kaput, fini—all because Tubby said the school now goes all over the damn world getting these damn geniuses—they get them literally from anywhere, Brooklyn, Tierra del Fuego, anywhere. They get them, take them in, and then they don't even have the decency to graduate. They just stay on—M.A., Ph.D., on and on. They just stay there and help each other or the damn Government or something, and all this time Tubby and the rest of us are supposed to *support* them while Little Tubby walks the streets. Tubby told the story very quietly—it was really very moving. He said it was all the Government's fault for helping such people. And when he got through, he just turned to the man and asked what he was going to do about that. And do you know what that man had the gall to say? He said it wasn't his department!

Well, Edgy Bull, as I've told you, doesn't hear very well with that damn hearing aid of his, and of course he didn't get the word "department"—he thought the man said "Dartmouth." Edgy doesn't like Dartmouth—he says they wear mackinaws up there. Anyway, when we finally got that straightened out, Fog Horne asked the man what the hell was his department. And at that the fellow went into a long rigmarole—all weasel talk, of course—and during it darned if old Foggy didn't fall asleep. The fellow saw it, of course, and when he finally finished he asked Foggy sarcastically if he understood now. Well, the fact that he stopped talking woke Foggy up, and Foggy, quick as a flash, said it wasn't his department. I tell you it was rich.

We all zeroed in on the dollar, of course. We told that bird that we were prepared to defend the dollar down to the last man, and if he didn't have the gumption to defend it in Washington, at least he'd learn there were people who would. Even the General got in on that. The General told the man that ever since the trouble about the dollar, he had never knowingly bought a single piece of foreign merchandise except the *New York Times*. When it came my turn I got up and gave the man a dollar bill out of my own pocket, I told him that when his Franklin Delano Roosevelt abrogated the dollar contract on that bill—to pay the bearer in *gold*—well, had welshed is what he had done. And ever since, as far as I was concerned, with all due respect to my friends in Wales, they've had nothing down there in Washington but one Welshman after another.

I next asked him if he had been to Switzerland lately, or Japan, or any other damn place. Of course he hadn't—they just hole up down there—and so I told him about Schermerhorn Fish's dinner and hotel room in Geneva. Skimmy, you know, paid $90 for his dinner and $160 for his hotel room. The man had never heard of Skimmy. But I didn't let him off the hook with that. I told him he ought to be ashamed of himself, that a tiny little country which makes watches, for God's sake—good watches, yes, but just the same, watches—could keep a decent currency and we couldn't. As for the Japanese yen, I told him, if there was anything that made my blood boil, it was all this talk about the damn yen. Yen, yen, yen, I told him. That's all you hear. Well, I said, when I wanted to hear about the yen, I'd let him know. And meanwhile he could stop printing money down there as if there was no tomorrow. Because tomorrow, in case he didn't know it, was yesterday.

The man asked me what business I was in. I told him I was in every business he could name. And then I asked him how long he thought he would be drawing his salary if there weren't someone like me keeping my money in stocks come hell or high water. My thin green line, I told him he could call my stocks. Out there on the firing line, fighting the good fight against him and labor and slovenly workmanship and no service and rotten deliveries and all the enemies of decent capitalism. And don't you forget it, I told him, they're getting damn tired out there on that line. After all, they've been there for damn near fifty years. I told him I was getting tired too. I said that he would probably think that a man like myself who had stuck to his guns and keeps his soldiers up at the front through thick and thin would be a multimillionaire by now. A multi! I said. Hell, I wasn't even half of one millionaire. I was practically a pauper. And meanwhile I had to sit and see those damn rock singers who couldn't hold a tune if their lives depended on it, and those awful movie moguls and those stars and athletes and the rest of them—I had to see them make more in a year than I had made in my lifetime. Why, I asked him, why? But when he started to answer, I stopped him. One thing I didn't want was any answers from him.

But the man broke in anyway. He said he didn't have anything to do with the stock market. I had to smile at that. Listen, I told him, you and your Government down there play with the stock market like a child with a toy. I told him that all his boys down at the Federal Reserve had to do was to just think of someone like me and they'd put up their interest rates and send me one step nearer to the poorhouse. Oh, he said, I was talking about the M1 figures. I stopped him again. Don't talk to me

94

about those Mi's I told him. That money supply, or money in circulation, or whatever it's supposed to be. Those figures are just nonsense. In my day, I told him, we had decent indices— your carloadings, your housing starts, things like that—things you could get your teeth into. I told him he had put out those damn Mi figures every Thursday night. All right, Thursday nights were never easy with the maids out. But today they'd made my Thursday night impossible. They'd come out with those figures Thursday night and bingo, Friday morning, down go my stocks.

At this the man said that I should realize that they were talking down in Washington about a "tax reform act." Again, I stopped him. I said all those tax reform acts of 1969 and 1976 ever did was to boost the rate on my capital gains from twenty-five to forty-nine percent. Forty-nine percent! Half my profit, mind you, for them. And, I told him, they weren't actually capital *gains* at all. I told him if he ever learned the rudiments of economics he could figure out that my capital gains were a hell of a lot more like losses—if you took into account the fact that the damn dollar wasn't worth anywhere near half of what it used to be.

Finally, I told him I had heard he was proposing a capital gains tax break for, if you please, the middle class only. Once more he started to interrupt. But this time I wouldn't even let him start. What the hell, I asked him, did he mean for the middle class only? I knew only too well what he meant. He was going to leave me out. Well, I told him, I'd tell him something. I would rather be left out than put in the middle—if he would pardon the expression—of something there wasn't any more of. I told him there was no more middle class in America than there was in Russia. There was just the Government and the unions on top and then there was me, the last of the peasants.

After I was through Fish Frobisher gave the man one of the clearest examples of Government meddling I ever heard. Fish really spelled it out. Fish told him very slowly, so the man would understand it, that three of the best known families in America—the Whitneys, the Wideners and the Ryans—all made their fortunes by transporting the public—with good, polite service, he emphasized—for a five-cent fare. And all in a day when there was a hell of a lot less public than there was today. Today, Fish told the man, New York City was going broke with a fifty-cent fare and the best thing he could do was give those subways back to the Whitneys, the Wideners and the Ryans, and be quick about it.

Witter Hardee came up with a beauty. Witter had been reading a study put out by the Brookings Institute. They had examined Government agencies for fifty years, Witter told the man, and said that of the 175 agencies existing in 1923, only 27 of them had, by 1973, disappeared. And meanwhile, 246 new agencies had been born. In other words, for every one that died, ten were born. Witter told the man he'd done some figuring on this and he figured by the year 2,000 everyone would be in an agency and the only answer he could see for it was birth control.

Well, that set us off on the population problem. And that Government man, if you can believe it, didn't come up with a single idea for a solution. Personally, I thought one of the best ideas was, of all people's, Tubby's. Tubby's idea was that they put the Pill into the hamburgers at McDonalds and Burger King, and also into the chicken at Kentucky Fried Chicken and places like that. We all agreed we wouldn't mind the everlasting advertisements of those places on television if you could be sure that with every bite one of those children took some day there'd be less of them.

Finally, Fog Horne, as I knew he would—he always does—brought up the question of a minimum wage. If there's anything Fog hates worse than people who tinker with the Constitution, it's that damn minimum wage. He told the man frankly that of all the examples of misguided meddling, the minimum wage was the worst, and if that man raised it once more, we might as well fold up the Club. He told him we weren't talking about William or Henry or any of those. But how in the devil could we afford to try to break in people when this damn Government was demanding that we pay them as if they were a finished product? Fog told the man that if anyone down there in Washington had the brains they must have had before they went there, they wouldn't have any minimum wage—what they should have for labor would be a maximum wage. Fog gave the man two choices—either he put in a good honest-to-God low maximum wage, or, Fog said, he was going to call a Constitutional Convention.

Fish Frobisher made the last and I thought best suggestion of all—that tomorrow morning the Government cut every wage in the country ten percent. I seconded Fish's motion, and then told the man that besides a wage cut they should also immediately stop these God-awful cost of living increases. What the devil, I asked him, was cost of living increase anyway? And then I held up my hand, because again the last thing I wanted was his answer. It was one more excuse, I told him, to "gimme" to some good for nothing at the expense of me. He gets the cost of living and I get the increase. Both Fish and I agreed that every time the cost of living index went up, they should cut wages by exactly the same percent. The minute you get those damned wages down, your inflation will stop, your dollar will go back up, the people will go back to work and all the troubles that plague us will go by the board. Once Labor got used to the idea that everything that goes up must come down—they've never lived through a real Depression, you know like I did—well, in no time at all we'd get the ship back on an even keel. And then we'd keep on rolling her back, inch by inch, if we had to, winch her back if necessary, but anyway get her back the way things were in the old days.

I tell you that fellow never knew what hit him. He was reeling by the time he was ready to leave. But at least he got some damn good advice that he wouldn't forget in a hurry. On the way out, however, as the man was saying goodbye to me he had the nerve to ask why, if I was having such a hard time, I didn't use my dividends. At first I just looked at him. I didn't trust myself. But then I let him have it with both barrels. I told him that even a newborn babe in arms knows that my dividends are not just taxed once—they are taxed twice. Once when the Government gets it out of the company before they give it to me, and then once more when the Government breaks down my door and gets it again from me. My dividends! I told him I might as well stuff them down the toilet—although I said that I wasn't sure but that that would be just the place where the IRS would be waiting to get them a third time. I told him I didn't know whether he had anything to do with the IRS people or not, but that if he did, that last little jackass who audited me —honestly, if you said he came out of the woodwork you'd be paying him a compliment.

Well, after the man had gone and we were holding our usual postmortems, I tell you it was a very solemn group. The Professor had some ideas about it, but naturally he was the last person we wanted to hear from, so we all joined the General in not speaking to him. After I was back in my room, though, I did some philosophical thinking. Here was I, I thought, an individual entrepreneur for half a century, and where was I? I go into a store and it doesn't make the slightest difference what price they put on anything, because whatever I want I have to multiply by five—that's about the size of it for someone in the eighty percent tax bracket. If I want to buy a camera, say, for forty dollars, do you know what that camera costs me? Two hundred dollars, that's what. So naturally, I can't afford to take pictures. And that's why there are no pictures in this book. Don't blame me—blame your Government.

The pathetic part of my situation is that no one understands it. Particularly women don't understand it. Women are hell about money, anyway. But tax brackets they just simply cannot fathom. You take one of them to dinner and you see a steak, say, which costs twelve dollars. Well, it just isn't polite of course, to point out to her that that's sixty dollars to you, and that obviously, if she really wants it, the best thing for her to do would be to buy for herself in that little tax bracket. That's one sensible thing women's liberation has done—let the women pay.

The other day, for example, I took a woman to the theatre, and made the suggestion—that we walk rather than take a taxi. She wouldn't do it—she said her hair would get blown—you know how women are. So what could I do? We took a ransom cab, as Witter calls them. Their rates are really awful. I took one to a funeral not long ago, just around the corner, really, but with the traffic and all when we got there, the bill was $1.80, so I gave the man $2.00, and told him to keep the change.

Whereupon he turned around and gave me a piece of his mind —which, even if he'd given me all of it, would, I assure you, have been no bargain. I tell you he practically flung that 20 cents back at me. Of course I took it, and when he got through his tirade, I very quietly asked him if he knew what 20 cents was to someone in the eighty percent bracket. He didn't, of course —I might as well have been speaking Greek. So, still keeping my voice down, I told him it was very nearly a dollar, and if he didn't want his twenty cents, I most certainly did want my dollar. And with that I put it back in my pocket and got out of the cab. That was one man, I assure you, who the next time he has someone in his cab in a high income bracket will at least show some consideration for him.

The long and short of it all is that, with taxes what they are today, there is no way to make enough money, even for the bare necessities of life, in the stock market or anywhere else, except to steal it. That's what those movie moguls and people like that have been doing and frankly, I understand it. But even if you steal it, you know you have to declare it. I'm not joking. I read an article about it. A fellow who stole $84,304—I kept the clipping—over a three-year period, from an amusement park. And then he quit his job. Well, the amusement park went after him and caught him and then the fellow really behaved very handsomely, I thought. He not only admitted what he had done and promised to pay it all back, but he also did pay it back—and with interest too. The only thing he didn't do was report the stolen money on his income tax. He said he didn't know you had to report stolen money. So then comes along the Government and gave him that usual "ignorance is no excuse" argument, and not only got its taxes from the fellow but hit him for a fifty percent fraud penalty, too. I tell you, that IRS ought to be ashamed of itself. That's not even robbing Peter to pay Paul. That's robbing Peter to rob Paul.

CHAPTER V

Women

BEFORE we start on this most painful of subjects, particularly nowadays, with this utterly damnable women's liberation thing, I think I should make it clear there will be several matters to be discussed in this chapter which should, on the whole, be kept from the eyes of the gentler sex. Not that we will be discussing matters of the boudoir—naturally we will place that chapter off limits. But the fact of the matter is, right in this chapter, we will be discussing not only very depressing things, but very emotional things, and I would like to bring to bear on it as much logic and as little emotion as possible. I think therefore it would be best for it to be done without people who are, after all, almost entirely emotions. I also don't want to have to explain myself every two minutes, the way you have to when you're carrying on almost any conversation, let alone one about women, at which women are present.

All in all, then, I think it would be best to do it as one would have an after dinner discussion among gentlemen with the cigars and the brandy after the women have gone off to wherever it is they go and discuss their children and their shopping and their servants and whatever else they like to discuss. Also, boudoir or no boudoir, there will even here be frank discussion of matters which, in the interests of delicacy, all decent women should wish to avoid. Therefore, without further ado, I'm going at this point to bid adieu to my fair readers. I suggest we meet again at the chapter marked "Children." Thank you.

To begin with, when you're talking men, you're thinking men—or at least men and gentlemen. But when you're talking women, right at the start, you're talking nice girls, and you're also talking the other kind. They're two entirely different breeds of cat. They always have been, and they always will be, I don't care how far this damn liberationing goes. Even your nice girl category, as a matter of fact, breaks down into at least four subcategories. At the top you've got your real ladies, and then underneath them you've got in order, your ordinary women, your shop girls and finally, your flibbertigibbets.

Don't ask me to distinguish between them—not nowadays. No, I'll take French leave on that. Which, if I do say so, is a pretty apt expression for it today. But no matter. Where was I? Oh, flibbertigibbets. Well, let me tell you something. Don't think for a minute your flibbertigibbets are just your actresses and your chorus girls and your models and so forth—they're not. Your flibbertigibbets today are in every walk of woman-life today. Believe me, I know.

Well hold on now. I want to amend that. *Almost* every walk. Cornelia, my first wife, was certainly no flibbertigibbet. As a matter of fact, I don't want to say one word against her. She wasn't the brightest woman in the world, and God knows she wasn't the prettiest, and she would try the patience of a Job, and she was a plain damn fool to divorce me—I am sure she knows that now—but the point is she was no flibbertigibbet. Now Muffie, my second wife, on the other hand, was a flibber-tigibbet. Honestly she didn't have the sense God gave little fishes. It wasn't so much she didn't think—she literally couldn't think. I used to ask her sometimes, when she'd lost something, to think where she'd put it, and then of course, I'd realize that I'd asked the impossible.

Why, I can hear you asking, did I marry Muffie? God only knows. Because love is blind, I guess, and I'm the marrying kind. But the only kind who ever should have married Muffie should have been blind *and* deaf. God, how that woman could talk. I don't think she ever had a thought in her life she didn't say out loud. And the trouble was, her little mind couldn't keep up with that voice of hers. You really can't imagine what it was like, trying to think what was going on in her mind, at the same time that awful little baby voice was going on and on.

But no matter. I don't want to criticize Muffie any more than I want to criticize Cornelia. Bygones are bygones. The important thing is not to get personal about women—that's the way they are, and the last thing you want to be is dragged down to their level. Which brings me to the other kind of women. As I said at the beginning, and I want to repeat it here so that there will be no mistake—there are two kinds of women—the kind you marry, or should marry, and the kind you shouldn't. All right, I said I wouldn't criticize Muffie. She's married to somebody else now—God help him—but I'll tell you one thing. I'll wager anything you want that by now even he knows that as far as being the marrying kind, Muffie's on the borderline.

But the point is, and I want this clearly understood too, I am not running down those other kinds of women. Quite the contrary. Indeed, I believe that what's happened to ladies and nice girls and flibbertigibbets is not nearly as important in the whole general picture of the trouble with nowadays, as what's happened to the other kind of women. All right, there are fewer ladies around than there used to be—in fact most of these young people today wouldn't know one if they fell over her. And I can prove that. Witter Hardee's cousin is a member of the California Club out in San Francisco—a pretty decent little place, as I understand it—and he wrote Witter that they had one of these sidewalk interviewers out there in the newspaper, and this fellow asked people what a lady was. And you know what the first person he asked said? He said it was someone who wears a funny hat. You know there was some truth in that. Some of Cornelia's hats wouldn't go through a revolving door. But the second man the fellow asked—asked—he was evidently a very young man—he thought the reporter fellow was referring to the girl he lived with. They have an expression for it, you know. I believe they call such a person "my old lady." Why I don't know, and frankly I don't care. But Witter also said that a few days later that same sidewalk interviewer asked people what a "gentleman" was, and one man said—Witter wrote it down for me word for word—here, I have it here. "You can find," the man said, "gentlemen in England and in parts of

France and especially in Italy and Spain, but there aren't any in the United States." Not any—isn't that rich? Just the same, that young fellow wasn't too far wrong, was he?

Where were we? Oh, about there being fewer ladies. Well, there are fewer ladies than there were, it's true. But, when you get right down to it, there are less of all the amenities. And while it's important, I suppose, to have ladies to keep up the standards and things, it really is more important, when you get right down to basics, to have the other kind of women. Those you just have to have. It's just a plain damn fact of life—life can't run without them, at least it can't run decently. No, I'll go further—it just can't run at all, as even this damn liberation thing is finding out right now. Why do you think we have all these Playboy Clubs and massage parlors and pornography right on the street? I'll tell you why we have them. We have them because they've ruined the other kind of women, that's why we have them.

It really makes me heartsick. They were wonderful in the old days, those other kind of women—they were there when you needed them, before marriage, and a few years after marriage, and that sort of thing. And they were, like so many other people in those days, damn good at their job. They were mistresses is what they were—it was just as important a word in the old days as lady was. Different, but just as important. It wasn't easy being a mistress, you know. There are a lot of damn lonely times, when they're just waiting around for you. But my point is that in those days, it was not only a place for everything and everything in its place, there was also a place for *everyone* and *everyone* in his or her place. And an important place for those particular ones was being mistresses.

I'll tell you something frankly. I don't think there's a single man at the Club—or a married man, either—who had a mistress who's even in the same league as the mistresses I knew in my youth. Today they're either always after you every minute to marry them, or if they're not, they're trying to take you to the poorhouse. Tubby's mistress, for example, runs Tubby ragged—honestly she runs him raggeder than Betty Bull runs Edgy. And that woman Fog Horne brought in here on the last Family Night, if they'd turned the lights up, poor Foggy would have run, let alone the rest of us. But Foggy had had champagne—Foggy's no good on champagne.

Remember, though I said I wanted to keep this thing impersonal, and I do. I also want to make clear that, despite my own personal misfortunes with women, I personally do not go along with some Members of the Club who believe that all women are dumb. All women aren't dumb. I've had some very intelligent conversations with women, not only at dinner parties but in other locations I don't care to mention. I have found, for example, that, generally speaking, women are better card players than men. They are almost as good backgammon players— indeed, if it wasn't for the numbers, and the counting and the doubling, I think they'd be just as good. I'll even tell you one more thing. I once lost a game of chess to a woman. I know you're not going to believe that, but it's the honest truth, as God is my witness. Of course, there was a perfectly good reason. If I may digress a moment, I will tell you the reason.

I read somewhere, and I have no reason to dispute it, that the average human brain acquires, from the time of your birth to the time of your death, ninety-eight million ideas. I don't remember for certain, but I assume that statistic was talking about the average male brain. But even the average female brain I would assume, absorbs perhaps forty-nine million ideas. Now the female head isn't that much smaller than ours, so what it means is that their brains are rarely as full as ours are. Your brain, you see, is like a cup. And frankly, my cup runneth over. If I get another idea, the fact is, I've got to discard one I've already got to make room for it. That's why I'm always forgetting names. A woman's brain, on the other hand, not being full, is always able to put another idea in. That's why it's so important, when you're talking to a woman —about politics, or economics or something important—that you put in good ideas. But in another way, it's exactly why I lost that game of chess. Her little cup probably not being even half full, she, of course, remembered that variation of the Sicilian Defense, which I had had to discard. It was just as simple as that.

But as I say, there's no use talking about it personally. And there is no use saying that nowadays has just ruined one kind of woman. Nowadays has ruined both kinds of women, that's what it's done. And the important thing is to find where the whole damn downhill slide began. Because it's no slide now— it's a damn toboggan ride.

Let's back up a little on this thing. What was your highest civilization? Right, Greece. Before Rome was even heard of, mind you. And what was the position of women in Greece? You don't even have to take my word for it—take Xenophon's. In my day, I read my Xenophon in the original Greek—that's another trouble with these young people today. They never read anything in the original anything. I could read it to you, out of my old college copy. But I couldn't find it. It had a lot better print than the one at the Library. I've told you they keep making the print smaller and smaller to cut corners—typical shoddy stuff. But the point is the same. Anyway, I found my old trot, and I'll give it to you from that. Let's see, where is it? All right, here it is: This fellow, Ischomachos—he was a well-born fellow and very well-connected, like myself, I guess. Anyway, Xenophon says he was educating his new bride. She was fifteen —that's the age brides were in Greece in those days. And a good age too, when you come right down to it, before any of this do-what-you-please stuff sets in. Anyway, up till then she'd obviously been brought up right—by her parents. Here it is: "The greatest pains," Xenophon tells us, "had been taken by her parents so that she might see as little as possible, hear as little as possible and, above all, ask the fewest possible questions."

Just picture that for a minute. Imagine today a girl brought up to ask the fewest possible questions. I tell you I sometimes thought that if Muffie asked me one more question, I'd strangle her. And the worst of it was, she asked all the questions to make conversation, and she didn't even listen to the answers, and so, of course, in no time at all, you'd get the same damn question all over again. But excuse me—I promised I wouldn't go on about Muffie.

Where were we? Oh, about that fifteen-year-old. Well, and this is a literal translation now, right out of my old trot. Here: "Once," it says, "his wife had been broken in, and had grown used to her husband's hand," well, then Ischomachos started his instructions. "Men," he told her, "are strong, and they must go out to contend with the elements. And, if need be, with other men to get a living for the family. Women on the other hand, are physically weak—therefore, God meant them to live in the house." And that isn't all. "They are timid," Ischomachos went on, "while men are bold. They are stewards, while men are acquirers."

Ischomachos was talking about your average woman, of course. I never thought of Cornelia as timid. But no matter. "Women," he continued, "are naturally fonder of babies than men are; by this discrimination, God beckons women to the nursery."

Of course what Xenophon and Ischomachos were talking about here is man and nature and the laws of nature, which nowadays people act as if they don't exist. One young fellow in the Club told me he actually looks after his children half the time. Just picture it—half the time. He said he and his wife went fifty-fifty on all the chores. Half and half, really! That's what we are nowadays, half and half. Nobody's anything—I don't care whether it's the cream for your cereal, or your laws of nature.

Anyway, after Ischomachos got through telling his bride about life, he told her what her duties were, and how she should organize her slaves. How she was to choose some for outdoor work and some for indoor—that sort of thing. But one thing here is especially interesting. He told her she would have one duty which he was afraid she would find disagreeable—she would have to look after any slave who fell ill. Ischomachos was sure she wouldn't like it. But instead she looked at him—"lovingly," it says—and then she said, "That will be the most pleasant task of all. Because it will make them fonder of me."

Well, Isomachos was very pleased with this answer, of course, and so he then went on and told her about looking after their household goods—again, that good old truth about a place for everything and everything in its place. But here he warned her that she must not think the slaves would do this since she shouldn't either expect or trust them to take the same interest in the property as she, the owner of the property. To this the wife replied that it would be as natural for a woman to look after her belongings as it would be to look after her children—that he would have given her a more difficult task if he had bidden her to take no heed in these matters.

Ischomachos was so keen on this answer that he went right over and told his friend Socrates about it. Isn't that interesting? I told you he was well-connected. Anyway, Socrates made a memorable comment. "By Hera, Ischomachos," he said, "your wife reasons like a man." It was typical of the man that he phrased it that delicately—with the oath not to a god but to a goddess.

Actually, just about the only trouble Ischomachos had with this girl was over the matter of cosmetics. His wife put a lot of powder on her face. Well, naturally Ischomachos was good and sore about that. But instead of doing nothing about it, as these damn namby-pamby modern husbands do, he went right to the mat about it. He told her that what she was doing was just as dishonest and dishonorable a thing as it would be for him to deceive her about the extent of his property. And then he added what I think was a wonderful touch—he told her that her deception might fool others, but how could it fool her husband, who would, after all, be sure to notice it either early in the morning, before it had been applied, or after her bath, or when she was crying.

The good wife, of course, saw the point—although she did express the worry that her skin might not look healthy enough if she didn't get out of doors. At this Ischomachos very properly, I think, informed her that there was no necessity for her to go out—that outdoor air was necessary for men but indoor air was all that was necessary for women.

I ask you, where would you find a girl like that today? You might as well save yourself the trouble of looking. Where are the snows of yesteryear? And, speaking of snows, Ischomachos talking about that powder brought me back again to Muffie. If there is anything that makes my blood boil, it's a painted peacock. I was brought up that lips that touch paint shall never touch mine. Honestly, Muffie wore so much paint I told her one day if she didn't take some of it off, I'd sell her as a piece of modern art.

But enough of Greece. It's Rome where this whole damnable woman thing really began to come apart at the seams. The Romans, to put it bluntly, really went berserk on the subject of women. Go back to Gibbon—you'll find the seeds right there. Rome was Rome, Gibbon tells us in crystal clear language, " 'til," and I quote, "female blandishments insensibly triumphed, and every salutary restraint was lost."

The irony is that Rome started out in great shape on this thing. In Stoic Rome, the Roman father—*pater familias*—was *pater potestas,* the absolute authority. And, mind you, not only over his women and children and slaves but specifically over his girl-babies. Naturally they weren't regarded as important as boy-babies, and in Stoic Rome's great days, the law stated very clearly that "if the child were deformed or female," the father was permitted to "expose it to death." I know it sounds heartless, and I don't necessarily believe it's the answer to today's problems, but again the point is the threat should be there. After all, it puts the whole man-woman relationship in the proper perspective.

When it came to marriage, Rome went Greece one better.

Ischomachos' wife was, as both Xenophon and I mentioned, fifteen—well, your average Roman wife was between thirteen and fifteen. Some were older, it is true. Cicero, for example, married a seventeen-year-old, but there was good reason for it. He was sixty-three. Anyway, the most important thing was that the father arranged the marriages of his sons, and well before the girls had gotten to that awful sexy age when they don't know what the devil they're doing anyway. A son could not marry without his father's consent, and even after he had, his wife still came under his father's power in every way until the father had given her special permission to marry *cum manu*— literally from his hand to his son's hand.

In your great days of Rome too, your whole divorce thing was beautifully handled. The way it worked was your husband got his divorce just by giving his wife a letter. Imagine. "Dear Muffie," I could have written, and that would have been that —instead of all these years of this damn alimony. Well, I'm digressing again. But the point is the father could not only divorce his wife, he could also divorce his daughter-in-law too if, in his judgment—not his son's, mind you—she didn't come up to snuff. Just picture all the trouble that would save in these modern marriages, and the father did it in the same way he did his own—just with a letter.

Before some of you modernists, however, start condemning Rome, remember something. Compared to Greece, it still represented an advance for women. Most of these so-called advances that I've seen in my lifetime are like that old game we used to play—one step forward and three backward. But no matter. What I'm saying is that your Roman wife was not like your Greek wife, confined to her *gynaecum.* I can see some of my younger readers reading gymnasium for that, and thinking

114

about these modern women athletes—it was *gyn,* not *gym,* like gynecology. I don't know exactly what it was, but anyway, it was where your Greek women stayed—ate there and everything. A Roman wife ate right with her husband, although of course, she sat, while he reclined.

What these modern fellows forget is that throughout history the most highly respected authorities always believed in the basic idea of male tutelage for women. Paul, for one. Paul stated very clearly that women should take a subordinate place. He was a particular bearcat on women being quiet in church. "If they want to find out anything," was the way he put it—in Latin of course—"they should ask their husbands at home." That's good advice—not only for women in church, but when they go out anywhere. All of Roman law, as a matter of fact, was based on the idea that your woman was never, as they put it, *sui iuris*—of her own right. She was always dependent on some male guardian. Gaius, perhaps, put it best. "According to our ancestors," he said, "even women of mature age must be kept in tutelage because of the lightness of their minds." That's a good word to remember—"lightness."

Don't forget that this book is based on the changes from Caesar's death to my birth vs. my birth to now. But I'll tell you that you can even go back to Caesar's birth on this woman thing. Caesar and I are particularly close on this. Caesar had a wife named Cornelia, too, you know. She was his second wife, Cossutia, his first wife, was the daughter of a knight. But remember in those days a knight wasn't a knight as we understand it today. Fish Frobisher, for example, is a real knight—with a right to a coat of arms and all the rest of it. But in those days a knight didn't have a thing to do with ancestral distinction. Your knight in those days was just your ordinary banker

—actually well down the social scale. For a young man like Caesar, who had bully ancestry, his marriage to Cossutia was little short of a misalliance. The fact is it happened when Caesar was very young, and when his uncle, Marius, frankly needed the money. Anyway, Caesar divorced Cossutia and married Cornelia, who was the daughter of Cinna, the head of the *Popularae.* When you compare his Cornelia with my Cornelia, it's apples and oranges. And remember, Cornelia was his *second.* When you compare his Cornelia with my Muffie, you're talking night and day. Actually Caesar liked Cornelia so much that even when Sulla tried to get him to divorce her, Caesar, much to his credit, refused. And then after Cornelia died, Caesar's wives, after her, were Pompeia and Calpurnia. *Two* more. Well, that's Caesar's business, not mine. I wouldn't have one more if you gave *me* alimony. But I can't help reminiscing about them. Talk about being above suspicion, and comparing Caesar's wives with my wives, it's heart-rending. But it's water over the dam now.

Well, as I said at the beginning of this chapter, Gibbon tells us what happened. When your men abdicate, your women fill the vacuum. Step by step, Rome went down the drain. The women might just as well have unlocked the gates, and let the barbarians in—they were that responsible.

Actually the parallel with our decline and fall today is frightening. You give your wife more freedom, then your children want it—your daughter, mind you, as well as your son—and then what do you get. Steady anarchy is what you get, and that's just what Rome got and that's just what we've got today. In Rome's great days, when you had your regular complaints about married life—everybody gets those—you went to a goddess. It was a mistake, of course, to have it be a goddess. It would have been better to go to a god—but your gods were probably too busy with more important things. Anyway, your goddess for marital complaints was obviously the right sort of goddess. They called her *Viriplaca*. Again, you have to know your Latin to get things right and know what I am talking about. *Viriplaca*, for your information, means "Appeaser of Husbands"—and that's why I say she was the right sort.

In Rome's great days too when a husband found his wife guilty of some sin—one of the ones often mentioned was getting ahold of the keys to the wine cellar—Muffie, you know, was impossible after that second cocktail—well, anyway, in those days a wife who did that was, as Gibbon clearly tells us, "stripped of all her wealth and ornaments, not even excepting the bodkin in her hair."

I don't want to imply that the women in Rome didn't have a perfectly respectable place. They did—as childbearers. In those days, remember, children were useful. But the wise Roman rulers realized that that was woman's place and not some other damn place, and they made no bones about it. The Censor, Metellus Macedonicus, for example, asked men to marry and beget children as a duty to the State, but he asked them to do it, in his words, "however much of a *molesta* a wife may be." Do you know what *molesta* means? Of course you don't. Well, it means nuisance—that's what it means. And if there had been more Metellus Macedonicii, maybe Rome wouldn't have gone down. But the fact is the seeds of Rome's destruction were sown right after the Punic Wars. Because right then, Gibbon tells us, the matrons of Rome started doing anything they pleased. "They defeated," he tells us, "the solemnities of the old nuptials" and even "kept their own names." So much for this modern thing women now seem to think they've discovered.

In plain words, dammit, they didn't bother about marriage anymore, they just up and cohabited, the way these young people do today—like rabbits in a warren. But it wasn't only in their personal life that women let go—they also ran rampant publicly. Your Roman women began to go about just as freely as men. Some women, it is true, went in the direction they should go—poetry and art and things like that. Frankly I have no objection to women even going into writing—some of them are remarkably good at certain kinds of writing, like letters. But I generally agree with Pliny about this. He said that his wife delighted to read his works over and over, and read few other people. Now that's a literarily inclined woman one could live with, and not all this everlasting criticizing.

But anyway, as I was saying, your Roman woman not only went into decent fields, she also up and went into everything you can shake a stick at—politics, law, medicine, sport. They even became gladiators. Clodia, the wife of Quintus Caecilius Metellus, was a particular troublemaker. She believed in women's rights—something as I say, these women today think they have discovered. The fact of the matter is it's always been around, like any other dark side of life. In any case one of the things Clodia did was to go around after her marriage, unchaperoned, with male escorts. The idea of doing something like that *before* marriage was, fortunately, unheard of. But even doing it after marriage was bad enough, and signaled the beginning of the end. Clodia, in fact, actually kissed her male escorts in public. Cato was furious about this as well he might have been for what it portended. Cato had already, you remem-

ber, banished Manilius for kissing his wife in public. Cato himself was beyond reproach on this thing. He once said he never
embraced his wife except during a thunderstorm.

That is, of course, extreme—after all there're not that many
thunderstorms in the winter—but my point is Cato stood four-
square for the old virtues. He told the Romans frankly that if
they had made it a rule and maintained, as he put it, "the
prerogative and authority of a husband," they would have had
—and I quote him again—"less trouble with the whole sex."
Cato also spoke of the awful habits women had gotten into.
"What sort of practice is this," he asked, "of running out into
the public, besetting the streets and addressing other women's
husbands?" And then he asked the question that should have
been asked of every such woman then and now. "Could not,"
he asked, "each of those same women have made the same
request to her husband at home?" And then he made his final
point—he had great logic, you know, something we have too
damn little of today. "Are your blandishments," he asked,
"more seductive in public than in private, and with other
women's husbands than your own?"

All right then, I assume we are agreed that the chief reason
Rome fell was because of women. But remember something.
Even Rome in all its awful decline and fall never fell upon the
kind of women we have today. And don't forget either I've seen
it all in my brief lifetime. As far as I'm concerned it's the
cornerstone of my argument that I've seen worse changes in
my lifetime than from Caesar's death to me. Honestly where
women are concerned, there's no comparison. I have problems
here Caesar never dreamed of. I tell you if Caesar could have

imagined the women of today he wouldn't have married at all, let alone four times.

You think I'm exaggerating? I wish I were. Rome never, for example, had a women's club—or even a woman *in* a club. Today I go to the squash court—the squash court, mind you, the squash court in a Gentleman's Club—and who sits down beside me? I'll tell you who—a sweaty woman, that's who. I don't like to use the word, but that's what they are today. In my day we used to say, "A horse sweats, a man perspires, and a woman glows." But what's the use of even thinking about things like that today? They'd probably put you in jail for "sexual prejudice."

Rome had a few women in sports all right, as I told you, even a few women gladiators. All right again. What have we got? We've got women jockeys, for heaven's sake, and women wrestlers, and women boxers. Boxers! I tell you. Do you know who's rowing on my old 150-pound crew today? Four women, that's who. Why, you ask, why? Well, I'll tell you why. Because I know women, and I know children, and I'll tell you something. Women are exactly like children. They always want to go wherever you don't want them to go, and they also want to go wherever they're not wanted. I said that way back when they gave them the vote. I was just a little tyke then, but I could see what was happening. I remember right where I was standing. I remember Tubby was with me, and Tubby didn't pay any attention. But I said, "Tubby, you mark my words. They won't stop with the vote." I said it then and if I said it once, I've said it a thousand times, and I'll keep saying it till doomsday— which, by my figuring is the day after tomorrow. Do you know what Tubby was doing the last time I saw him at his house? His own dishes, that's what he was doing. While his wife, if you please, sat and talked to me.

Well, we all realize it now, of course. They got the vote and then they brought their friends, as I knew they would. And they just kept hounding and pounding away, day after day, and worst of all, night after night. Honest to Pete, all you have to do nowadays is put up a sign, "Men Only," and you'll have the place crawling with women. Men's Bar, Men's Grill, Men's Room—I don't care what it is, it's the same damn thing. We used to have a sign in the bar "Accompanied Male Guests Only." Do you know where it is now—some woman thought it was so funny she took it home as a souvenir—and now of course they're cackling around that bar at all hours of the day and night. They are banging down the doors everywhere is what they're doing. Not even a "Keep Out" sign does any good. And the irony is that women are supposed to be the guardians of manners. Well, how do you think manners started? Good manners are good etiquette is what they are. It started right in the reign of Louis XIV. Louis had an old master gardener, a Scotsman, who couldn't get people to stop tramping on newly seeded lawns. So he put up warning signs or tickets—*etiquettes* is what they were called. But still the courtiers paid no attention to them, so finally the old Scotsman went right to Louis. And Louis—bless his soul—up and issued an edict commanding everyone at Court to, as the edict was worded, "keep within the *etiquettes.*" And in no time at all, the word came to cover all rules of decent behavior.

That's what we need today for these damn women—another Louis XIV and more "etiquettes." I tell you women are barging into the very last places you'd want them. Look at your men's colleges—it's not just your freshwater colleges, it's Harvard, Yale and Princeton. Some damn fool in the Middle West, I've forgotten his name, thank heaven, even gave a coed dormitory to Harvard. Imagine, a coed dormitory in Harvard Yard! You might just as well kiss Harvard goodbye. Which is an unfortunate expression, but there it is. A friend sent Fish Frobisher a clipping for his Society to Put Things Back the Way They Were —an item from a Boston paper that college girls in increasing numbers were saving money for graduate school by working as strippers. In *increasing* numbers, if you can stomach that, for *graduate* school. The Professor just got back from a trip to all the Eastern colleges, and he told me women out there go literally anywhere. Look at Tubby and that new wife of his. They spend just about every weekend at some college or other, trying to get Tubby III in somewhere—well, Tubby told me he went into the bathroom in a dormitory and who do you think came in? A girl.

Whoever decided that girls were going to get into those colleges anyway? God knows I didn't decide it, and nobody I know decided it. I'll tell you who decided it—they decided it. They weren't wanted there, so they wanted to get in. It's so ridiculous. They have perfectly good colleges of their own, and now, of course, since they've gone and gotten into our colleges, our boys have gone to their colleges. One of the colleges Tubby and his wife visited was Vassar. Can you picture it? Vassar. Next I suppose he'll have to tell us he's a member of the Daisy Chain. One thing is certain, he'd be elected a Member of the Club over my dead body, Tubby or no Tubby. I talked to Tubby about it, you know. Not about Vassar—I didn't have the heart to mention that—but I mentioned the woman thing at Harvard and Yale and Princeton. And you're not going to believe what Tubby told me. Tubby told me that with all those girls around, the way he heard it, there was less going on today than there was in our day. Of course there is. I could have told him that. If it's around all the time, it doesn't mean anything. It's just like what happens to sex in marriage. But of course these new types of professors and these new kinds of people they've got running these colleges are just too inexperienced to know anything about it.

What do these damn women want ultimately? I'll tell you what they want. They want me out of my Club, that's what they want—and one of these days I'll oblige them. I tell you the day one of them gets into the Fortnightly, you can just say good night to Fortnightly. Actually, this Club is a textbook example of women trying to get in where they're not wanted. We had the very devil of a time with them. In the old days, we had a perfectly good once-a-year Ladies Day in the main dining room —and that was that. And then there was that famous meeting and somebody said they should be allowed in more than that. I remember it as if it was yesterday. I said no. I warned them. But they didn't listen to me, of course. A new generation had arisen, which knew not Joseph. I might as well have been shouting into the wind. And the next thing you know, there were Sunday nights, and then there were Sunday nights and Thursday nights. That was when Witter suggested they let maids in. No matter. After that came the separate entrance and the ladies' dining room, and then they abolished the separate entrance—it was a perfectly damn good entrance—and let them in the main door, and today the only goddam place you're absolutely safe is . . . no, I won't mention it. Because the next thing you know, they'll be in there.

I suppose one of these days women will be manning boats

—womanning them they'll probably call it. I bring this up because yachting is such an excellent example of a place where you don't want women. At least in a breeze of wind, in a close race, you don't. Believe me, I know. I grew up in Marblehead. And I want to tell you I've met precious few members of the fair sex in my lifetime who have ever understood even the rudiments of beating to windward. Women don't understand that if you want to go somewhere in a sailboat, you can't just go there. And, of course, since they don't understand beating to windward, they also don't understand coming about and not getting hit with the boom.

I remember a fellow captain I knew in Marblehead. He took his wife on a race and it was blowing a gale and he was coming up on the finish line, fetching it easily, leading the field, when all of a sudden the wind shifted and he had to tack and sure enough his wife got hit by the boom and went overboard. It was a question of going back for her or losing the race. He made to my mind the only possible decision. After all, somebody else picked her up and after they got the water out of her she was perfectly all right.

This whole women take-over thing they're trying is so utterly ridiculous. Do you know there has been, in all of recorded history, just one matriarchy? There have been matrilineal societies—you're going to have to pay attention now: A matriarchy is not necessarily matrilineal. Your matrilineal society is one which traces its ancestry and property through the woman—I imagine they're pretty well washed up by now, and probably broke too. And there have even been, briefly, matrilocal societies. That's where the husband moves into the wife's house, or some such nonsense—I imaging they were very brief. But there's only been one society which was a real matriarchy—

124

both matrilineal and matrilocal. The Hopi Indians!

Now I have nothing against Indians—they got a very raw deal in some respects, although we've gone awfully overboard on them now. Honestly, these youngsters today go for anything that's red or black or brown—anything but good old-fashioned white. But before anybody, young or old, takes up for the Hopi, they should remember that even among the Hopi, they had an avuncular system. I don't suppose my younger readers will even know what that means. But avuncular is uncle, is what it is. And let me tell you very simply and clearly so that there will be no mistake—your Hopi avuncular system is a system whereby all power in the family is vested in uncles. So the woman may think she is running the show, but in point of fact, all actual power is in the hands of the woman's brothers—her mother's brothers and even her mother's mother's brothers.

We were talking about the Hopi the other day at Fortnightly and the General brought up the question of the Amazons. Well, I'd just had enough of the woman thing that night, and I told the General that frankly I couldn't think of a single subject that there had been more bilge written about than those Amazons. I don't like to quote myself—I like to rewrite the well-known things I've said—but sometimes I have to. In the first place, I told the General, the Amazons were a myth. I remember I told him that first and then I said that's all they were—just a damn myth. Nobody knows where they came from or for that matter, where the hell they went to. In the second place, I said, they never did any of the things that people are always claiming they did. And then I mentioned that nonsense about cutting off the right breasts of their children because it interfered with their shooting their bows. The General asked me how I knew that, and I told him there were just some things I knew because I know what makes sense and what doesn't make sense. In those days—whenever the damn days were—they would have bled to death. In the third place, I told him, Hercules never got the girdle of their queen for Eurystheus, for the simple reason that Hercules and Eurystheus were myths too—and two myths, to coin a phrase, don't make one truth.

The General said he's been told that the way the Amazons kept their race going was by keeping men just for mating purposes—and having them do the jobs that, in other societies, women did. I told him that was just bushwa. I told him, the race didn't keep going—where are your Amazons today?—and in the second place the way I'd heard it, the Amazons didn't keep any men around at all. I told the General that I'd heard that from time to time they were supposed to go to a place where men were and then mate with them and keep the girl babies and let the boy babies go. And then, of course, I told him I didn't believe that either. But at least my story made some sense. The General got very hot under the collar about it, and said that his story made just as much sense as mine, and then I told him it didn't. I told him it was purely and simply an old wives' tale—perhaps he'd gotten it from one of his. And then, of course, he really got on his high horse, and I apologized. Actually, the General's wives weren't half bad, as wives go, particularly for Army ones, who so often think they made the earth.

But let's stop talking about the Amazons. Really, I couldn't have less interest in them. I like my women dainty and I like them demure. When was the last time—honestly now—you saw a demure woman? I tell you, I don't think they make them anymore. Speaking of that, Witter Hardee told me he'd re-

cently seen where a restaurant switched from serving fab-
ricated roast beef—beef with binder—to real roast beef, and
their stupid modern customers, if you can believe it, were
furious. Well, according to Witter, that's just what has happened to us—it's been so long since we've seen a real, old-
fashioned girl that if we did see one, we wouldn't like her.
We've gotten used, Witter said, to girl with binder.

I want you to pause here and think about something. Were
the relations between the sexes doing so well that we could
afford, let alone need, this ghastly liberation thing? Of course,
they weren't. I don't believe I know a man from this Club who
doesn't have either a son or daughter who's divorced. With
children all over the place—just like puppies in a kennel. And
any man in the Club who doesn't have a son or a daughter
divorced has either a son or a daughter, or both of them, living
with somebody without benefit of—never mind your clergy—
without benefit of anything except their poor father's support.
And this was all, as I said, before this liberationing thing came
along and not only ruined the last vestiges of your marriage
vows, it also made no distinction between your nice girls and
the other kind. They just lumped both kinds of women together in a big, badly cooked pudding, and all they succeeded
in doing was ruining them both.

Now I'm sure everyone realizes it—they've killed the goose
that laid the golden egg, that's what they've done, and they've
made life for the gander absolutely impossible. How could it
be otherwise? The minute you have your nice girls doing what
they're doing on the one hand, and, on the other, you have the
other kind of women so damn blatant that you might as well
go to bed with a computer—well, what's left? I'll tell you what's
left, homosexuality is what's left, and that's just what we've got.

Running rampant. And I want to say here and now and out loud that I don't blame them one damn bit. I've never even thought about homosexuality for myself, but let me tell you something. Compared to going to bed with some of these new modern women I see today, I'd take anything else that came along.

But let's get off a very unattractive subject. I tell you today we are literally bathed in propaganda about these "new women." To begin with, there's this awful "Ms." thing. I tell you the day I put "Ms." on a letter of mine, it'll be either to someone else's mistress or the Bureau of Msing Persons. And I'm not sure I'm joking about that, either. Edgy Bull left a clipping in my box about the Bureau of Missing Persons—it said that nowadays they are asked to track down more missing wives than they are missing husbands. If that doesn't show you right there what's going on, I don't know what does.

They have a whole new language, these people. It's not just that "Ms.," it's "chairperson," and all that tommyrot. Can you imagine a chairperson at Fortnightly? One article I saw about this at least had the decency to admit that there was, and I quote, "awkwardness" in some of their damnable substitutions. The example they gave was, for "manhole," "personhole." Personhole! Can you beat that? But the same clipping went on to suggest that it would be "fairer"—fairer, mind you —not to use either man or woman, but use instead "heman" and "sheman." Heman and sheman! Sounds halfway between characters in a morality play and a shyster law firm. Betty Bull told me to stop using the word "girl." I told her that I'd use it as long as I wanted to—that to me a girl was any female younger than I was. I couldn't resist it. Betty's at least a year older than I am.

The newspapers are just as bad. Fog Horne wrote every newspaper in the Club one of his Concerned Members letters. They didn't publish it, but he got a letter back from one of them telling him, if you can believe it, that when a woman's name was mentioned for the first time, it was to be Mrs. or Miss or even that Ms. but that after that, it was to use just the last name. Honestly, just the last name, without any identification. So, the first time, I suppose, when they were talking about, say, Grandma Moses, the first time it would be Mrs. Moses, but after that just Moses. I tell you it makes me ill—particularly in the morning paper.

Fish Frobisher was sent two examples of this modern nonsense for his Society to Put Things Back the Way They Were. One was a clipping from a women's group out West somewhere, that they didn't even want history anymore—they wanted "herstory." And another one, I think it was from the South—you'd think they'd have more sense—was a letter written to one of these advice women, and the writer wanted to know why no woman's face had ever appeared on our currency. Well, Fish did some looking up on that one, and the fact is women's faces have appeared on our currency. Martha Washington's face appeared on a silver-dollar certificate, and Pocohontas' face appeared on a twenty-dollar banknote. And good old Fishie found out what happened to them, too. Martha Washington's silver-dollar certificate disappeared from circulation—and so did Pocohontas. Hotfooted it for England.

Now they've put Susan B. Anthony on a fifty-cent piece. The idea of putting women's faces on money is just plain absurd. It's just like this idiotic thing about women trying to pay their share of the check. There are exceptions, as I mentioned, but most of the time it's just a kick in the teeth to the man, that's what it is. Anyway, have you ever seen two women lunching together and trying to figure out the bill? Their share? They never can figure out what their share is. If I've heard them once, I've heard them a hundred times. "No, you had the tuna salad, and I had the chicken supreme."

Even the Professor found me a clipping. The Professor, you know, is very self-conscious with me about these girls in the men's colleges—after all, he was there—anyway, the clipping he found was a "Rule"—if you can believe it—in an article for girls in offices. "Have whatever lifestyle you want," the article said—that almost stopped me right there. If there's one word that makes by blood boil, it's the word "lifestyle"—the people who use it wouldn't know style even if we allowed them to come into the Club and see some. But anyway, the article went on about having this damn lifestyle, and then it said, "But if you are living with a man, don't tell your boss if he's over forty-five." The final "Rule" was "Be assertive with sons and lovers and husbands." My answer to that is that they better be assertive with the sons, all right, because they're not going to have any lovers or husbands. Assertive, forsooth. They don't just write lies, these modern new women, they write the exact plain damn opposite of the truth.

But Witter Hardee found the best one. It was not a clipping. It was a whole article, in one of these women's magazines. And what it said was that there was no conflict between women's liberation and those God-awful high heels women are always sticking into sidewalk gratings and places. Witter gave me the article and I'll quote it to you. "By wearing those heels," the article said, "it shows you're not afraid to be equal and sexy too." Can you beat it? Equal and sexy too. It's just one more plain damn modern contradiction in terms.

130

When we scheduled our Fortnightly on Women, and announced that we were going to have a woman speaker, I tell you all hell broke loose. We had more criticism than we'd had in the entire history of the Club since we had that Democrat back in the '40s—I forget his name. And all this, mind you, before we even had our Speaker picked out.

I want to be blunt about this. At first we had no idea of a woman doing it. We'd never had a woman as a guest, let alone a Speakeress, in the history of Fortnightly, and the last place you'd want to start would be by having one of them on the subject of Women. Witter Hardee suggested Edgy Bull. After all, he said, just being married to Betty qualified him, if not as an authority, at least as a saint. Witter was, of course, joking but somebody took him seriously—that's the danger of a joke—and the next thing I knew Edgy came to me, as sober as a judge, and said to me he couldn't do it. He said—and I'm going to repeat this exactly as he told it to me—"Betty wouldn't hear of it." Betty wouldn't hear of it! In my day, women heard what we wanted them to hear, not the other way around. And then, if you please, out of a clear blue, Edgy suggested Betty. Well, that was too much for me. I told him I didn't mean to be unkind, but just because we wanted to hear about the subject didn't mean we were masochists. I told Edgy he couldn't get one vote in the Club for Betty. I begged him to look at the thing objectively. If you want to hear about the F.B.I., I told him, you'd have J. Edgar Hoover, you don't have John Dillinger.

Well, anyway, we went through a lot of other authorities on Women, both in and out of the Club, and we were getting desperate—after all, the deadline for the Club bulletin was coming up. Anyway, one day I was talking about it with Marjo-

rie, the girl from the publisher who comes to pick up my manu-
script—I keep forgetting she's a full-fledged editor—and she
gave me that curious look she gives me and said she would do
it. I thought she was joking too, but I suddenly realized she was
serious. She even said she was a member of their party—or
whatever those liberationists have—and she would like to come
and speak from their point of view.

Well, I was so shocked about her being one of them that at
first I couldn't think of anything to say about her idea of speaking. But, as I told you, by then we were desperate and I thought
what the devil, you only live once, and the hair of the dog that
bit you and all that sort of thing. Not that I did it unilaterally.
I put the thing to the boys, and darned if Fish Frobisher, who's
seen her with me—she's a pretty little thing as I've told you—
didn't say he thought it was a bang-up idea. Well, after Fish,
Tubby chimed in, as you can imagine, and Tubby was all for
it—Tubby's for anything in skirts—and then came Fog Horne.
Fog said it was all right with him as long as she didn't say
anything against the Constitution, so to make a long story
short, Witter and Edgy and the Professor and the General went
along and, sure enough, we had our Fortnightly. And our
speaker, this little slip of a girl who, I tell you, sitting at the end
of that long table with me, didn't come over the soup tureen.

When I stood up to introduce her, something happened that
had never happened to me before—I had forgotten her last
name. She had told it to me and I'd written to her, but I just
forgot it. And so I had to stop right there, as I was standing at
the microphone, and ask her what her whole name was. "Mrs.
Marjorie Moore," she said. Well, I wasn't going to let that pass.
Not in this Club it wasn't, I said. She might be Marjorie Moore

somewhere else, but in Fortnightly she was not Mrs. Marjorie Moore.

The poor girl didn't even understand what I meant. So then, of course, I had to ask her what her former husband's name was —she was divorced, I told you—and what, before that, her unmarried name was. She told me Peter Moore and Marjorie Huntley. All right, I told her, and I did it slowly because she was obviously a woman of limited range, that she was Marjorie Huntley when she was a little girl, and then when she married Peter Moore she was Mrs. Peter Moore. I told her she could be Mrs. Huntley Moore now that she had divorced Mr. Moore, but she could never be Mrs. Marjorie Moore. At least not in good company, and certainly not at Fortnightly. It was just cheap-john, I told her. It meant you were either lower class or didn't know any better, or both.

Finally, she got it straight—these young people today are not dumb, they're just not taught anything—and then she began to speak. She first told us that while Women's Lib, as she called it, wasn't really her "bag," I think she said "bag"—whatever that meant—and that she wasn't really all the way "into" it— they really speak very badly, you know—just the same she was for it. Imagine? *For* it. In any case, she said, she wanted us to know exactly where she was "coming from." Well that was just plain silly—she had obviously just come from her job. Nowadays, none of them know enough to go home and dress properly, even for something like Fortnightly.

From there she proceeded to tell us that she had never, for example, joined something called "S.C.U.M." Well at this point, Edgy, whose hearing aid gives him the very devil of a time with *s*'s—they whistle you know—thought she said dumb.

He told her he didn't think she was the least bit dumb—she seemed to him very bright for a girl. And then she burst out laughing. After that, of course, she had to repeat S.C.U.M., which, as I understood her to say, was a "Society to Cut Up Men." I gathered it was kind of a joke—a paper doll sort of thing. Anyway, then I heard Edgy tell Fish that he had often heard the expression "scum of the earth," but this was the first time he knew they had a Club.

The girl also told us that she had never joined something else either—something called "W.I.T.C.H.," which, she told us, stood for "Women's International Terrorist Conspiracy from Hell." Well, that woke up the General. In a loud voice, he told Tubby they had them in the Great War. They were, he said those Scottish Highlanders, who wore kilts, only they called them the *ladies* from hell. But the girl paid no attention. The WITCHers, she said, were the ones who went around burning their bras.

Well, you can bet that Tubby was all ears on that. He'd always wanted to know, he told her, why they did that. She told him that it was because they didn't want to wear them, that is was like binding your feet in the old days, and it was a symbol of oppression. And then without so much as a pause, she said, "As a matter of fact, I'm not wearing one." Tubby was really fascinated now, and of course, just couldn't take his eyes off her. But I'm happy to say the rest of us remembered our manners, curious as we were, and looked straight at her face. Good old Witter broke the ice by asking her what else WITCH did. "They picket things," she said, "like brides' fairs and brides' fashion shows. They dress up as witches and carry broomsticks."

Well, I'll tell you, any kind of picket is a red flag to Fortnightly. But picketing brides! It was just plain anarchy. This was one time when we all agreed with the General's solution. You shoot the ones in the front rank. But when this was explained, the girl burst out laughing. "Listen," she said, "we seem to have different headsets on." That was silly too, of course, she wasn't wearing anything on her head. Anyway, at this point she said that what she would really like to do was try some "consciousness-raising." That was hopeless for Edgy—so many *s*'s. He thought she was hissing. But he wasn't the only one who wanted to know what she meant. The girl looked from one to another—all around the table. "What I propose," she said, "is that we try a little role reversal." Everyone wanted to know what that was too. It was now as if she were talking to herself. "Yes, that's what we'll do," she said, "role reversal. We'll make a game of it." Well, none of us had ever played it before, but if there's one thing Fortnightly is known for all over the Club, it's games. We've got both the bridge champion—Fish—*and* the dominoes champion. That, if I do say so, is yours truly.

Everyone wanted to know how to play. "Well," she smiled, "we'll have two teams, the boys and the girls." Tubby didn't like that, to begin with—he said there weren't enough girls. "That's all right," she said, and then she explained that she would be a whole side by herself. Tubby didn't like that either —he wanted to be on her side and so, curiously, did Fog Horne. "No," she said, "we have to reverse sides. My side is really going to be your side and your side is going to be my side. That's what role reversal *is.*" She paused. "Only," she said, "to get it started, I'd better speak for both sides at first."

Well, it just didn't make sense at all. It sounded like one of those children's games where they make up the rules as they go along. But we were sports, so we gave it a go. "Let me start out by saying," she said, "suppose I'm tired of all this hair I have on my head. It weighs too much and it's a damn nuisance, and I have to fix it all the time, and it's impossible in the wind."

We couldn't make head or tail out of that—or perhaps hide or hair would be a better expression. But she went right on. "Now," she said, "let's suppose I don't like all this lipstick and foundation and eye makeup and my false lashes and all the rest of it." She paused again. "Put your hands right over the top of your eyelids," she said. "All right, how would you like to have to peer out at the world through long, false lashes?"

We told her we'd hate it, and that she shouldn't do it. I told her the story of Ischomachos and his bride, and said that it was just as dishonest of her as it was of Ischomachus' bride. All the time I was telling her, though, she just kept staring at me. After I was through she said, "May I ask you all something—do you feel threatened by me like this?"

Well we didn't understand that at all—and it didn't help to have Edgy think she'd said deafened. I told you he is very sensitive on that subject. Anyway by now everyone was getting restless. "All right," she said, "let's let it all hang out." I shook my head—I hate that expression—but she ignored me. "Very well," she said, "let me put it to you this way. Let's suppose that I am sick and tired of the whole masquerade of being—well, a girl—which incidentally you insist on calling me even though I don't like it, because I'm twenty-nine. How would you like it I called you 'boy'?"

Again, it was just plain silly, we weren't boys, we were men and she was a girl. She waved her hand. "Let's say I'm sick of it," she repeated. "That I don't want to have to try to be pretty all the time and smile all the time and when I don't want to—

136

that I don't want to have to keep my voice down and, when I do speak, speak in a sexy, throaty voice." We shook our heads —she didn't have to worry about that, she had a very nice voice. But this didn't stop her either. "Let's say," she continued, "I don't want to have to show you little peeks at my bosom or looks at my legs. Like this." She stretched her legs. They were a very fine pair of limbs, too. "Say, instead, that I want to cross them any way I want to." She paused again. "And above all," she said, "let's say I'm sick of trying to be pretty and sweet and gentle and dainty just to please you. Because, all my life, it seems, I've had to please some man. First it was my father, and then it was every boy I ever went out with and then it was my husband. I had to look up to all of them and bat my eyelashes at them and say how wonderful they were and how mean everybody else was to them and what brilliant ideas they had, even when it was just some fatuous old bore."

It was so sad—we all wanted to pat her on the head. We told her that one thing she wouldn't have to worry about at Fortnightly was fatuous old bores. We kept them out. I told her myself we kept out any of those non-stop talkers or opinionated liberals or in fact anyone who wasn't a good listener and didn't have the same standards and values and decent opinions we did.

She looked me right in the eye when I said that. "I give up," she said. "Good," Tubby said. "Then it's our turn." "All right," she said—although I didn't think she said it too enthusiastically. "We'll try." She paused, again looking from one to the other of us, and sighing. "Well," she said, "let's suppose you're tired of being men. You're tired of playing little soldier and not being allowed to show your emotions, and having to be macho."

The General didn't like that little soldier thing. Trying to be what? he wanted to know. "Macho," she said. "Macho, macho. You're tired of virility—that's the whole point. Men have female hormones and women have male hormones. In this role reversal thing, you've just got to let your female hormones all —whether you like the expression or not—hang out." She said that looking at me.

"Okay," she continued. "Let's say you have a very fixed opinion about something." Well, that was easy for me—if there's anything that makes my blood boil it's a fellow with a wrong fixed opinion. The girl was looking at the General now. "Well," she said, "you suddenly and completely change your mind. That's your feminine prerogative, you know. Let's say the General here suddenly says he likes the Professor, and the Professor says he likes the General. All right, say it," she said to them. "Now talk to each other. Really communicate."

Of course it was hopeless. I pointed out to her that she was barking up the wrong tree this time—they communicated only, I told her, through a third party. She didn't believe it. She asked the General what it was about, and then when he told her, she asked the Professor—and before you could say Jack Robinson they were not only talking to each other, they were both talking to each other at once. That little girl had been able to do something in one night none of us in Fortnightly had been able to do in years—get them to talk to each other. It just shows you there is truth in that old saying, "And a little child shall lead them."

But that wasn't all this remarkable little girl Marjorie had in store for us. "Now," she said, "I'm coming to the really big one. I'm going to count to three. When I say 'three,' I want all of you to burst into tears." That was too much for Witter. "For

138

crying out loud," he whispered to me. Well, I couldn't help laughing at that. So there we were when we were supposed to be crying, laughing. You've got to give the others credit, though—they all tried. But again, of course, it didn't work. I don't think a man in Fortnightly has ever cried since he was a baby. After all, that's why you have the expression, "Cry like a baby." Still that girl wouldn't give up.

"Last but not least," she said, "I'm going to count three once more. When I say 'three' this time, I want you to turn to the man on your right and give him a great big kiss."

Again, those *s*'s. This time they set off Edgy's aid for a fare-thee-well. "A great big what?" he asked. Well, I was going to be damned if I would explain it to him—Edgy was on my right. Anyway, that part, like the crying, was also a failure. You just don't kiss other men unless there's something very wrong with you.

One thing that kissing did was end it all. And the fact is all of us agreed, when we said goodnight to Marjorie, that we'd had a very stimulating evening and she must have learned a lot. We called Henry and had another round of drinks and we were all in a fine humor when we drank the song and sang the Fortnightly toast—I mean the other way around—and adjourned.

CHAPTER VI

Children

FIRST off I want to welcome back my readers of the fair sex. Which reminds me that though I want to be fair, they might as well know at the outset they bear a heavy responsibility here. That old hand-that-rocks-the-cradle-rules-the-world thing unfortunately is true—and the plain fact is you women have rocked the boat here, that's what you've done.

From Caesar's death to my birth there was nothing to compare with what I've seen in my lifetime in the steady decline of youth. It's so damnably over-emphasized and made the focus of everything. Youth, youth, youth. It comes at you from everywhere. Look younger, be younger, that's all you hear. What is youth, for Pete's sweet sake? It's children, that's what it is. It's so bad that sometimes I don't think any of us can stand the gaff. But the awful thing is we have to. Remember, children are, no matter how much we detest them, the you and me of tomorrow. And so, whether we like it or not, it behooves us to take a good, long, objective view at the whole awful problem.

Let us begin by defining our terms. A child is, let us say, anyone under thirty. All right, remember what they used to say in the sixties, "Never trust anyone over thirty." What malarkey! Never *trust.* What is the first thing you think of when you say that word "trust"? Your fiduciary responsibilities, right? Can you imagine trusting *that* to anyone under thirty? Of course you can't.

Having defined our problem, we come straight to the solution. And I'm sorry to say the only one I see is the obvious one staring us in the face—don't have children. I myself have never had them. I was very fortunate in that regard. But as I've told you, I've always been a very careful person, and I've always had discipline. In any case, the very fact that I've never had any children of my own means that I can be totally objective in my objections to them. And so I can tell you frankly that in my considered opinion, based on a lifetime of objective observation, people who have a lot of children are not very good at anything else. There are exceptions, of course. Take Edgy Bull, and Tubby. Edgy could have been a success at anything he chose and Tubby wasn't just a drop-kicker—he could pass, too, and he often did, even in a field goal situation, when he got a bad snap from center. But what happened? Edgy just got trapped by Betty—she's just had one child after another—and Tubby, what can I say? You give Tubby that third martini, and he doesn't know whether he's having another martini or another baby. Fog Horne drinks more than he should, but I don't care how many Foggy's had, he has his code. He doesn't mix his drinks to begin with, and he never mixes his drinks and his women.

Let's face facts—the wrong people usually have children. I don't care whether it's natives or religious fanatics—the less children they should have, the more they have. All right, you have exceptions—Johann Sebastian Bach, for example, had eighteen children. But generally speaking you don't find a Witter Hardee or a Fish Frobisher or a me having children all over the place. Witter's had none. Fish had Fish IV to carry on the line, of course—but that was that. And Little Fishy, as we call him—he's in his forties now—had Fish VI. But just one, of course—although I think there's a girl or two. But what difference does that make? In the old days, as I've said, there was a need for big families down on the farm. But nowadays, if you've got a grain of sense, you have one boy, and then you stop. If you have a girl first, all right, you try again, but once you have a boy you stop. Think of it for a moment—one Fish among the three of us, Witter, Fish and me—and yet we're the very ones who should be having them, if anybody should.

I remember in the old days we used to say that some child or other was at the age when only a mother could love it. Frankly, I can't remember what that age was. And it doesn't really matter. Nowadays there are so many things wrong with children of all ages—that it's hard to know where to begin to correct them. The really young ones are ghastly. They make so much damn noise on these damn Family days. What do they think the SILENCE sign right here in the Library means? Everybody except children, I suppose. They're either crying or yell-ing or shouting for something. Or else they're laughing like hyenas. Why in heaven's name can't they be taught to laugh quietly?

Whatever else they're doing, they've always got those awful runny noses. That's really all those young children are, when you get right down to it—noise and nose. They're terrible carriers you know—they've always got colds. They go snuffling and sniveling around, never using their handkerchiefs, and giving everyone else pneumonia. I myself have been at death's door maybe ten times in my life, and at least nine of those times it was directly attributable to some runny-nosed little monster from whom I couldn't possibly get away without offending the feelings of his mother.

Teenagers are just as bad, and by teenager today I mean anyone up to thirty. Anybody in his twenties is to me a teenager, that's what he is. I told you about that "Rock Brunch" they had at the Club. On Sunday morning, if you please. I actually tried to listen to some of that music. No wonder they call it "rock"—it's obviously what they found it under. And their lyrics—they're not lyrics at all. Do you know what one of them told me was the latest among their singers? It's eating worms. That's right, eating worms. One of their singers named Jack Jones, the boy said, started it—no relation to our Jonesey here at the Club, of-course. But what this Jones person said, the young fellow told me, was that birds sing well after eating worms, so he decided to, too. I told him to ask that Jones how many rock birds there were. And a bird, I told him, would at least sing the lyrics the way they were written—and sing them so that you could understand them. I told him you didn't hear a bobwhite singing "Baa-waa . . . baa-waa." You hear a beautiful, clearly enunciated "Bob White! Bob White!" I don't sing

"Taa-walla . . . taa-walla," for example, I sing a very clear "Tit willow, tit willow, tit willow."

I studied those teenagers at that damn brunch. Frankly, I didn't know which one was a hippie or a yippie or a beatnik or a peacenik—or probably all of them together. I didn't even know which one was smoking "grass," as they call it. Heaven knows, I smoked grass in my day—we put it in our corncob pipes. But we didn't make a drug of it. And, above all, we were patriotic. Why do you think we don't have patriots anymore? Because the children don't love their fathers—that's why. What do you think the word "patriotism" comes from? Look it up. From your *pater,* father—your good old *pater potestas.* And one way he stayed *potestas,* believe you me, was by making his children love him—by force, if necessary.

Another thing I noticed at that brunch—and remember, we probably had the best of them there—is that they're dirty. All of them were just plain filthy. And they don't pick up anything, even their feet. Long hair—don't speak to me about it. It's unspeakable. And those beards. I have no objection to a beard on an older person, after he's distinguished. But on your young person, before distinction, it's presumptuous and preposterous, and poor form to boot. A lot of my best friends had or have beards. I had a beard myself for a while. But then Muffie . . . well, no, we had enough of her in the last chapter. But speaking of girls, the really amazing thing about looking at all those young people together was again I couldn't help thinking how much more attractive they were than the boys they were with and wondering what on earth they saw in them. Actually, as I said before, any one of them if they spruced up a little would be perfectly able to attract an older man—someone with at least a modicum of maturity. Marjorie, the girl from the publishers, whom we had at Fortnightly, is a good example of this. I myself have seen the steady improvement in her mind just from our talks together.

Another thing, children are a divisive influence. Not just on marriages, but in other ways. Do you know the real reason the Professor and the General didn't speak? I'll bet you don't. Well, it was all over children. Remember, the Professor was there—teaching in college at the very worst of that children thing. At Yale, too—can you imagine? The Professor never went haywire on the thing, either. He knew why the damned children couldn't read, I've heard him say it a thousand times, They couldn't read because they didn't want to—that's why they couldn't read.

Well, the Professor and the General got to arguing over what could be done about the damned students trying to take over the university. And the Professor said the General's only answer to every problem was to shoot it—and at that of course, the General got mad. He insisted he never said shoot them *all* —only the leaders. The General knows riots—you shoot the ones, he said, that are in the front ranks. That's all you ever will have to shoot, he says, because pretty soon there wouldn't be any front ranks. Well, then the Professor said how would the General feel if his own son was in the front ranks? And at that —I'll say one thing for the General, he stands his ground and he's got the courage of his convictions. He said that if his son was in the front ranks, he wouldn't have the slightest compunction about shooting. You have to shoot, he said, to teach 'em a lesson. And then he said that after all the Professor was there, and if he'd been doing his job properly, there wouldn't have been any necessity for shooting. Well, that was too much for the Professor. And one word led to another. And then, as the poet tells us, all words stopped together. And then, as I told you in the last chapter, Marjorie, bless her little heart, got them back, if not together, at least on a speaking basis.

Of course, looking back at that idiocy in the universities, if there's one thing I've learned in my lifetime—and I'm sure Caesar learned it in his—it is that there's nothing new under the sun. You take those damn students. Well, I'll wager you a brandy and soda right now you don't know when the first time was that students seized control of universities. It wasn't five years ago, or even ten years ago or even fifty years, or for that matter a hundred years ago, or two hundred years ago, it was seven hundred years ago, in the thirteenth century. And it didn't happen at just one university, either—it happened at two universities. It happened at the University of Bologna and it happened at the University of Paris, the students even took charge of the renting of rooms. They rented them on one side of the university to students and on the other side to prostitutes. So there's nothing new about these girls getting into men's colleges, after all.

It's interesting how it ended, too. It was ended by the King himself. In 1450, right at the University of Paris, the record reads, King Louis XI first restrained the students' excessive feasting, and then he imposed a loyalty oath, and finally he did what he should have done in the beginning—he prohibited student strikes. And how did King Louis XI do it? I'll tell you how he did it, by telling the students if they struck he'd draft them. Imagine! All that time between Caesar's death and my birth just that one trouble with students, compared with what I've had to cope with in my life every single day.

Actually, there's no use beating around the bush between Caesar's death and my birth on this thing. Go back to your Bible. Open it to Ecclesiastes. "Woe to ye, O land, when your kingdom is a child." And that's exactly what we've done today —made kings of these damn children. And if you don't believe me or the Bible, all right, I'll give you Lord Chesterfield. "The young leading the young," he said, "is like the blind leading the blind—they will both fall into the ditch." Well, that's exactly what we're in today, the ditch.

Rome had the same thing. Who do you think said *"Pietas fundamentum pravulorium est omnium virtuum?"* Cicero said it, that's who. But I suppose the very people who need it most won't know what it means. So I might as well tell you that what it means is, and I quote, "The dutifulness of children is the foundation of all virtue." And how do you get that dutifulness? By filial piety, that's how. Filial piety was, as a matter of fact, the very cornerstone of the Roman Empire in its great days. Gibbon tells us that the whole foundation of Roman jurisprudence was, and I quote again, "the exclusive, absolute and perpetual dominion of the father over his children." Indeed Gibbon goes so far as to tell us it was, and I quote a third time, "coeval with the foundation of the city." And I guess even the people who don't know Latin will know who founded the city. Romulus, that's who. I don't know where Remus stood on this thing, but Romulus is quite good enough for me, thank you.

"In the Forum," Gibbon tells us, "the Senate or the camp the adult son of a Roman citizen enjoyed the public and private rights of a *person.*" Those are Gibbon's italics, not mine. "In his father's house, he was a mere *thing.*" Again, those are Gibbon's italics. The son was right there, Gibbon goes on, with the "movables"—you know, the cattle and slaves and things—and the father could banish him or even kill him without—and this is the important thing—"being responsible to any earthly tribunal."

Actually, as Gibbon very wisely points out, the slave was better off than the son, because the slave regained, by his first manumission, his alienated freedoms. Not so the son. If he was disposed of—exiled or sent to some unnatural father, or whatever, it was not, Gibbon clearly states, "until after the third sale and deliverance that he was enfranchised from the domestic power." Furthermore, the absolute control of one's offspring went on and on until one's own death. Listen to these ringing words:

> Neither age, nor rank, nor the consular office, nor the honours of a triumph, could exempt the most illustrious citizens from the bonds of filial subjection: his own descendants were included in the family of their common ancestor . . . without fear, though not without danger of abuse, the Roman legislators had reposed an unbounded confidence in the sentiments of paternal love, and the oppression was tempered by the assurance that each generation must succeed in its turn to the awful dignity of parent and master.

Well, of course each generation didn't succeed, and each generation succeeded less and less. No wonder things have changed more in my lifetime than from Caesar's time to me. Why I would no more have thought of talking back to my father, let alone disobeying him, than I'd have thought of flying to the moon.

It is true there were, here and there, as Gibbon tells us,

abuses. Erixo, for example, whipped his son, we are told, "until he expired"—the son, not Erixo. And the "multitudes" got so exercised about it—you can count on those damn multitudes to take the wrong tack every time—that the Emperor himself had to save Erixo, as indeed he should have. You just don't throw the baby out with the bathwater. But other Emperors just caved in, and down came your temple, stone by stone.

Augustus really started it all. Augustus had his points, as I've told you, but domestically he was just a plain damn liberal is what he was. Those Julian Laws, for example, *Lex Julia de Pudicitis et de coercendix adulteris.* The net result of them was that for the first time in Roman history, marriage was brought under the protection of the State, instead of leaving it where it belonged, in the hands of your *pater potestas.* Of course your father still had the right to kill a daughter who had a lover—that would take care of this modern living together thing in short order—but your basic trouble with your Julian Laws is that they were designed to have people have more children. Imagine, *more* children. Though in those days, as I've told you several times, children were much more valuable than they are today. Anyway, Augustus made marriage obligatory for all males under 60, and women under 50. If you were a bachelor or a maiden aunt or something, you couldn't even inherit a will, unless you were married within a hundred days after the person who willed you the money died. Even widows and divorcees could inherit money only if they remarried within six months after the death or divorce of the husband.

The whole motive, as I say, was the frightening one of increasing the population, and it was carried to utter absurdity. Of the two consuls, for example, do you know which one was to take precedence of the other? The one, if you can believe it, who had the most children. At that rate, we'd be governed by Roosevelts and Kennedys forever. No wonder Rome fell.

Recall once more that Tacitus himself called the Augustan or Julian Laws a failure. Recall too that the Julian Laws were only binding on what were called the "orders"—the two upper classes. After all, if you've going to have a lot of damn children around, at least it would be comforting to know that they were all your kind. And there's another point here too. They were decently brought up.

In Rome, for example, a child entered his elementary school accompanied each way—to school and home from school—by his *pedagogus,* or child leader. We've absolutely slandered that word today—into something like stodgy. Well then, I tell you what we need today is more stodginess. Your good old *pedagogus* in those days just had one duty—to guard the safety of the child *and* his morals. That's important. He had nothing to do with your schoolmaster or your *ludi magister,* who was in charge of play and games, and the less important stuff. Your *pedagogus,* as I say, had the big job—safety and morals. Boy howdy, how we could use a couple of million *pedagogi* today.

Other countries besides Rome have known how to raise children. Saxony, for example, or Scythia. In Saxony, newborn babies were plunged into icy water to harden them. In Scythia, your warrior was so well-hardened that by the time he went into battle he could even fight in snow and ice without a stitch on. The General is my authority for that. The General also told me that one of these Scythian warriors was questioned by an Athenian, who asked him how it was he didn't feel the cold. The Scythian pointed out the Athenian's face and said he wore nothing on that and yet his face didn't feel the cold. "Just think of me," he said, "as face all over."

From the time of Caesar's death to my birth, there was really none of this modern nonsense about childhood. Take these rules from a book which Witter Hardee found for me, about little children—one written as recently as 1475, about that time they were having that trouble at the University of Paris. Read this slowly now:

> Little children must not speak till spoken to, they must not chatter or stare about, they must stand till they are told to sit, they must not look sulky, they mustn't pick their noses or scratch their ears, pick their nails or teeth, they mustn't drink with their mouths full, mustn't lean against posts or doors, mustn't put their elbows on the table, nor wink or roll their eyes.

Rules like that make your mouth water today. But just as important in those days there was none of this everlasting talk about childhood—as if it was a damn separate state. Childhood wasn't a damn separate state—it was simply a period of miniature adulthood, out of which children had to be trained as rapidly as possible. And that, friends, when all of this modern pap is said and done, is still the case—children are underdone adults, and damn underdone, if you ask me. I've been accused of being partial to any century preceding my own. Well, I'm guilty. I admit it and I'm proud of the charge. And the reason is that all those centuries right up to mine just handled things like children better. Well into the twentieth century, mind you, children weren't even dressed like children—they were dressed as tiny adults. I'm not necessarily advocating this, I don't give a tinker's damn how children are dressed, as long as they're decent and neat and clean and don't have a cold and stay out of the Library.

Looking back over the history of children—which is a very depressing piece of history, by the way, there are actually three terrible ages of childhood—one to ten, eleven to twenty, and twenty-one to thirty. The one to ten years are, of course, best handled by nurses. Indeed, I believe that we should take it as a rule of thumb--a particularly apt simile there, if I do say so —that nobody should have children who can't afford nurses. And, mind you, I don't say nurse, I say nurses. In my day, we always had wet nurses. I don't suppose your modern child would know a wet nurse from a dry nurse if they were both together in the nursery. Probably think they had something to do with swimming, like a wet suit. Well, I don't mean to offend anybody's sensibilities, but on the other hand I'll be damned if I'll beat around the bush—your wet nurse took care of the baby's milking—that's what she did. The best description I ever read of a wet nurse I found in the locked closet in the Club Library—a book of instructions by Jacques Guille. He was a man who, among other distinctions, was *chirugien* to such French kings as Charles IX, Henri III and Henri IV. I can hear some of you saying what is a *chirugien.* Look it up, son, look it up. I'm not a dictionary. Anyway, here is the description of your old-fashioned wet nurse:

> She must have an agreeable face, clear eyes, well-made nose, red mouth, white teeth, strong round neck and a deep chest. The shape of her breasts was immensely important, and minute particulars must be given as to their

size, shape and colour, and on how they are to be prod-
ded and felt for firmness and resilience. The wet nurse
should not be pregnant; she should speak well and should
be neither a drinker nor a glutton. She should feed the
baby whenever it likes, and frequently unswaddle it and
wash it. She should not desire the company of her own
husband; as to her employer's husband, if possible, she
should have an actual aversion to him. She should be able
to sing pleasantly.

Frankly, I don't remember mine singing, but the point is she
did her job, and it was a very important job, and it's one that
has no business being done by a young wife. In the first place,
it is very unattractive. Even when it's done in total privacy,
which, of course, is the only way it should be done, the idea is
unattractive. In the second place, it ruins sex—and right at the
crucial time for most marriages when sex is rapidly becoming
not what it's cracked up to be. Many a young husband has in
fact been so repelled by it, that he just up and abdicates the
domestic scene altogether, and while this probably means he
spends more time in his Club—which, if he's the right sort in
the right kind of Club, is probably a good thing—the fact
remains it raises hob with the family. All in all, there's no
question but that your wet nurse was the best solution. I'm not
making a joke here, because it's too serious a matter. And I'm
in no mood for a joke. It's just one more example of a good,
old-fashioned thing that's gone with your wind.

After the wet nurse, there comes the question of day nurses.
Again, mind you, I say nurses. The minute a nurse starts to
spoil your child, you might just as well have spared the rod. So

what you have to do is get another nurse, and never let her get too fond of the child.

The best nurse was, of course, your English Nanny. Your Nanny, incidentally, was called a rocker, in the days before she was called Nanny. The Club's old Webster says that the word "nanny" is, and I quote, "elliptical, for nanny goat"—which certainly suggests a rather coarse derivation. But this is nonsense. Dictionaries are often wrong—particularly on social matters. I don't suppose whoever writes them has much social experience—how could he if he was busy writing a whole dictionary? In any case, I don't give a damn what the word came from. I just wish she'd come back from wherever she's gone to. God knows these modern children need her.

The Nanny taught the child the basics. Sticky fingers—how Nannies used to scold about that, and how right they were—runny noses; eating up, too. I can remember Nannies telling children to eat up and make a Hoover plate. These modern children never eat anything they don't want to, and wouldn't have the ghost of an idea what a Hoover plate was. They probably think it has something to do with a vacuum cleaner. Well, let me tell you it didn't. What it had to do with was Herbert Hoover—one of the best Presidents since George Washington, in my humble opinion. Anyway, before he was President, he fed the starving Belgian children after the Great War. And if you didn't eat what was on your plate, your Nanny gave you what Paddy gave the drum.

All my good old Nanny's words—how they come back to me. But what use are they to me—it's *today's* children who need them. "You can, but may not." "Ask me no questions, and I'll tell you no lies." "Good riddance to bad rubbish." "Never trouble trouble till trouble troubles you." "Waste not, want not." "Eat it up, wear it out, make do, do without." "Fine feathers don't make fine birds." "Laugh before breakfast, cry before supper." "If you can't play a sport, be one." "Patience is a virtue/Virtue is a grace/Both of them together/Make a pretty face." "Patience and perseverance brought the snail to Jerusalem."

Ah, that snail to Jerusalem, that really takes me back. I wish my Nanny were right here, to see the progress I'm making, slow but sure, on this book. But your Nanny did more than give you the positives—she was also very careful about her negatives. Above all, she never overpraised. I remember one day when I was going to a party and I'd cleaned myself to the nines and wore everything she told me to wear and was going out the door—well, she just gave me that inspection she always did from head to toe. When she was through, she gave me the tiniest little pat and said, "You'll do." I tell you I can still remember how I felt. Just wonderful. Better than any time I've ever felt after any effusive silly-ass modern compliment I might get today. Because a Nanny's compliment meant something— you knew she didn't throw them around.

Strict? The modern child doesn't know the meaning of the word. Fish Frobisher's Nanny was so strict that if he didn't eat everything on his plate, it was brought back to him, cold, at the start of the next meal. His Nanny also had a spiked back put into his chair at the table—to make him sit up straight, of course. It sounds medieval today, but it didn't do Fish the slightest harm—indeed I believe it's one of the things that made a man of Fish. And the General told me his Nanny always insisted that when he started out on a walk he advance the left foot first. Harm? Nothing. I'll wager it's what started the General on his military career.

Another thing Nannies did—and this is a ticklish subject, and I want to phrase it as delicately as possible—was to stop you from taking, well, too much interest in yourself. This is just as important for girls, apparently, as it is for boys, although I never knew it was until I got married. But Cornelia used to say that when she was a little girl, her Nanny always made her go to sleep on her side, with her arms crossed and folded against what the Nanny called "her potential bosom." Cornelia said she remembered the rest of her body feeling "left out" when she was in what Nanny called her "safe" position. But you can certainly see the Nanny's point. And the same thing, of course, goes for us. Tubby's Nanny caught him playing with himself one night and Tubby himself told me the next night his Nanny tied his hands to the bedpost. Didn't do Tubby a bit of harm, of course.

What Nannies did, in a word, was give you the rules for life —and the plain fact of the matter is that nowadays nobody does. Husband and wife literally compete for the affection of the little monster—they're so afraid he won't love them—and of course what does he do but just trade on this and do what he damn pleases. On top of it all, there's a great vogue today of making fun of anyone who makes rules. Even in England they're doing it. Jonathan Gathorne-Hardy, for example, in his *Rise and Fall of the British Nanny,* has a paragraph which is, to my mind, pure codswallop:

> If you make a great many rules for a child and then always reward him for conforming, and punish him for

breaking them, if you never allow him to behave spontaneously, never, say, at the age of two, let him crawl by himself and climb dangerously and untidy the house, if you never let him do things on his own and find out that there is a value in questioning authority, a value and reward in experiment and exploring and poking about, then he will grow up, in the vast majority of cases, to behave like this in adult life. He will behave well, he will conform, he will want and need rules, conventions, recognized authority. He will want clubs . . .

He will want clubs! Well what in the devil is wrong with him wanting a club? If he's the right sort and behaves well, what else could he want? Honestly, no wonder they no longer call the whole damn thing child *rearing.* They don't dare, because that's exactly what they're doing—raising them backwards.

Actually, in this whole children thing, a lot of bad blood came from our own country. The really damnable thing is that we started out in great shape, right on the right track. In New England, for example, disobedient children were publicly whipped. It was good for them and it was good for their parents too—taught them both a lesson. And in Virginia, in the early days, they were bearcats on discipline and proper education for children. Take Thomas Jefferson. Now I don't hold with Jefferson on everything—he was too far to the left for me. But on this children thing, he was as sound as a nut. I'll give you, as an example, one of his letters to his daughter, Patsy—written in 1783:

> With respect to the distribution of your time, the following is what I should approve. From eight to ten

o'clock, practice music. From ten to one dance one day and draw another. From one to two draw on the day you dance and write a letter the next day. From three to four read French. Four to five exercise yourself in music. From five till bedtime read English, write, etc. I expect you will write to me by every post. Inform me what books you have read, what tunes you learn and enclose your best copy of every lesson in drawing. Take care that you never spell a word wrong. Always, before you write it, consider how it is spelt, and if you do not remember, turn to a dictionary. It produces great praise to a lady to spell well.

In the nineteenth century, there were a lot of other sound books on bringing up daughters—all of them written by their fathers, of course. You just can't let mothers into it. When it comes to raising daughters—there's that competitive thing, you know, for your affection. We have this book in the Club library, for example, an excellent book called *A Father's Legacy to His Daughters*. It was written in the eighteenth century by John Gregory, a British clergyman-author—that's a good combination, the eighteenth century and a clergyman-author. That's one thing we should have a lot more of today. Anyway, this Rev. Gregory wasn't even afraid to take on the question of how a girl should look. This is always a ticklish subject, but he really knew, as the youngsters say today, "the score." "When a girl ceases to blush," he says, "she has lost the most powerful charm of beauty." He also advises them to remain "rather silent" in company, particularly mixed company. "If you happen to have any learning," he says, "keep it a profound secret, especially from the men." Above all, he advises them not to try to be funny. "Humor," he said, "is often a great enemy to delicacy." And then he adds, "Wit is the most dangerous talent you can possess."

Fortunately, that isn't too much of a problem with most of the young girls today. But Dr. Gregory has some excellent advice on how to handle some things that of course in a decent day wouldn't have happened but do today. Take this awful thing of girls actually calling men for dates. They do do it, you know. Well, Dr. Gregory handled that with the flat statement that, and I quote, "Love is not to begin on your part." He also tells them exactly what to do if they should fall in love with a man. "If you love him," Dr. Gregory says, "let me advise you never to discover to him the full extent of your love; no, not although you marry him; that sufficiently shows your preference, which is all he is entitled to know." Finally, of course, Dr. Gregory condemns "violent love" altogether. "It would lead," he said, "to satiety and disgust," and it was a woman's job to avoid it.

Even in my day, of course, we were brought up either by Nannies or mothers who used good, sound books like that—and not this terrible Dr. Spock. My mother's favorite was Dr. John Watson. "No mother," he writes, "has the right to have a child who cannot give it a room to itself for the first two years of infancy. I would make this a *conditio sine qua non.*" I don't blame my mother for liking him—I like any author who's at home with Latin. But this Dr. Watson was really a philosopher about children. "It is a serious question in my mind," he wrote, "whether there should be individual homes for children, or even whether children should know their own parents."

Well, my mother didn't go that far, but I know she admired Dr. Watson very much. She even did her best, I remember at one period, to follow what was perhaps the strictest of all of his admonitions to mothers. "Never hug and kiss children," he wrote, then, "never let them sit in your lap. If you must, kiss them once on the forehead and then say goodnight. In the morning, shake hands with them."

My mother sometimes kissed me, but to his dying day my father shook hands with me. And we would have both been embarrassed had he done anything different.

It wasn't easy deciding on a speaker on the subject of children for Fortnightly. This time Edgy's wife, Betty, came up—via Edgy, of course, that's the way she does things—with the suggestion that we have a child. Well, we gave that idea the deep six, of course. Just because we'd had a woman speakeress didn't mean we didn't have some standards. Actually, I had a sneaking suspicion that what Betty really had up her sleeve was one of those damn Bull terriers—that's what Witter Hardee calls those Bull children—and I told Fish that if one of them got past the Fortnightly door, I'd do a Gauguin and go to Tahiti.

The real trouble was that when it came to considering decent adult guests, there wasn't a man Jack of them who didn't feel exactly the way we did about the whole awful subject. Then, just when we were at our most depressed, good old Fish Frobisher, who was filing some stuff for the Society to Put Things Back the Way They Were, came upon an incredible article about some nut who believed in children's *rights.* No, I'm serious—the man really did. He was a psychiatrist—boy, I loathe those birds—and he'd written a whole book, if you can believe it, about rights for children. Picture it, a book about something you should be able to write in one word—and that word is "No."

Well, I don't know quite why it was—maybe we were just ready for a real farce—anyway, the idea appealed. Still we were careful. We sent out feelers on the fellow. Actually, what we were doing was finding out if he was really in the pay of the Kremlin, or something like that. That, of course, would have reflected very badly on Fortnightly. He wasn't, as it turned out, but he couldn't come anyway. He was, he said, too busy. That was a hot one. But at least he had manners—what he did was to suggest another psychiatrist. I guess they breed them like flies, those fellows, because of course they have no morals at all. Well, when we asked this second bird—this was really something. He said he was a disciple of the first bird. A disciple, if you please.

To make a long story short, we got him. And when he walked in there that night, everyone thought the same thing. One look at him, and a child would know he was pro-child—he was nothing but a child himself. Really a holy terror he was—the long hair, the beard, the pipe—every single thing you don't want in a Club wrapped up in one man. Hell's bells, I promise you, you wouldn't let him in the house, even if it was raining. And he looked at me as if I was a dinosaur. And once he mumbled—that's all these young people do is mumble—that I was something out of a book. So, after he said that, I told him he would shortly be in my book. And he never even smiled. Well, then somebody said something mildly amusing, but not nearly as funny as what I had said, and he guffawed. I never trust a man who's got nothing between a smile and a guffaw.

One thing that made my blood boil was that that young man didn't call me "Sir" or "Mister," but "Man" Imagine a guest at Fortnightly calling me "Man," and yet if I called him "Boy," you can picture what would happen. Finally I asked him to stop calling me "Man," that I wasn't his man and that, as a matter of fact, the last man I had had was before World War II. He was a fair valet, too. But during the war you couldn't get them anymore, and after the war, my butler told me not even to try getting one. The war he said, had totally ruined them.

The young man, incidentally, was wearing a waistcoat, which I complimented. And then, of course, he pronounced it "waist coat," so I had to correct him. I thought he might as well learn something. I told him it was either a vest or a weskit, and if he didn't know how to pronounce it, he shouldn't wear it. That young man, incidentally, wore it with the bottom button unbuttoned. I thought that was very bad form. In my day, you didn't leave the bottom button unbuttoned until after you'd made your first million.

The very idea of that fellow making a million, of course, was a laugh. By the time we got through with dinner, we all had him pegged. He kept smiling that supercilious half-smile of his, which wasn't surprising because he did everything by halves—particularly his thinking. And at that I'm giving him more credit than he deserves. Actually, he wasn't even half right about anything. He was just 100 percent wrong. For example, right at the beginning of his speech, he said we were in "an era of 'age-ism,' " and that we "venerated the old at the expense of the young." Well, none of us could believe we had heard him right. Witter Hardee said to me he wondered where the man had been lately—Witter's guess was in outer space. Then he said that instead of accepting children for the individuals they are, we "patronize them as 'adults-in-training.' "

Adults in-training, I remember we all thought at the same time, what the devil was wrong with that? What else were they? But we didn't even get time to finish our thought before the man went right on and said we were using this as an excuse to "dominate, segregate, program and ignore them." I had to interrupt. "Look here, boy," I said, "what do you mean by 'ignore'? I told him that I had missed the Children's Crusade, but one thing I was certain of—we were living in the most child-oriented *un*ignored society since then.

Well, if you can believe it, even that didn't stop this bird. He said we "incarcerate" children and that most of them have not done anything that would be considered a crime if it was done by an adult. And then he gave three examples. The first two were running away and truancy. I wanted to ask him what was the difference, and when was the last time an adult was a truant. What was the use? Anyway, at that point, he up and gave his third example of something that wouldn't be considered a crime if done by an adult. And what do you think this one was? Sexual promiscuity, as I live and breathe. Honestly, if I ever thought I'd live to see the day.

Up to that point, the other Fortnightly boys had been fairly quiet. Frankly, I figured they had been struck dumb. But that "sexual promiscuity" woke them all up. Sexual what? Edgy Bull wanted to know. Edgy has trouble with all those "s" words, as I've told you, they whistle in his aid. He thought the man said something about a promissory note.

Sometimes Edgy can get way off base. Anyway after we got that cleared up, the bird said that what he proposed, and this time I know I am quoting him exactly, was that no children be punished without counsel and jury trial.

I tell you that that piece of intelligence, and I am using the word in its most sarcastic sense, fell on our group like the shelling of Fort Sumter. Tubby wanted to arrest the man, and you can guess what the General wanted to do. Witter tried to smooth the whole thing over with a joke. He asked if it would be like reading your kid his rights before you let him have it in the seat of the pants—but I don't think anybody but me even heard that. I didn't hear exactly what the fellow said at the very end, but Witter told me afterwards, it was something about extending full citizenship to children, including the right to vote. Vote, mind you. First, the servants, then the women, then the children. *O tempora, o mores.*

After he had sat down for a long time no one said anything. But we couldn't just sit there, we realized that, and finally we pulled our socks up. Good old Fog Horne started it—he ordered one more double and then asked at what age did the man propose the damn children should vote? "As soon," the man replied, "as they could talk." Well, I caught Edgy Bull's eye and I thought of his grandchildren and judging by the way they talk —they really mumble—they wouldn't be voting until after they do now—at 18 or 16 or whatever it is. Edgy once told me that he figured his grandchildren apparently determined to go through life on just five expressions—"right on," "with it," "far out," "get it all together," and "let it all hang out." And that, as he understood it, "right on" meant "with it," "with it" meant "far out," "far out" meant "get it all together" and "get it all together" meant "let it all hang out." Witter came next. He asked the man how many children did the man figure there would be voting? "About eighty million," the man said. Well, Witter didn't bat an eyelash. Witter covers his sarcasm with such politeness that the other fellow never recognizes it until it's too late. Anyway, Witter said he was picturing those eighty million little minds at the polling booths, and wasn't the fellow afraid they would vote in blocs? The fellow shook his head. Perhaps, Witter persisted, looking right at the man, with them.

But the rest of us were in no mood for humor. Fish Frobisher got the thing down to facts and figures. He had brought some of his STPTBTWTW file right with him. This country, he read the fellow, "is spending more on grammar and high schools than ever before in its history. Seventy-five billion dollars last year," Fish pointed out, "despite a 400 percent increase in 1960. And yet our students entering college have the lowest Scholastic Aptitude scores in half a century." Could the fellow please explain that? Well, of course, he couldn't. He just smiled that supercilious half-smile again. And Fish just went right on. The chaplain of Washington & Lee University had told him, he said—Fish really has a wide circle of acquaintances —that the students there didn't know how to do anything from completing an assignment to writing a decent paper.

Well, we all sat up at that. Washington & Lee isn't exactly Harvard or Yale, but it's not one of those tiddlywink colleges either. The chaplain had told him, Fish continued evenly, that the simple inability to do a job had replaced sex and religion as the Number One problem in the colleges.

That was so good we didn't wait for the fellow's answer—by then he wasn't giving any answers anyway—in fact it was so good that we asked Fish to repeat it. All of us agreed that it was no good to have anything replacing religion, but to have something replace sex was, nowadays, at least a step in the right direction. Of course, one could wish it was something more substantial than the simple inability to do a job, but still.

At this juncture, the General brought up an interesting point —that over sixty-three percent of our men in Congress are children. Almost two thirds of them were thirty-eight years old, or younger, and as if that weren't bad enough, they were getting younger all the time. And at the same time, he said, the general level of trust in government, based on a Gallup Poll, had fallen from seventy-six percent, in 1960, to thirty-three percent today. The General's answer, of course, was a coup. But as I pointed out, you couldn't get at your children problem with just a coup in Washington, you'd have to have coups all over the country. Children were, after all, everywhere—movies, television, everything was for children. The rest of us simply didn't matter. I told him it was what they called "demographics," that they even used it for products. I told him no wonder the children didn't have an education. If they went around watching all the movies and television that was put on for them, and buying all those products they were supposed to be buying, they wouldn't have time to go to school.

Edgy Bull showed that psychiatrist fellow a book that Betty had made him bring along. *What to Tell Your Child About Sex,* it was called. Of course it was pure hogwash. Typical Betty stuff. Edgy showed me one page he had marked. "Don't be negative," it said. "Avoidance, repression, rejection, embarrassment and shock are the most negative forms of sex education." Edgy said Betty wanted him to show the book to the fellow. I threw up my hands. It was coals to Newcastle, I told Edgy, but go ahead. What difference did it make? Anyway, Edgy did, and what do you know? Sex obviously made that psychiatrist fellow nervous, because right after Edgy showed him the book he said he had to go, excused himself and left. And that at least cleared the air. From then on we decided we ourselves had been too negative and that, in the future, we'd admit only positive suggestions. And if I do say so, we came up with three really exciting ones. The first was Fish Frobisher's again—it was from a clipping someone had sent him. It was about a couple out in East Lansing, Michigan. What this couple had done was to put an advertisement in a magazine offering to trade in their teen-ager. "Have 14-year-old boy," the advertisement read, "who wants to try different environment. Would like to trade for boy or girl." Do you know how many replies they got? Over two hundred!

The second suggestion was, of all people's, Tubby's. I never think of Tubby as an authority on children. But Tubby said a friend of his had come up with a terrific idea—Rent a Kid. The way it worked, Tubby told us, was based on the idea that obviously, when you have company, or your boss or someone coming to dinner, you don't want your own children, dressed the way they do, and looking the way they do, and acting the way they act, and making a terrible impression. So what you do is send your own children away and order, from Rent a Kid, good children. Good, old-fashioned ones, the way we were—who come in politely, shake hands, bow or curtsey, answer a few questions with a smart "Yes, sir," or "No, sir," and then get out and stay out.

The third and last suggestion, and the most helpful of all, was supplied, as you might expect, by Witter Hardee. Over in England, he said, there was a medical health officer—from a place called Darlington, I think it was—anyway, he was working on something that could revolutionize the whole problem. What it was, Witter explained, was a pill to delay the onset of puberty. Witter explained it very carefully. It was a hormone preparation to delay adolescence—in other words, to extend the period of childhood, between the age of six and puberty, that period when children are not quite as impossible as later on, when they turn into teenagers. According to Witter, the pill, when fully developed, might even be able to delay the onset of sexual maturity until the students had left college and could earn their own living. We all broke into spontaneous applause at that.

It was a wonderful end to a trying meeting. And, on that happy note, we drank a toast, sang the Fortnightly Song and adjourned.

CHAPTER VII

Foreign Affairs

F OREIGN AFFAIRS," Witter Hardee told me, "they're the
only ones to have if you want to keep peace in the family."
Witter is a card. Anyway, here I am, at the last of the Big Three
of the troubles with nowadays. I've given you women and children—the Harvard and Yale—and now we have Princeton.
Which reminds me of that bloody Woodrow Wilson. I've told
you about him when he was President of Princeton going after
the clubs there. Now that's exactly the kind of man you don't
want on foreign affairs, a man who would do a thing like that
is basically anti-American. "No entangling alliances," my
Uncle Bagnalls wrote him. But what good did it do? Every
damn President since I can remember has been so in love with

171

foreign policy that they're just like a schoolboy with a new girl. They go mooning around trying to save the world while our domestic economy goes to rack and ruin. But no, with these Presidents, it's that grass is greener thing—which it always is, of course, after they've been in office a while. And then they're off on that damn Air Force One from here to hell and gone, to do anything except what they should do, which is, of course, mind what's left of the store

And when they're back in Washington, they're just as bad. Let someone like me go down there and I'll cool my heels while they're entertaining some banana boy from Latin America or some tinhorn dictator from the Middle East or the King of Timbuctoo. You name them, and they'll roll out the red carpet —it would be red, of course, wouldn't it?—and give them a damn State dinner. And the next thing you know, they're giving them another billion of my money. They serve just wine, they say, at those dinners. Well, I never did trust a man who drank nothing but wine. This Carter, they say, is one of them —nothing but wine, no hard liquor in the White House. Well, I'll tell you something—that's why his foreign policy is soft too. The final straw was that give-away of the Panama Canal. And who did we give it to? Some two-bit one-star general who wanted it because it wasn't his. Those birds always want what the other fellow has. They either want to tear it down or grab it for themselves. And the worst of it was we not only gave it away, we gave them money to go with it.

People say we stole the Panama Canal. Nonsense. We offered those Panamamies a perfectly good deal and they turned it down—Colombia it was then—so then they revolted. We didn't "engineer" the revolution. That's pure bunkum. Those people love to revolt. Revolutions are mother's milk to them.

They have them like we have holidays. Stole it my foot, we paid for it twice. We paid the French for it, after they'd failed—the French never were very good builders—and then after we'd built it, we also turned around and paid Colombia for it, whom we didn't owe anything to. That Canal was built with good old American knowhow and stick-to-it-iveness—that's how it was built. Those Panamamies didn't do a damn thing to build the Canal. They just watched us build it. They sat around on their backsides and had siestas—and now we give it to them. I tell you it's sickening.

They say we had to do it because of our "image" in Latin America. Our image in Latin America! In the first place, it's not Latin America. They don't speak Latin down there anymore than our young people do up here. And, in the second place, it's not America. It's either Spanish or else it's Portuguese, which isn't much better. In the third place, what the hell do they mean, *image?* I suppose every time I want to do something —or, worse still, when somebody has done something awful to me, like grab my property—I go whining around and looking at myself in the mirror and wondering what my image is. Let me tell you what your image is—and I don't care what kind of a reader you are—your image is the sum total of what you are as a man. That's your image, son, and that's all you need to know about it. It's your breeding and your background and your education and saying what you mean and keeping your word and having the gumption not to take any guff from anybody.

Never mind Gibbon—go back to Lord Acton. He was a Catholic but he had some good ideas, just the same. He was an English Catholic, you know—they're very different.

Young people today unfortunately only know Lord Acton for

that "Absolute power corrupts absolutely" thing. Well, our Presidents should read that—over and over. But Lord Acton said a lot of other things. "Learn as much by writing as by reading," he said. And I can vouch for that one myself. I'll tell you I've learned as much from writing this book as you will from reading it. I know it's hard for you to believe, but it's true. And Lord Acton also said, "Be not content with the best book, but seek sidelights from the others." What that means very simply is you should not only read my book, but you can also pick up some additional little helpful hints from others. We have the right ones right here in the Club Library—books by Alexander Hamilton, Hamilton Fish, Fish Frobisher. They won't take the place of mine, of course, but they'll supplement it.

Another thing about Presidents that galls me is that when they go to one of those countries they try to speak French or Italian or Spanish or Urdu—I don't care what it is. Well, that's wrong. An American should speak English, and that's that. French used to be the diplomatic language, all right, but it isn't anymore. The French just didn't have the discipline to keep the job. They're weak, you know, and they're always thinking about sex. Anyway, I say nowadays your diplomatic language is English. And I say people abroad either learn to speak it or, if they can't do that, then at least they can learn to understand it when it's spoken to them.

Take me. I made the Grand Tour, like Fish and Fog and Tubby and Edgy and everybody else. But I didn't have to learn every damn language I ran into. I found that just by speaking loudly and distinctly in your native tongue you can make the dumbest person in one of those countries at least get the idea. But you do have to speak really loudly—I think a lot of foreigners are inclined to deafness anyway. Just very simple broken English, at the top of your lungs, will do the job in nine cases out of ten—although one trick I have I'll offer you as a tip. I learned it in France with Mamselle Terrier—I think that's what her name was, although it was Frenchified. Well, she undertook to teach me French and I can still remember her trying to get me to get that "eu" sound right. I can see her as if it were yesterday, pursing those pretty little rouged lips of hers and saying "Eu, eu." "Comme des *oeufs,*" she'd say, "pas comme les *oafs.*" But when I couldn't think of a French word, what I'd do is just say the word in English and give it that "eu" sound. If I was late, for example, and I couldn't think of the word for "sorry," I'd just say "seuré," and give it that accent sound, and everyone would be perfectly happy. I tell you if foreigners would just make as much effort to speak our native tongue as I make to speak theirs, we wouldn't have this "language barrier" people are always talking about.

The other day the General and I were reading the *New York Times* in the Morning Room and something got my goat and I put down the paper and said we hadn't had a decent foreign policy since John Paul Jones. I said it quietly, of course, because I didn't want to wake the General—he's getting as bad as Fog Horne about going to sleep, particularly when he tries to read the *Times.* Actually he would have been basically in sympathy with my Jones idea, but he wouldn't have liked my choice of a Navy man for the job. You know how the General is—he has very little use for the Navy or the Marines or the Air Force or the ROTC or the National Guard or draftees or women in the Army or whatever. But if he'd woken up, this time I would have called him on it. I would have told him to forget his inter-service rivalries—hell, I'd have said, we're all Americans.

Looking back on it now, I wish I had woken him up. Because by Jove there was a lot of truth in what I'd have said. What is foreign policy, after all? Define your terms, as I've said before, if you're going to argue with me. Foreign policy is first foreign —the trouble with your foreigners—and second it's policy. And what does your word "policy" come from? From your "police," obviously. And that's exactly what we want in our foreign policy—a policy that will police your foreigners. That's what we want and that's exactly what we haven't had since good old J. Paul J.

Jones was just a boy, you know—your boy then was very different from your boy today—when both the captain and the mate died on his first ship and he brought her home himself from halfway around the world. He was still a young man on the *Bonhomme Richard.* God, how we need some of that *Bonhomme Richard* philosophy today. Why, do you know that in that famous engagement with the *Serapis,* it was so bloody that neither Jones nor his opponent on the *Serapis* ever issued a complete casualty list? Later, another officer estimated that 302 men were killed or wounded on the *Richard* alone. And don't forget that when Jones was older and more mature, he still had time for Witter Hardee's idea of foreign affairs—he had one with Catherine the Great.

There were plenty of other Navy boys, too, besides Jones who knew how to handle foreign policy. General or no General, your Navy always was a cut above your Army socially anyway. I was in Naval ROTC, and there was just no comparison between us and Army ROTC. Those boys were just a grab-bag really. And, speaking of boys, do you know how old

Farragut was when he took command of his first ship in the War of 1812? Twelve, that's what he was, twelve. Today I wouldn't trust a boy of twelve to bring me my newspaper, let alone command a ship. It's been just steadily downhill, as I told you in the last chapter. Remember, Alexander the Great conquered the world at the age of twenty-one. I know there was no income tax in those days, but still.

Besides Jones, I give you Dave Farragut. Did you know that at Mobile Bay when Farragut said "Damn the torpedoes! Full speed ahead!" the ship in front of him had just been blown clear out of the water? Sometimes, when I'm writing this book, I tell you I feel old Dave Farragut's ghost at my side. And make no mistake. There are minefields being laid in front of me too. And some of them, I might add, by my own Clubmates.

"Damn the torpedoes! Full speed ahead!" "Millions for defense, not one cent for tribute!" Those are ringing cries. Today? Don't make me laugh. We pay billions for tribute and we haven't got a defense good enough to let me take my constitutional in broad daylight. After dark, forget it. I carry this little blackjack up my sleeve and I have it right here with me now. It's like a shillelagh. It's double-backed up there but when you swing your arm down it comes down and all the weight extends to the head. Like this. You crack a man with this, and he'll stay cracked. But I'll tell you something. Even with this, I don't believe your Government today can protect me against foreigners right here in my own Club. I could get up and go to the Club kitchen right now—our kitchen is crawling with foreigners, you know, men who literally don't speak a word of English—and I could disappear in there and I tell you your Government wouldn't do one damn thing about it. Any more than they'll do anything about these diplomats and students

177

and businessmen who disappear all over the place. I don't mind the diplomats disappearing—that's part of their business, and I certainly don't care about those students. They just smoke drugs and get into trouble anyway. But when business-men abroad start disappearing all over the place, well it's just damn bad for business, is what it is. And one of these days, we'll just pull in our horns and stop our Grand Tours altogether. Just wait till that happens, and you'll find these foreigners will stop this nonsense, pronto. Not one of those countries would last through the night without our American tourist dollar, and don't you forget it.

Remember, I'm not just talking about ordinary trippers. I'm talking about your Grand Tour boys. But what's the use? Today, you can't take a Grand Tour to your bathroom in safety. You think I'm joking? All right, take all the places everyone used to be able to go in the winter—places like Bermuda or Nassau or Jamaica. You go there today and you'll wake up some morning garroted. And it isn't just you, either, it's your prop-erty. Don't forget that. I would no more build a house in Jamaica today than I would build one in Cuba. And, speaking of Cuba brings me to the Bay of Pigs and Vietnam and all the rest of it. What in heaven's name was our Navy doing at Guan-tanamo Bay? I'll tell you what they were doing. Sitting on their backsides, that's what they were doing. In Vietnam, it was the same thing. And Korea, and everywhere else. Everything we've done in my lifetime in foreign policy has been done by halves. We even go around dividing countries in halves—we give the good half to the Bolsheviks, of course, and we take the have-not half. But never mind Cuba and Vietnam. It really is sicken-ing that we can't give a well-respected businessman abroad the protection that Caesar gave his slaves. And all we need is a

President with a modicum of guts. The last one we had—no, I can't even think of one, with the possible exception of Teddy Roosevelt. There was James Monroe, of course. Monroe was all right—he was a good man on defense. But I'm talking about your offense. Remember Teddy Roosevelt's "Perdicaris alive or Raisuli dead!" Now that's foreign policy you can hang your hat on. And we got that fellow Perdicaris back—from those pirates too—in two days.

But it isn't just your pirates. Today your average pirate would look like Little Lord Fauntleroy compared to your hi-jackers and all the rest of them. Look at your "Third World" and your "emerging nations." Don't talk to me about Third World. As far as I'm concerned, we'll have a Third World when there's a Second Coming. And "emerging" nations—I hate that word "emerging." Let me tell you something. Everytime one of those babies *e*merges, I'm just that much more sub-merged. It is simply absurd. A nation has no business being free and independent unless it's been a good, hard-working colony and helped its mother country for a good, long time. They talk about "developing" countries. Well, that's what "de-veloping" is. I hate that word too—the way they've corrupted it. Developing is developing, that's what it is. It's exactly the same thing as a good boy on a farm. He just doesn't run off to the city and holler "I'm independent"—not until he's done his work as a big boy to help pay back his family for when he was a little boy and no damn use.

How many generations do you think it took to develop me? At least ten—and there were a lot of shirt-sleeves to shirt-sleeves in three generations in there too. And there was no disgrace in it, either. But these natives today, they're nothing but shirt-sleeves, generation after generation, for one single reason—they won't do a day's work let alone a generation's. Do you realize that this country was founded in 1607? That's Jamestown. All right, when did it become free? 1776, right? Add that up now. That's 169 years of good, hard-working, sensible growth, and then, after that, we had a perfectly decent revolution. But all those years, before we had that revolution, we were developing landed gentry and top drawer people—the people from whom you draw, or at least you should draw, your leaders. Do you know, for example, how many members of just one family, the Lees, there were at one time in the Virginia House of Burgesses? It was long before our Revolution. Seven, that's how many, seven out of a House of just a hundred—and good, able men, too.

Compare that to your average "emerging" country today. They emerge them right out of the cocoon. "I want to be free," they shout from someplace you never heard of, and then we give them the country and they haven't even got the decency to keep the name that God gave them. They change it. Actually, to me, that's the worst—the way they change their names. In my day we had decent geography books and maps and globes with all the countries decently colored—pink for England, green for France, I don't remember what Italy was, brown, as I recall, but no matter. Those were your countries and there you were. Today you'd need a jigsaw puzzle to keep up with them.

Why in the name of all that's holy do we let them do it? Good old solid names like British East Africa, German East Africa, Portuguese East Africa, French West Africa, the Belgian Congo, the Dutch Cameroons, and so forth. Now what are they? They are Zaire and Zambia and Gambia and Namibia—honestly, Gambia is now calling itself "The Gambia," as if there was one called *"A* Gambia." And they admitted they did it because they said people get mixed up. Mixed up with their own changes over there, that's a good one. But look at all the other changes—Dahomey, Djibouti, Mali, Malawi, Rwanda, Togo and God knows what else. All right, your stamp collectors like it—I used to collect stamps myself—but who else? It's change for the sake of change, that's what it is, and it ought not to be allowed. And of course we don't allow it here at the Club —not with our Society to Put Things Back the Way They Were, you can bet on that. If there's one thing that makes my blood boil, and Fish Frobisher's too, it's some damn country changing its name. We discuss Africa the way it was meant to be discussed—with the names God gave it. If you think we're going to call Rhodesia "Zimbabwe," you've got another think coming. Honestly, what kind of a name is that? It sounds like something some native would yell in the middle of a war dance if he didn't feel well.

The whole African thing, you know, never really needed to happen. What you had was the last of the British Empire, on the one hand, and, on the other, the collapse of gumption by us. What did we get after the Great War, anyway? The *Leviathan,* that's what. The *Vaterland,* she was. All right, she was a big ship, but use your bean, boy. When you've won a war you don't want ships, you want territory. Who did we give the German colonies to? We gave them to France and people like that. And yet even a schoolboy knows that your French race is rotten with colonies—they've just never been any good at it. The Dutch aren't much better. Or the Belgians, or the Portuguese, for that matter. As for the Spanish—well, the trouble there is that they're Catholic and therefore opposed to birth control. You can't get any colonizing done properly if you don't have birth control. Your Anglo-Saxon race, when you come right down to it, is your premiere colonizer. And England, of course, is your textbook example.

Take England—I mean my England when I was a boy. I used to play with soldiers day and night. I had a dandy regiment of Grenadier Guards and one of Highlanders and my Light Horse too. They came eight to a box for your Infantry and five for your Cavalry. And when I had the croup, my mother would get the croup kettle out and I wouldn't have to go to school, and I'd set up my soldiers on the rug and have a real war. I'd put the savages on one side—I had some very well-made savages —chiefs with their tomahawks whose arms went up and down —and then on our side I had English and Americans. I particularly remember the American Marines with their bayonets. We fought not only on the rug, but in the bathtub, where we floated them on rafts. And then during the Easter vacation, we'd go out to the big pond and we'd set up mother countries on the main bank and on the other side we'd set up colonies. We dredged those little colonies' harbors and everything. The point is we loved those colonies. They were the savages on our side. And we took care of them when they were attacked by other savages, and sent in our Marines.

How it takes me back! But we must press on. Look at the map in 1918. Now there was a map for you. Pink for England, as I told you, and just look at it—there was pink all over that map. Start with your self-governing dominions—Canada, Australia, New Zealand, South Africa. Then look at the new territories— Mesopotamia, Trans Jordan, Tanganyika, the Cameroons, and Southwest Africa. And besides India all over Africa, the outright Empire—Egypt, Anglo-Egyptian Sudan, British Somaliland, the East Africa protectorate or Kenya, on and on—Northern Rhodesia, Southern Rhodesia, Uganda, Nigeria, the Gold Coast, Sierre Leone and Gambia. Not "The Gambia," of course, just Gambia. Even the little islands all around—Ascension, Tristan da Cunha, Mauritius and Zanzibar, which was the gateway to all the African territories. It had, of course, been an Arabian sultanate, the center of the slave trade, but now it was under British protection. These modern historians—they make me sick. We didn't start the slave trade, or the British either. The British abolished slavery in the Empire a hundred fifty years ago. But tell that to your Africans today. They think *I* had slaves. Slaves hell, I can't get a civil waiter.

The thing we should have done right after the Great War was sink our teeth into a real Colonial Empire of our own. Train men for the job—from the private schools, the second sons. That's the place for your second sons—colonial service. I'm not casting aspersions on second sons. A second son had a very important position. He never learned to carve the roast or things like that—that was your first son's job—but since he had no claim on the family estate, he was expected either to marry well and establish new landed lines of his own or else go into the Army or the Navy or, as I say, go into the colonial service.

In England the core of your colonial service was the old boys from your Public Schools. Public Schools, of course, in the best sense of that word "public"—in other words, from the private schools. What you learned at those schools, or at our better private schools for that matter, was how to be what we used to call an "all-rounder." You learned that from Latin and Greek —you learned how to reason. You could always hire a little expert to build a bridge or get rid of the tsetse fly or whatever your problem was, but in those days, remember, an expert was

183

your inferior. That's something we've totally forgotten today. We make tin gods of these damn experts. We make tin gods of them and build them up to the sky and then wonder why, not having the background, they fall flat on their backsides when they try to do the job of an all-rounder.

Besides Latin and Greek, the other thing those English boys learned at their public schools was the playing of games. There were cricket and rugby, of course, while ours would be football and baseball, but, above all, you learned sportsmanship and fair play. Remember your Great War was won on your playing fields of Eton. But how would you teach our boys that sort of sportsmanship today? The first thing you'd have to do would be to turn off that damn television. Sportsmanship today—tell it to the Marines. Look at those dances they do after touchdowns. Or that "spiking" of the ball they do in the end zone. Incidentally, where was The Game on my television? The Harvard-Yale Game, for Pete's sake. Instead they gave me Michigan and Ohio State. I know people go to those colleges—the people who live there—but where is your tradition? And your sportsmanship? Did you see that Woody Hayes punching that boy from the other team? Those television reporters never even mentioned it. Couldn't find the instant replay, they said. Couldn't *find* it—they just didn't want to find it.

I tell you sportsmanship went out with all this awful professionalism and big salaries and players' agents and even unions, for God's sake. Honestly, it makes my blood boil—but I won't let it. Because the essence of being a gentleman in sports is not to take them too seriously. But in my day, goddammit, the very word "professional" was suspect. Today, if you're an "amateur," you're not very good. If you're a "pro," you're, well, a pro. Well, do you know what the word "amateur" means? It

184

means "lover." It's from your Latin *amare*, "to love." It doesn't mean "lover" the way the young people use the word. It has nothing whatsoever to do with sex. It meant lover of the game. *Lover of the game,* as compared to your lower class players, who played for pay. Why, I remember in tennis and golf and horse racing and any sports you could name, if the man was a professional, you never used the word "Mr." That was the difference between you. Either you were Mr. So-and-So, or you were just So-and-So. Last name only. And yet I was watching that awful Ilie Nastase—he and Connors are a pair, aren't they? Anyway, I was watching him on the television the other day and he had done something wrong, as usual, and the referee called him on it and said, "Nastase, will you please serve?" And Nastase, if you please, shouted "Call me Mr. Nastase." I tell you I couldn't call Nastase Mr. Nastase if you paid me. Which is just my point. He *is* paid, so you shouldn't.

Where was I? Oh, I hate to keep doing that. Oh, about sportsmanship. "Play up, play up and play the game," we used to sing. "On to the walls, on to the walls, on to the walls—and over." And with it all we had humility. We learned it from the hymns and the poems we had to commit to memory. There should be much more committing to memory in schools today than there is. I, for example, can still recite Kipling's "Recessional" completely from memory, without missing a word, just the way I used to do it at school. I often do it at Fortnightly:

> If, drunk with the sight of power, we loose
> Wild tongues that have not Thee in awe,
> Such boastings as the Gentiles use,
> Or lesser breeds without the law—

185

Lord God of Hosts, be with us yet,
Lest we forget—lest we forget!

And now we've done just what Kipling tried to warn us about. We *have* forgotten. And look at what it's cost us. Kipling, by the way, didn't use the word "Gentiles" the way we use it —as a religious thing. By "Gentiles," Kipling meant all Europeans, and then by his "lesser breeds." he meant Asians and Africans and so forth. Your British racism, you know, was like my racism. It's never been a color racism. The true Anglo-Saxon, no matter how modest he is—say one like me—feels he's just as much a cut above other Europeans as he is above Asians or Africans or South Americans or anybody else. Don't forget, then Kipling praised Gunga Din, he said Gunga was a better man than *he* was—Gunga, in Kipling's words, was "white, clear white, inside."

The whole British experience in Africa was something from which, if we'd only had the will power, we could have learned a lesson. And today we'd be running our empire just as the British did until they ran out of gas—or, as they say, out of petrol. Freddie Lugard warned us, just like Kipling did. Dear old Freddie—he was a close friend of my father's and the real pioneer of British penetration into both West and East Africa. There's never been a better book on Africa than Freddie's *The Dual Mandate in Tropical Africa.* I was brought up on that book and I gave it to the Club Library and I have it here in front of me now. Freddie was a very fair man—he believed that both colonizers and natives had their rights. Here's exactly what he said about those rights:

The tropics are the heritage of mankind and neither on the one hand has the suzerain power a right to their exclusive exploitation, nor on the other hand have the races which inhabit them a right to deny their bounties to those that need them. The merchant, the miner and the manufacturer do not enter the tropics on sufferance or employ their technical skill, their energy and their capital as interlopers or as "greedy capitalists," but in fulfillment of the mandate of civilization.

That says it all right there—the mandate of civilization, and we've let it all go down the drain. But you don't have to get Africa out of books. I'll give it to you straight from the horse's mouth—Tubby's mouth. I told you Tubby knew Africa. He's played polo over there, I told you, and he's gone back twice—once to get servants but another time out of sheer love of the place. Tubby says that where we made our big mistake in Africa was in not getting behind their tribal thing. We never should have let them have countries at all—just keep their tribes. We should have sent in the Marines if we had to keep those tribes. Tubby has told me many times that we're plain wrong, not only in Africa but all over the damn world, when we think of a native and you and me as basically the same. We're not and we never will be. The fact is, between even the best of your natives and an average me, it's night and day. As for some of your lesser tribes, we're not even shaped the same. Tubby points out that in one of those tribes, your average native head, although it's bigger than my head, has only a 35-ounce brain. While a brain like Tubby's probably weights at least 45 ounces. Tubby also points out this same tribe has an exceedingly thick cranium.

The good Lord evidently made them that way and it's very useful, because they use their heads, you know, not just the way you or I use them, but actually as weapons of attack. In other words, the way I understand it from Tubby, when you get exasperated with a native over there, and say "Use your head, man"—and he's angry with you—you'd better look out.

But never mind Tubby. Talk to the General. Talk about knowing real Africans—I tell you the General was in Africa in the Great War. How many people can say that today? The General was attached to the British Army under Meinertzhagen—Meinertzhagen was on our side, remember, despite his name—against Colonel Paul von Lettow-Vorbeck. Mark that name well. Von Lettow-Vorbeck was a German of the Old School—they don't come any better than that, you know—and he knew your African natives. To von Lettow-Vorbeck, for example, your Hottentot wasn't just a joke or a symbol for a give-away program. Far from it. Von Lettow-Vorbeck had had two years of bush warfare in the Hottentot rebellion of 1904, and he really knew those bush babies. He had practically no help from Berlin in the Great War, and when he finally surrendered in 1918, he had exactly 30 officers and 125 men left, not counting his Porks. The Askaris, of course, were English-trained Africans, and the Porks were Portuguese. Anyway, for four years, von Lettow-Vorbeck held off an army of over 30,-000 in a war in which the English lost as many lives, if you count natives, as they did in the whole Boer War.

I was going to have the General write the whole story of the Great War in Africa. I don't want to hurt the General's feelings, but frankly, he's just not up to it. The General, bless his heart, just doesn't know how to tell a story—he's too full of facts, and he never comes to the point. I've spent many a drink listening to him and, take my word for it, you're better off getting it from me. The first and most important point is that the African native, then, or now, or in 4,000 A.D.—you name the time—just isn't worth a damn in combat unless he has good tough training and a good tough Anglo-Saxon officer—I don't care which side he's on. Meinertzhagen himself got so discouraged with the natives that he told the General he wished to heaven he could get back to the Western front and fight in the trenches. Imagine, trench warfare. You had everything there—mud, slime, lice, gas. Why your modern soldier wouldn't last a day in one of those trenches. Yet Meinertzhagen so despaired of the lack of discipline of those natives that he *wished* for it.

Now I'm not one of these people in the Club who are prejudiced, who says that all natives were bad. They weren't. On our side, for example, you had Ghurkas and your Punjabis from India, who were first rate, once you had them trained. They were your Gunga Din types. And the Germans, don't forget, not only had their Askaris, some of whom were surprisingly good, but they also had their Rugga-Ruggas. They were top drawer too. They were primarily used as runners, but they could trot for hours, carrying messages in split sticks.

The second point is that both sides really fought a bully war —it was the last real gentleman's war. There was good form on both sides and real sportsmanship and they observed all the amenities. Von Lettow-Vorbeck, for example, had an agreement not to fire his artillery against the British position Sunday afternoon at cricket time. That's where we get our expression "It isn't cricket." Well, according to the General, one day they did fire a round at four o'clock in the afternoon, for heaven sake, and needless to say the British commander, Brigadier General Wapshare—they called him "Wappy"—was furious.

189

He sent over word demanding to know whether or not von Lettow-Vorbeck was a gentleman or wasn't he? Well, naturally, von Lettow-Vorbeck apologized. And of course it turned out it was some half-trained Askari who had fired the round.

On the reverse side of the coin, when the British, by mistake, put a six-inch shell from the cruiser *Fox* into a German hospital, good old Wappy sent Meinertzhagen himself over the lines with a flag of truce to apologize. On the way over, Meinertzhagen came across the body of one of his best friends, which had been horribly mutilated by the Askaris, but that didn't deter him from his duty. He apologized profusely to the Germans. And afterwards he told the General the Germans were "kindness itself." They not only gave him an excellent breakfast but went out of their way to praise the fighting spirit of the North Lancs. The General said Meinertzhagen told him that both sides discussed the war as freely as if it had been a football match—which, of course, is just the way a good war should be.

On another occasion, the General also said, Meinertzhagen was out on reconnaissance one night when he saw a German officer coming down the path alone. The German was unarmed but so was Meinertzhagen, and Meinertzgahen told the General he remembered thinking should he spring out and try to strangle the man or should he just say "How do you do?" and let him pass. Well the answer was obvious. It was a gentleman's war and there was certainly no necessity for two gentlemen to have it at each other out there in some kind of undignified personal contest. Actually, what Meinertzhagen finally did was he not only jumped up and saluted the man and said "How do you do?" he also said it in German—which was really a nice touch. By the same token, however, when a somewhat similar situation occurred later, and a German officer sprang out alone and attacked him, Meinertzhagen was so furious with the man for breaking the code that he cracked him on the head with his knobkerrie and killed him dead as a dodo.

Of course there were some lovely bits of humor in that war. The General couldn't tell a humorous story if his life depended on it, so I'll do it for him. My favorite was the story of that dear old Brigadier Wappy, as I told you they called him. He was about to be transported on a rickshaw in Mombasa pulled by little Swahili boy who turned around and asked, "Wappy? Ju?" —which meant in Swahili "Where to? Up the hill?" Whereupon Wappy jumped out and walloped the boy with his swagger stick. He thought the boy was asking if he was Jewish. I don't see how even the General can miss on that story, but he does. Time and again he does.

So much for your Africa. We've still got the Far East and the Near East and God knows where else to cover. Take Asia. I mentioned John Paul Jones. Well, I'll tell you we haven't had a good foreign policy in Asia since Matthew Perry. There was another Jones for you. Perry literally opened up Japan single-handed. He concluded that—and I'm quoting from a Club book on this—that "the only way to break Japan's intransigent isolationist attitude was to approach them with resolute attitude." He sailed right into Japan with just two frigates and two sailing ships and said he wanted to give them some documents. And he didn't just ask them to take them—in fact he said he was "not soliciting it as a favor"—that it was an act of courtesy which was due from "one civilized country to another." When was the last time you heard one of the namby-pamby members of our striped pants set say something like that? 1854, right? Right then with good old Perry. And when the Japanese ordered him to leave, he replied that if the Japanese Government did not delegate a suitable person to receive the documents in his possession, he would—and I'm quoting from the Club book again on this—"go on shore with a suitable force to deliver them personally, be the consequences what they might." Whereupon, the Japanese hopped to it, of course and sent the official out to collect the documents and the next year the President got the treaty he wanted. Incidentally, Millard Fillmore was President then. I've never rated him as highly as I perhaps should. But I'll tell you one thing—I'd take him in a minute over one of these whippersnapper Presidents today.

That was foreign policy for you. Compare Perry in Tokyo Harbor to our position in the Far East today. All we do everywhere is worry about Russia. Let them worry about us, for Pete's sake. The minute they went into Hungary, for example, we should have gone right into Ceylon, or someplace like that. You could use as your excuse that they changed the name. Sri Lanka! It shouldn't be allowed. All I've seen in my lifetime is appeasement—all the way from Czar Nicholas to Henry Kissinger and this Vance fellow. They gave in to Lenin, they gave in to Stalin, they gave in to Hitler, they gave in to Mussolini and they gave in to Tojo. And when we were all through giving in to all of them, we started giving in to anyone who wanted anything as long as he was black, or brown, or yellow or young or a woman. If I painted my face and said I was a native of somewhere, they'd give me Fort Knox. I remember when Cabot Lodge was at the United Nations and said something in reply to, as he put it, "the gentleman from Russia." "I am not a gentleman," the fellow replied, "I am the delegate from the Soviet Union." "I did not know," replied Cab, "the two were mutually exclusive." That said it all, right there.

I tell you, your giving programs are bad enough—they sap your pocketbook. But *give-in* programs, they sap your very fibre, your moral fibre. And we've given in so much, there isn't enough fibre left in our young people today to make a doll-house rug. We've given in until we've caved in, That's what we've done. Take Asia. Who was the greatest authority on Asia in history? Douglas MacArthur, hands down. He was also top military man in Asia, or for that matter all history. I wouldn't even put Genghis Khan above him, although MacArthur himself did—he was that modest. And don't forget that besides his military genius, he also ran single-handed the greatest occupation in history—the occupation of Japan.

I'll tell you something. The Japanese people were so crazy about MacArthur that they actually petitioned to become the 49th state in the Union. Only a handful of people know that— my Uncle Bagnalls is one of them—and of course it was hushed up. But just imagine—the 49th state! If we'd had the brains of a she-goat, Japan right now, as I'm writing these words, would, instead of competing with us all over the world, with their damn Sonys and Toyotas and Datsuns and Fuji Film and all the rest of it—why they'd be selling those things all over the world *for* us. Right now, I'd be not sitting here worried half to death about my General Motors and my Eastman Kodak and even my IBM—instead, I'd be out cheering those little Japs on. Honestly, it makes you sick how dumb we can be. Instead of taking them up on their offer and making them the 49th state, we made it Alaska. We already had Alaska, for Pete's sake. They didn't need statehood—there's not enough people up there to put in Rhode Island. But with Japan, statehood was the only way to get them. And MacArthur had not only saved them from the Bolsheviks, he had made first-rate little Capitalists out of them. But now, of course, since we missed the boat, too damn first-rate Capitalists. Oh, the ironies of history.

I remember right where I was standing the day that damn Truman fired MacArthur. In the bar, we were, when we heard the news. And I've never seen a pall cast over that bar like that one. The General wanted to march on Washington right then. But Fish stopped them. That would play right into their hands, he said. As for Fog Horne, I tell you he was purple. But I can't go into that. The point is I have here two books of MacArthur's speeches from the Club Library. You know, there is more demand for these two books by MacArthur than any other author in the Club, save Goldwater. And we elected them both Honorary Members of the Club, too. In Goldwater's case there were some objections from our more prejudiced people, but as I said at the time, the man had just lost a bid for the Presidency and he needed something to buck him up. But never mind that. As far as I'm concerned, Douglas MacArthur wrote the book on appeasement. Go back and read that "Old soldiers never die" speech. Read the whole thing now. Young people today just skim—it's that awful speed reading thing. I can speed read too—I can even speed write for that matter. But you don't speed read Douglas MacArthur. I wish every internationalist, every Bolshevik appeaser, every U.N. worshipper, even all these damn Europe firsters, would read that speech every day. I want you to read this part of it right now:

> There are some who, for varying reasons, would appease Red China. They are blind to history's clear lesson. For history teaches with unmistakeable emphasis that appeasement begets new and bloodier wars. It points to no single instance where this end has justified the means,

where appeasement has led to more than a sham peace. Like blackmail, it lays the basis for new and successively greater demands until, as in blackmail, violence becomes the only other alternative.

And now we recognize China and turn our back on Taiwan. Well, that's just what's been done to me in my life. Blackmail, in all senses of the word. And many's the time it's occurred to one of us at Fortnightly that violence is the only answer. Honestly, if there's one thing that makes my blood boil, it's what we've let happen in Asia. You have the same damn thing you had in Africa—England abdicting all over the place and us not having the common or garden sense to pick up the pieces. We never had to pick up the whole thing, you know. Who wants all of India or all of China or all of Japan or all of any of those places? What you want are just certain parts. We'd want Hong Kong, of course. It's a fine city and a great trading port. And Singapore. You never let natives run something like the Raffles Hotel. They don't run things, you know—they just run things down. India is a perfect example. You wouldn't want all of India, of course—you'd just want part of it if England was going to be fool enough to give it up. Simla, for instance, up in the mountains, where the English colonial government used to go to escape the heat of the summer. What earthly use was it to give it back to the natives? They don't even feel the heat the way we do. They don't even go to the beaches—they're already tanned.

There are a whole lot of other places we ought to have over there. Places like Katmandu and Tibet. We should never have let China take that. We could run it and let the Dalai Lama be the figurehead. And we also ought to pick up Bali and Fiji and places like that. They'd be fine colonies because they'd be self-supporting, thanks to the tourists. It's really so simple. All you have to do in foreign policy is go at the thing establishing top-drawer clubs all over the world. I don't mean Fortnightlies —you couln't hope for that—but you could establish perfectly decent run-of-the-mill clubs. The basic trouble with our Presidents and Secretaries of State is that they're not club men and they can't see the whole picture. They just run around the world putting their fingers in the dikes and trying to plug the little leaks, and not realizing the whole damn dam is bursting. When Kissinger was Secretary of State, I tried to tell him my Club theory. I wrote him a very simple, easy-to-understand letter about it. But all I got back was a thank-you note from an Undersecretary. Imagine—and those boys are supposed to know protocol. Of course Kissinger probably wouldn't have understood it anyway. He's bright enough and he's traveled all over hell and gone, but the man, as I understand it, had a very limited social life before he got married. Just movie stars, and people like that. He was a professor, you know—that's the basic problem. A professor is the last man you'd want for your top job at State.

I don't mean to take off just on Kissinger. There hasn't been a single damned Secretary of State in my lifetime who was worth his per diem. Marshall was the worst. He really started the Santa Claus thing—he and Truman—the two of them together would give away your mother. And the dumbest thing about them was the way they didn't see it wouldn't make us popular. All right, Santa Claus is well liked. Well, why is he well liked? Because he's a myth, that's why—there isn't a word of truth to him. But the way we gave away money, there was no myth about it. And of course everybody got cross. The ones who didn't get as much as the ones who got the most were just as furious as the ones who didn't get anything.

Remember that wonderful movie, "The Mouse That Roared," about the little country that decided to declare war on us so they could lose the war and then get millions of dollars afterwards—only they made, as I recall, the mistake of beating us. Well, that picture came too close to the truth for comfort, if you ask me. I've been looking over the money we've been ladling out since the end of the Second World War, and I tell you "The Mouse That Roared" was an understatement. Germany, 5 billion; Italy, 6 and 1/2 billion; Japan, 7 billion; Austria, for Pete's sake, a billion and a half. Anyone who fought us got billions—"loans," they called them, though of course they never repaid them—while a decent little country like Finland, the only one which paid its debts from the Great War, remember, got the back of our hand. The only one which has paid us over a billion back is Germany, and they, with the richest economy of all, still owe us 4 billion. As for Italy, it still owes us 6 billion. And if you think we're going to get it out of those Bolsheviks, you're very much mistaken. As for Japan, don't make me laugh. They've paid us exactly 2 million back, out of 6 billion. Meanwhile, they're running around the world putting my General Motors and my Eastman Kodak and my Bethlehem Steel out of business.

I beg you, don't talk Marshall Plan to me. That was supposed to be for Europe. Europe, my eye. We've been doling out money to every corner of the globe. India, over 10 billion, out of which they've paid back less than one billion, Turkey, 7 billion. They've paid back a few paltry million. Yugoslavia, 3 billion—the same thing. We might just as well have shipped the money right to Russia. Remember, I'm just mentioning the big countries. There are countries on the list you've never heard of. You don't believe it? All right, try Upper Volta for size. Maybe we gave to the Volta Boatmen.

My favorite though is 3 billion dollars to Iran. Iran and Iraq and Saudi Arabia—I never can remember which is Persia and which is Mesopotamia and which is just good, old-fashioned Arabia. But no matter. Imagine giving money to those people! Why they've got more money than we have. All that damn oil money. That Shah of Iran was obviously a man of substance, though I speak of him in the past tense. Certainly he was a man we would have been happy to invite to Fortnightly. But you have to ask yourself—where was our CIA? Really, sometimes I think it isn't our CIA, it's somebody else's. Just by the law of averages you would think they would be on the right side half the time, but they're not. Honestly, it's so discouraging. When it comes right down to it, I'd give money to the Israelis any day in the week before I'd give it to the Arabs. I know this isn't going to win me any popularity contests with the fuddy-duddies around here, but at least the Israelis have got gumption.

Take these OPEC nations, and I wish you would. Here we sit, like scared rabbits, wondering when they're next going to hold us up with a new boost in the price of oil. Scared rabbits, in front of a bunch of desert Bedouins, sitting on their backsides, waiting for their oil to come in while some tinhorn Sheik sits in his harem waiting for my dollars to come in. We haven't even got the nerve to walk in there and say "This is what we'll give you, Buster, take it or leave it." And if they don't take it, well and good. We'll take them. Or rather we'll leave them alone—who wants them anyway?—and take their damn oil wells. Wells, remember, which we drilled to begin with, with your and my money. And one of these days they'll take them over, you mark my words just the way Mexico did with our wells there. Just up one night and took them, while we sat and took it. This time what we should do is tell those OPEC boys the shoe is on the other foot.

We are running out of oil—all right. Does that mean we have to sell the Club to the Arabs? Of course it doesn't. But I tell you the last time I was in England the only place I could go which wasn't owned by an Arab was White's Club. I came back and told Witter about it, and Witter agreed it was sickening. He told me that the ruler of Abu Dhabi had a bullet-proof Rolls-Royce and a bodyguard with a silver-plated machine gun. That bodyguard would need it, I told Witter, if I ran into him.

It's so absurd, this whole Arab thing. The minute you learn you're going to run out of oil, you take every oil well you've got and shut it down. Cap it—caput—and sit on it. And then you import every single solitary barrel you need from them. You run *them* out of oil. You don't run yourself out. And then, when they run out, you open your wells, and turn around and sell them oil—upping the price every time you feel like it. A child could figure it out. But not our Government, of course. They can't figure anything out, because they're no good at figures.

I asked Fish Frobisher to get me the facts on this oil thing. And Fishy did. At the rate we're using oil now, he said, we'll run out of oil on December 10, 2008, at 9:22 P.M. When Fish does a thing, it stays done. All right, those are your facts—billions of barrels of oil in the world, and at the rate we're using it, 9:22 P.M., December 10, 2008.

Very well then, if that's what it is, that's what it is. I believe in facing facts. On December 10, 2008, I'll be 100. And, with any decent luck, I'll be the Oldest Living Member. It's going to be me or Peabo Parsons and, the way I figure it, with Peabo never going out of his room right now, or taking any chances at all, it's going to be nip and tuck right down to the wire. But if you think I'm going to be like Peabo, you've got another think coming. I'd rather not win than win that way. And I have no intention, thank you very much, of being immobile on December 10, 2008. I've been doing a good deal of thinking about it, and what I am going to do is go out with my boots on. I'm going to hie myself down to the Automobile Museum and get my mother's electric car. She left it to the museum but she left a codicil that if I ever wanted it, I could have it. I remember that car, and I loved it. It was a good, old-fashioned decent sensible machine. Easy to drive, too.

For our Fortnightly on Foreign Affairs, everybody had a different idea on whom to have. Early in the game someone, I've forgotten whom it was, said we ought to have one of the United Nations people. And you can imagine the reception that got. None of us, of course, were against the basic idea of nations getting together, the Congress of Vienna, the League of Nations, whatever. But United? What in heaven's name gave them the effrontery to call it that? After all, I'm not uniting with one damn more thing in my lifetime, not even a woman—why would I expect my country to unite with another nation?

Anyway, I think mostly because we were sick and tired of Washington people, we decided to have a go at it. But who at the United Nations to ask presented a problem. Everybody had very different ideas about that. Witter Hardee wanted an Englishman, of course, and the General naturally wanted a friendly dictator. But I told him they didn't have the actual dictators at the U.N.—they just had their representatives. Fog Horne suggested we get a man from Switzerland who could tell us what to do about the dollar, but Fish Frobisher said we'd already had one dollar talk and this time, if we were really determined to have a U.N. type, we ought to go whole hog and really bite the bullet and get ourselves a Russian. Edgy thought he said "Hessian," but when he learned that it was to be a Russian, he felt we should at least have the decency to get a White one. I told Edgy we couldn't do that—they weren't in the U.N.—and then Edgy said he would be willing to settle for a White Chinaman. Fish pointed out that the Nationalist China people weren't in the United Nations anymore either. The long and short of it was the Russian won out—I think it was because none of us had ever seen a Bolshevik in person. But I'll tell you one thing—no one wanted to be the one to extend the invitation, you can bet on that. So we played golf dice for it and I, if you please, lost.

I had the devil of a time on the phone with them, but I kept at it, and I got my man. I never did get exactly what his job was there, or exactly what his name was. It sounded though like Isomovich. Well, you can imagine what that did to Edgy's hearing aid. Every time I said the name, Edgy looked shocked. The odd thing was the fellow looked just like an old-fashioned Russian, except he had less neck. And I promise you, he had the same facial expression for everything—as if he had just eaten and it had disagreed with him. Which reminds me, we gave him a first-rate dinner. We gave him just as good a dinner as we gave anbody—for which, of course, he didn't even have the common courtesy to thank us. But of course if we hadn't done it, we'd have never heard the end of it. That's how these fellows are—you're damned if you do and damned if you don't.

Well, the Bolshevik made his speech all right—about something or other, it wasn't important—but one thing he said was that just because the United Nations was in this country didn't mean we had more rights than anybody else. I tell you that did it. I started the question period myself—I don't usually do it, I usually wait for some of the little questions first—but this time I couldn't. I told the man I wasn't one of those people who believed we ought to take the United Nations and throw it into the East River. I told him I took the middle ground—I was for putting it in Switzerland or on some relatively friendly island like Bermuda or Greenland. I also reminded him that he and his other U.N. people could park anywhere they pleased, and yet they had their own perfectly good parking places outside their embassies and consulates. I told him the law can't touch them—that they were a law unto themselves. Well, after I got all through, he asked me if you please what my question was. I tell you they just don't listen.

Anyway, Fog Horne came next. Fog brought up the subject of money. He said that ten countries paid 80 percent of the budget for the U.N., and his question was what the hell were the other 140 doing in there? The Bolshevik got on his high horse about that. He said that both Russia and the Ukrainian SSR were in the top ten. Those *s*'s killed Edgy's hearing aid, of course—he thought the man said something about the Tsar. And when he finally got it straight, the Bolshevik made the incredible statement that Russia and those Ukrainian birds paid as much as the U.S. did. Well, that was too much for Fish Frobisher. Typical Fishy, he had a list of exactly what everybody in the top ten paid and he passed it right over to the Bolshevik. I copied it down, country by country, right here:

U.S.	25.00 percent
Russia	12.97 percent
Japan	7.15 percent
West Germany	7.10 percent
France	5.86 percent
China	5.50 percent
Great Britain	5.31 percent
Italy	3.60 percent
Canada	3.18 percent
Ukrainian SSR	1.71 percent

Never mind the Ukrainian SSR, Fish said, it's still a total of close to 80 percent from just ten countries—and yet we let 140 others in. The Bolshevik immediately said he couldn't comment on that, and then he looked at his watch—which was a good gold watch, by the way—and said he had to get back. Which you can bet was the best piece of news we'd had from that bird. Because from the moment he left, we all relaxed. We got hold of Henry and got another round of drinks and resolved to get down to brass tacks on this thing.

Fish Frobisher went to the Library and got a complete roster of the U.N. nations. When he came back we started on our complete reorganization of the membership. We all agreed first we'd take the ones who were paying their share, and to kick out Russia and China, we decided to substitute Taiwan for China, and then we also voted to throw out Italy, which was too damned Communist, and also that ridiculous Ukrainian SSR. We were pretty evenly divided on Japan—we finally decided, though, to leave it out.

That left us with our basic core—U.S., Great Britain, Canada, West Germany and France. And then we started alphabetically on the others. You really can't believe who they let into that United Nations. I tell you if anyone ran a Club on that basis it would go out of business tomorrow. Here's the way the list began—just the *A*'s on the list, mind you—Afghanistan, Albania, Algeria, Angola . . . I wouldn't let a one of those boys in on a bet. But your *B*'s, with the exception of Belgium and Brazil, were just as bad. Take your Bahamas and your Barbados —fine as resorts in the old days. But as nations? In our U.N.? Certainly not year round. And look at the others. Bahrein—I tell you not one of us had ever heard of it before. Nor half of the others, either. Benin, Bhutan, Burundi. And then, if you please, there was another of those Russian SSR undercover countries. This one was called, if you please, Byelorussian SSR. No, I'm not kidding.

Well, right away we saw we couldn't do the thing alphabetically. We'd have to do it by the map. We all picked out places and nominated them. Switzerland was first, of course—everyone wanted that. And then we started on the Scandinavian countries. Of course even though they weren't on the Grand Tour, everyone had been there on cruises. For our kind of United Nations, we wanted Norway and Denmark and Finland, the way we wanted Holland and Belgium. But there was very divided opinion on Sweden. Witter Hardee said he'd bet anyone even today you couldn't make a right turn on red there— and nobody took him up on it, either.

Actually, we all felt pretty good about letting in almost any northern country except Sweden. But the minute we moved south, we were very, very careful. Ellsworth Huntington was entirely right, you know, about the influence of climate on history. Uncle Bagnalls told him so. My Uncle Bagnalls had a saying that nothing good ever came out of a warm climate—

and everyone agreed that that was mighty good advice. Greenland, Iceland, places like that, fine. Hell, we'd have let in the North Pole, if they'd had a country. But South—chest your cards, we all agreed. They're lazy is what they are. And all they ever think of is siestas. Siestas! It's just one more excuse to breed. Anyway, Spain, we finally decided, we'd let in—Franco really did a superb job there. And Portugal too—you really have to give credit to that Salazar. And don't forget, he also provided a place for all the ex-royalty. When we came to Latin America, though, we drew the line. We passed Mexico by a hair, but none of us saw any real reason for taking in any of those countries south of that. Central America, for example, or any of those damn islands. The good ones you want as colonies, and they could perfectly well be spoken for by their mother countries. The others even their own mothers wouldn't want.

A great many of us were for taking in Greece—remember, it was very important once, and at least it's not communistic. We had quite a fight, though, over Turkey. I've forgotten what the upshot was—whether we voted to take them in but watch them carefully or watch them carefully and then see whether or not we'd take them in. But east of Greece and Turkey, let me tell you, again we moved very, very slowly. We took in Israel 4-3, but your A-rabs, as the General called them, they were a different story. Actually the only one for any of those countries was the General. He was for Persia, but we told him to wake up, man, there wasn't any Persia anymore. Whereupon, he agreed to settle for Mesopotamia. I tell you the General doesn't know what century it is.

But no matter. The Arabs were out. When we moved from the Near East to the Far East, though, we had hard sledding.

Tubby was for the Philippines, but I am glad to say that wiser heads prevailed—you just can't make exceptions, MacArthur or no MacArthur. In the end, we all agreed we wouldn't touch any Oriental country with a ten foot pole, except for White China, Australia and New Zealand. Those are good examples, incidentally, of your colonies earning the right to be a country. And remember, Australia was once a prison colony. But they were the right sort of people, prisoners or no prisoners, and they pulled themselves up by their bootstraps without running around and begging other people for money every two minutes.

All in all, we ended with a damned decent little United Nations. The U.S., Great Britain, Canada, West Germany, France, Switzerland, Norway, Denmark, Finland, Holland, Belgium, Greenland, Iceland, Spain, Portugal, Greece, Mexico, Israel, White China, Australia, New Zealand and Turkey with a question mark. Twenty-one or twenty-two countries, and not a single Russian bloc or Third World or emerging or any of that nonsense in the lot. It was a hard night's work, but we all agreed we'd done it to a T. And we were in a very mellow mood, if I do say so, when we drank the toast, sang the song and adjourned.

CHAPTER VIII

These Damnable Religious Changes

AFTER THE servant problem and your government, and women, children and foreign affairs, the next biggest change which has occurred in my lifetime is religion. In my day, everybody went to church. They went to their little Catholic Church or their synagogue or whatever—but dammit, they went. I went too, of course—I was made to. My mother was a very religious person. She made my father go too. I remember when he became a vestryman and passed the big silver plate. When he came to our pew, my mother put in a dollar and my brother and I both had to put in a quarter. It had to be a quarter, too—my father never let anybody make change from his plate. And then he and the other two vestrymen, who worked the other two aisles, and still another vestryman, who worked the balcony, where the servants were, would march up the aisle and we'd all rise and sing;

> Praise God from Whom all blessings flow,
> Praise Him, ye creatures here below,
> Praise Him above, ye heavenly host,
> Praise Father, Son and Holy Ghost.

I tell you it was very moving seeing the back of my father's head and him and the others holding those plates full of money. You really felt your religious account had balanced and come out even, the way it was supposed to. Also, on that score, my brother and I got a quarter from my mother every time we learned a hymn. We'd go through the hymn book, look for the shortest ones, and copy them down. And then when we'd learned them, we'd say them to my mother. We wouldn't get the quarter either, until we had it perfect. But it was damned good training and paid a dividend too, for someone like me who, even though I didn't know it then, would eventually become a writer. I can still quote from those hymns today.

We had to learn the Creed too, so that we could say it perfectly when we stood there in church. And we believed it. But my brother and I were always worried about that part that said "I believe in the holy catholic church." We didn't want to say that, and we wouldn't, until my father explained to us one day that it didn't mean the Catholic church, it meant the church in general. And that's why it was a small "c."

Anyway, to this day, I do believe in the church in general—particularly for the masses. I don't think you'd have nearly the trouble with your masses today and the young people and all the rest of it if they were made to go to church the way they used to be. That's one thing I've always admired about the Catholics, by the way—they *are* made to and, dammit, they go. For people like myself—all right, we're in a different walk of life. But, not to put too fine a point on it, we should go too. After all, if my father's generation could do it, we could. Remember, in my father's day, they worked Saturday morning. So they were giving up the one morning off they had. And when golf came in, that was a real sacrifice. These young people today—hell, they could play their golf Saturday mornings and Sunday afternoons too if they had the gumption to keep the women off the course, the way we did.

Talk about changes from my birth to now as opposed to those little ones from Caesar's death to my birth, and I tell you the changes in my lifetime beat Caesar's to me forty ways to Sunday. And Sunday, too, for that matter. I tell you these young people today have ruined Sunday. They don't know the meaning of keeping the Sabbath, as the Bible tells us to do. Not the Jewish Bible—their Sunday is Saturday—I mean the real Sunday Sabbath. Nowadays, Sunday is just one more excuse to do what you damn please. Why half the stores you see are wide open, and everybody either plays sports or watches them on television. You tell them it's Sunday, and they don't know what you are talking about. Why, I can remember when we couldn't start an inning after midnight Saturday. Today the only thing the young people do on Sunday morning is sleep. All right, Caesar's boys weren't great about keeping Sundays. They fed the Christians to the lions in arenas that day, just like any other day. But you have to remember, it wasn't the Roman Sunday, and in those days, don't forget, your Christians were your troublemakers.

In my father's day, as I told you, they not only really gave up things, on their one day off, to go to church. They also made another real sacrifice. After giving up half that day, they would then have to sit there and listen to some pantywaist minister go on and on, half the time preaching half-baked leftist ideas. I remember once a minister in our church preached a whole sermon on the idea that it was easier for a camel to go through a needle's eye then for a rich man to go to heaven. Imagine, saying a thing like that from the pulpit. Of all the decent things in the Bible he could have chosen, he had to pick that one. Well, my father never said a word while he was preaching—I can remember though, seeing his jaw muscles working. He didn't even say anything about it after church, or at Sunday lunch—my father never believed in talking about things like that in front of the servants—but that night he called a meeting of the other vestrymen, and the next Sunday we had a brand new minister.

My point is that my father's generation kept on going to church through thick and thin, and so, to a point, did my generation. But these new generations, honestly, you can count on the fingers of your hand the really regular churchgoers—and I mean even here at the Club. Fish Frobisher goes, of course, and Edgy Bull goes—Betty Bull makes him. On the other hand, Witter isn't very good about it, and Tubby doesn't go at all, and neither does the General. I don't know about the Professor, and frankly I don't care. Of course I go, even though not as regularly as I should. But I usually go Easter, unless I've got a special card game or a dominoes match or something like that.

Never mind us—the trouble again is your young people. And I don't mean the young people outside the Club, I mean right here in it. I think when all is said and done, the real reason they don't go to church is they don't like the discipline. It's God the *Father,* don't forget that—that was the way I was brought up— to respect first *my* father, and then God *The* Father. These young people today aren't brought up to respect anything, particularly fathers. And your God and my God does demand obedience, don't forget that. A merciful God, yes—all right. But don't forget, mercy isn't weakness. And this everlasting mollycoddling of criminals. The next time anybody gives you that balderdash about a merciful God, just remind him of that good old expression, "wrath of God." You remember, "bring down the wrath of God." It's a damn good expression, and they ought not to forget it. And on top of that, He's a jealous God. The Bible tells us that very definitely. And if He was a jealous God in those days, He's got one hell of a lot more to be jealous about in these rotten times when the young people won't even give Him the time of day.

I can get myself very worked up about this. I'm telling you right here and now that this change in attitude toward God may be the biggest change of all from my birth to now—bigger than anything from Caesar's death to my birth that you can name except women and children and foreign affairs. All right, Caesar had more than one god, which is not what you and I believe in. As a matter of fact, he didn't believe in them too much either. He was pretty much of an agnostic. But that didn't mean they weren't perfectly good gods who were around when you needed them but didn't bother you all the time when you didn't. Jupiter, the head god, was father, of course—I think of him pretty much as a man in my position here at Fortnightly. He had Mercury as his messenger—I see Mercury as my Tubby, sort of slimmed down—but remember Mercury was not just Jupiter's messenger, he was also the god of Business. And there were not only temples to him, there were also Clubs. "Clubs of Mercury" they called them—businessmen's clubs, which I presume were tax deductible. Anyway, after Jupiter and Mercury, you had Mars, your God of War and Saturn, who was guardian of the Treasury—God, how we could use a god like that today. After that, there were the household gods, Lares and Penates—they were really little gods for little people, the lower classes. I've always thought that was a good idea—they really should have their own gods, separate from ours. And finally, you had women gods—Juno and Venus and so forth. Even in those days, I suppose, you had to have them. It was probably the same damn token thing you have today. It's a shame, but there you are.

Well, as I say, all those gods are a long way from your religion and my religion. But it was a perfectly good religion for Caesar, who, as I think I told you, wasn't much of a church-goer anyway. The point is that it was a religion nobody messed around with, the way they do today. They say there's been a revival in religion. Revival, my foot. They have all these ministers nobody's ever heard of on the radio raising money and everything. And they have this scientology and all these other damn ologies—which is really just messing around is what it is.

I'm not blaming these other religions and beliefs, mind you. I'd be the last one to do that because people are messing around with my religion too. I don't know how long it's been going on, but I can tell you exactly how I found out about it. I found out about it from the horse's mouth—right at church. I told you I go almost every Easter. Well another time I go is to funerals. Frankly, I'm very fond of funerals. I go first of all to every classmate's, of course, whether I knew the man or not. I'm also partial to an older fellow's funeral, a fellow, for example, who led a full life and you can say it's a blessing and really mean it. And, besides those boys, I'll tell you I can't help getting a kick out of funerals of some of these younger ones, particularly when it's one of these birds who's always jogging or in the gym—you know the type, always priding themselves on keeping themselves in perfect physical condition. When they go, of course, you can't really use the word "blessing" but for my money it's a blessing in disguise.

People ask me what makes a good funeral, and I tell them the most important thing is your man in the casket. If you have a man of substance in there, you have the makings of a first-class funeral. There's a nice continuity to it. You feel you're not at the end of something—it's more like you are a kind of way station. You're part of an orderly transition—between the man's life here on earth and his proper station tomorrow in the hereafter.

A lot of these young people today don't even go to funerals. I really don't know what's the matter with them. I suppose it's that silly thing that when you're young you think you're going to live forever. Well, you're not. They should be taught that— and while they are young too. I remember my Uncle Bagnalls had all young people as pallbearers at his funeral. He left it right in his will. I even remember the wording. It was beautifully put—"So that they might better appreciate the brevity of life." Uncle Bagnalls always saw things clearly, right to the end. Sound as a nut.

A good funeral should make you think about your own place in the hereafter. I know I always do—particularly from a good rousing rendition of that wonderful hymn, "Ten Thousand

Times Ten Thousand." You know—"Ta *tum* ta *tum* ta *tum* tum"—and the rest of it, "the armies *of* the ransomed saints throng *up* the steeps of light." I remember I learned that and got my quarter for it when I didn't have the slightest idea what the devil a "steep of light" was. I assumed it was a kind of step. Anyway God knows since then I think I've climbed every one of them, whatever they are. I tell you there is no religion that can hold a candle to the Episcopalian when it comes to hymns. That "Ten Thousand" is tops. I'm singing it again right now as I write these words. "The armies *of* the ransomed saints . . ." Frankly, I don't think of myself as a saint, but dammit all, with the taxes today, I'm ransomed all right. However, I do want to say here and now that I think that "Ten Thousand Times Ten Thousand" is stretching it a bit. Ten Thousand times ten thousand by my figuring—let's see, I'll do it out for you. It's ten thousand, and carry four zeroes. That's a hundred *million*. Well, I don't know what your idea of heaven is, but I'll tell you one thing. I don't want any hundred damn million people up there—you might as well stay here.

The whole idea of where we're going when the good Lord calls us is interesting. But frankly it's not as complicated as some people seem to think. Take me, for instance. I feel I am about as good—whatever the standards they apply up there— as Witter and Edgy and Tubby, and almost as good as Fish Frobisher. I shall go where they go, and that is where I wish to go.

So much for that. To get back to funerals, the point is it was at a funeral I first learned the real truth about all these changes. It was some time ago and I've even forgotten whose funeral it

214

was. Anyway, the man's name is of no consequence—he was a perfectly nice fellow, and that was about it. And the turnout was pretty higgledy-piggledy, if you know what I mean, even in the front pews. But the moment the service started, I tell you I couldn't believe my ears. This little whippersnapper of a minister—they're too young anyway, nowadays, most of them, but he was an Episcopalian, I checked on it—started out, and I give you my word he didn't even get the first sentence right. He said, "I am resurrection and I am light." I am resurrection, I am light! It's "I am *the* resurrection and *the* light," for God's sake. And then he said, "Says the Lord." Says the Lord, my foot. It's *"Saith* the Lord."

At first, I just couldn't figure out what was the matter with him. You get a lot of ministers who lisp—you're about to in a profession like that—and I suppose they have trouble with those "eths," and "ests" and all those. But dammit all, that's no reason to change them. Anyway, this damnfool went on to say "whoever has faith in me shall have life, even though he dies . . ." I remember thinking what the devil was he up to. It's "He that *believeth* in Me, *though* he were dead, *yet* shall he live." It's like a poem—it has cadence, it has rhythm. Well, from then on, every damn word he said was wrong. Even about the Redeemer, for God's sake—you'd think he'd go easy with changes about the Redeemer. And then at the end, if you please, he didn't say "We brought nothing into this world and it's certain we can carry nothing out. The Lord gave and the Lord hath taken away, blessed be the Name of the Lord." Can you imagine not saying that? Instead of that, he went on with some drivel about "For none of us has life himself and none becomes his own master when he dies." His own master when he dies!

What the devil does that mean? That there aren't going to be any servants up there? That sounds like one hell of a heaven to me.

Then came the Twenty-third Psalm. "The Lord is my shepherd," he started out, "therefore can I lack nothing." Imagine! Therefore can I lack nothing! Instead of "I shall not want." That's just typical of nowadays. They want to make everything sound the way they talk on television. Then he went on, "He shall feed me in a green pasture." It's not pasture, it's pastures, for heaven's sakes, and and it's not "He shall feed me," it's "He maketh me to lie down in green pastures." He shall feed me in a green pasture! What does he think I am—the Borden cow? As if that weren't enough, the fellow went on and said, "Lead me forth besides the waters of comfort," instead of "He leadeth me beside the still waters." He made it sound as if they were looking for the washroom. Honestly, the fellow couldn't even say "Thou preparest a table before Me in the presence of mine enemies." He said, "In the presence of them that trouble me." Trouble me, for Pete's sake. They're *enemies* is what they are, and as far as I'm concerned, this bird was one of them.

The final straw was when the fellow came to the Lord's Prayer. No, I am not making it up—the Lord's Prayer. They'd even changed that. "Our Father in Heaven" the fellow said, "hallowed be *Your* name." And then it was "Your kingdom come" and "Your will be done." Dammit, if the Lord had wanted "Your," he would have said "Your." He didn't. He said "Thy." Honestly, you've reached the bottom when you get to changing the words of Jesus Christ. But they've done it, make no mistake. Right straight through the whole prayer they've done it. "Forgive us our debts," he said "as we forgive our debtors." It's not our debts, dammit. We don't have debtors' prison anymore, which is probably a mistake, but that doesn't mean we should let them go scot free. It's nothing to do with our debts anyway—it's our trespasses, dammit, our trespasses. And it's the trespassers against us whom we are supposed to forgive. And God knows nowadays we do. We live by the Lord's Prayer every damn day. Finally, the fellow didn't even say "Lead us not into temptation." He said "Save us from a time of trial." A time of trial! What in God's name is a time of trial? It's temptation, that's what it is. And I tell you my temptation right then was to boil that bird in oil. Literally the only thing he said right in the whole Lord's Prayer was the word "Amen." And at that I figured I was lucky. After what he'd said before, I expected "Awomen."

Well, I tell you that was the first funeral in my life I ever left early. I went right back to the Club and got a hold of Fish Frobisher, and we called an emergency meeting of the Society to Put Things Back the Way They Were. We didn't even call a whole meeting—we just met in executive session. And all of us agreed it was the most important meeting we've ever had. I read them my notes about that funeral word for word. And then I told them point blank that it was one thing to have people going around and changing things like servants, foreign affairs and women and children and fountain pens—it was something entirely different to mess around with the Bible and the Book of Common Prayer. You allow them to change the Bible and the Book of Common Prayer and you might as well say goodbye God. This was religion we were talking about, dammit, the very foundation of life. Life, hell, I told them—we were talking about the *after*life. Where we were all going ultimately.

All of us, of course, knew there had been some changes in

217

the services—that the Catholics, for example, weren't having theirs in Latin anymore, and things like that. But that was their problem, after all—I imagine Latin has always been a very hard language for them. But this was Episcopalian! And actually, if the truth be known, none of us before that meeting, had realized the full impact of what was going on right in our own church. Fog Horne kept saying over and over that we might have figured it—first the Constitution and then the Bible. Fish was wonderful, I thought. Cool as a cucumber. Just paced up and down with his head bowed and didn't say a word. When Fish is doing that, you know he's really thinking. But Tubby flew off the handle. I thought he was going to have apoplexy. Tubby isn't much of a churchgoer, and he really hadn't known the first thing about what had been going on. Neither did the General. He just sat there stunned. "I tell you," he said over and over, "it's the Reds. That's who it is. They always go for the foundations of your way of life." Well, Edgy Bull hadn't even adjusted his hearing aid and he thought the General said "Feds."

Witter, I thought, had the best suggestion. He suggested we start with the Bible and see what they'd been doing with that. Fish seconded that—he remembered we'd already thrown out a Bible from the Club Library which had the word "New" in the title. If there's anything you don't want mixed up with your Bible, it's something New. Anyway, we sent Edgy up to the Library for our King James version. The Professor, as usual, had an objection. He started some long song and dance about the history of Biblical translation, but when he got as far as the Venerable Bede I stopped him. He could say what he wanted to about economics and history, I told him, but when it came to the Bible, compared to him, *I* was Venerable Bede.

Well, one thing led to another and in no time at all we had a Committee—I agreed to be chairman, Fish took the vice-chairmanship, and we had Witter as secretary and Edgy as treasurer. And we instructed Edgy, as treasurer, to go out and get his hands on every damn "new" Bible he could—beg, borrow or steal. None of us were really in favor of stealing Bibles, of course, but if there was no other way, we told him, so be it. This was a national emergency. Edgy did a bang-up job, too. Within a week he had five of them. Five of them, mind you—every one of them different. The first one was something called *The Revised Standard Version of the Bible.* It was a contradiction in terms, of course. How can anything be a *revised standard*? But there it was. The second was called *The New English Bible*—again, that damned word "new" was enough to tell you what it was. The third one was something called *The New American Bible.* Just picture that. The New *American* Bible. Not satisfied with their blasphemy, they were obviously trying to drag patriotism into the thing. Imagine, patriotism vs. King James I in 1611. Really, it was absurd.

The fourth Bible Edgy brought back was just as incredible. It was called, if you please, *The Good News Bible.* I know you think I'm making that up, but I am not. That was the title. And it's right here as I write these words. *The Good News Bible,* published, if you please, by The American Bible Society. You would think they of all people, would know better. But the foreword of this miserable Bible really showed they don't. I've written it down word for word. "This translation," the foreword says, "does not follow the traditional vocabulary and style found in the historic English Bible version. Rather, it attempts in this century to set forth the Biblical content and message in standard, everyday, natural forms of English."

Everyday natural! Why don't they publish the Bible in four-letter words and be done with it. And don't fool yourself, they just about have, too, because the fifth and the last Bible Edgy brought back was called *The Bible in Basic English.* None of us knew what the devil they meant by "basic English" but there was something called "basic English," we recalled, some years back, and sure enough, when we looked into this silly Bible, it was it all right. A note at the beginning said, and I quote, "Basic English, produced by Mr. C. K. Ogden of the Orthological Institute, is a simple form of the English language which, with 850 words, is able to give the sense of anything which may be said in English."

I tell you, if my life depended on it, I wouldn't even take an oath on a Bible like that. What they'd done was to put the Bible into 850 words—I don't mean into just 850 words in all, but using just 850 different words. Imagine! The sense of anything which may be said in English! Can you picture doing that to the King James version? What my dear old English professor, John Livingston Lowes, called "the noblest monument of English prose in history." In 850 words. It simply shows you that nowadays there's absolutely nothing sacred. I suppose next those boys will be doing that to this book. With all the time and trouble I've gone to to pick just the right word for you, they'll up and without so much as a by my leave substitute the nearest word they've got out of their measly little 850. Honestly it damn well makes my blood boil just thinking about it. And I hope that sentence will make it hard for them. I'll bet they don't have a single "damn" or "blood" or "boil" in those 850.

In any case, after we had all these five new Bibles, we made a plan. We decided to take the bull by the horns and invite one

of these new ministers—revisionist, or whatever they call them
—to Fortnightly. That was my job, of course, and so I called
my church. I've gotten a little out of touch with them, but I
finally got their number and of course I got some dumb bunny
secretary who didn't know me from Adam. But I'm used to
that, so I just spoke to her slowly and clearly, using small words
and enunciating carefully. I told her that I was chairman of the
Emergency Committee of the Society to Put Things Back the
Way They Were, which I carefully explained, was part of Fortnightly. But even that she couldn't handle—they just aren't
taught to listen nowadays. So finally I just gave up and told her
I was a prominent parishioner—by then I knew that was really
the only thing that would sink in. Then, when I had her attention, I explained to her just what the Fortnightly was. Honestly,
I did it so that even a child could have understood. I told her
every single one of our members was sick and tired of all the
changes that were going on down there, and we had voted
unanimously to have one of their ministers come over to one
of our meetings and tell us what the hell was going on.

I remember after I had said that there was a long pause.
Then finally she said that their Reverend Anderson handled
that sort of thing, but that Reverend Anderson was in a meeting. Every damn person you ever want to call nowadays is
always in a meeting. I don't know why they don't hold meetings
the way I hold meetings at the Club. If there's somebody I want
to talk to, I answer the phone, meeting or no meeting. But not
these modern meeters. Of course, they're just an escape, is
what they are. People go into meetings or else have their secretaries say they're in them—because they don't dare make any
decisions by themselves. Anyway, as I say, this dumb bunny
secretary finally got all the details straight, and went away for

what seemed like an hour. When she came back and said that Reverend Anderson would be happy to attend our meeting.

I tell you one thing—we were ready for that bird. We had really done our homework. We had already decided that each of us would take one of the new Bibles and have our notes and face the fellow with the damned desecrations, chapter and verse, and, in this case, that's exactly what it was—chapter and verse.

And we were there too—all of us, with our Bibles at the ready. Fish Frobisher had the King James, I had taken the *Revised Standard,* Witter had the *New English,* Edgy Bull had the *New American.* Fog Horne was too mad to take any of the new ones, so we gave the Professor the *Good News Bible* and Tubby got *The Bible in Basic English.* Tubby, of course, is no reader, but at least we figured he'd be able to handle 850 words. The General didn't have a Bible, but the General didn't need one —honestly, he was so sore, he could have ad libbed a Bible.

As I say, we were waiting, both for the damned minister and our dinner—nowadays, people are always late—when in he walked, as I live and breathe, not a he but a *she.* A *woman!* "Hello," she said, without so much as a by your leave, "I'm Reverend Anderson." I tell you, nobody said a word. We were in a state of shock. Of course, it wasn't the first time we'd had a woman to Fortnightly—after all we had Marjorie, the girl from the publishers, but that was a meeting *about* women, so there was some excuse for it. This was a whole different ball game. This was about religion. And to have an ordinary woman show up wearing the collar and tell us she was Reverend Anderson, without an inkling of advance warning—well, it was something, I assure you. And, of course, I figured I'd be the one blamed. So I started to say something about never having spoken to her, but they weren't even paying attention to me. The reason was that Reverend Anderson was a mighty fine-looking woman under all that black, and what she had on, and not old either. She was a little too thin for my taste, but she had perfectly well-coiffed hair and good-sized eyes and all the rest of it. The only thing I didn't like was her smile. It was a little too knowing for me. I don't like knowing smiles from women —they know too much nowadays as it is. It seemed to me she knew perfectly well what a difficult position she was putting us in, and, frankly, was enjoying every minute of it.

Witter Hardee recovered first—Witter really has beautiful manners—and he stepped forward, greeted her and shook her hand as if he meant it. Well, that's Witter for you. Of course, it wasn't Witter's job to introduce her to the rest of the group —that was up to me. And dammit I did it. All around the room—after all, she was our guest. The only thing I wasn't sure of was whether or not to offer her a drink. But I motioned to Henry, and he asked her what she wanted, just as if she was a member. She chose a Manhattan—which was typical. Nobody but women and children and an occasional servant drinks Manhattans. But Henry didn't say a word. He just fixed one for her. Henry's a trouper. In no time at all, thank God, it was time to sit down, and so down we sat. But I want to tell you, that was the most stilted Fortnightly dinner I can remember.

Fish Frobisher of course wanted to know exactly what Anderson she was. Fish always wants to know that, and I tell you she didn't even know what he meant—so we got off that in a hurry. Really, as I remember, we were just casting about for anything to get us through the meal. Fortunately, she wanted to know all about Fortnightly, so I gave her the basic facts. And that took us through most of the fish course. Then, during the meat

223

course, Fog Horne took over and did a bang-up job on the history of The Society to Put Things Back the Way They Were. There were times when I thought she was going to laugh—but there wasn't anything funny about what Fog was saying, so we put it down to the fact that she was probably very nervous. Then out of the clear blue, during dessert, she suddenly turned to the General, and asked him what he was general of. Well, that took some telling—it always does—and the General wasn't the man for it. It really is hard to explain the Knickerbocker Greys to a woman. After all the General was a General of them when he was fifteen years old. I also remember Tubby trying to talk to her about women in sports. Tubby will talk to women about anything, but that subject is a favorite of his. He hates women in sports.

All in all, we talked every topic under the sun, *except* religion. Until finally, if you please, when we were having our coffee and cigars—thank God she didn't take one of those—*she* brought it up. I thought it was in very poor taste. But she launched into this tirade about how she had wanted to be a minister from the time she was a little girl. None of us had had any idea how many girl ministers there were nowadays, and frankly we were shocked. But we were too polite, of course, to show it. At that point, during one of the embarrassing silences—of which I assure you there were many—I leaned over to her and asked about her background for my introduction. To my amazement, she had graduated from a very decent seminary. So then I got up and made my introduction just as if she was a regular male speaker.

After I sat down, she got up and started talking. She said she understood we were concerned about changes in religion, and particularly changes in the Bible. And so she wanted to begin with a little history of Biblical translation. She spoke without a single damn note—women have very good memories, you know, that's what makes them such good card players, their memories. It's easier for them, of course, because they don't have as much on their minds as we do. Anyway, whether she had notes or not, I decided I'd take some—just to show her later where she was off base—and so, I noted, did the Professor.

As a matter of fact, she started, just as the Professor had, with the Venerable Bede. She told us that Bede translated the four Gospels before he died, which, she said was in 735. That was interesting—I'd always thought of the Venerable Bede as a much younger man. Anyway, then she went on to tell us that the first translation of the whole Bible into English was John Wycliffe's in 1382, but that neither Bede nor Wycliffe had used the original Greek or Hebrew, but had used the Latin Vulgate. I thought that was interesting too, and was just making a note of it when up piped Edgy Bull, who said he was sorry to interrupt her, but he couldn't hear and wanted to know who we should be grateful to. You just know Edgy wouldn't get a word like Vulgate. But no matter. The point she was trying to make, apparently—and making points was not her long suit—was that the first man to make an English version of the Bible by a direct translation from the original Greek and Hebrew was William Tyndale in 1525. And there was so much fuss about his that he was burned at the stake.

All of us exchanged a glance at this. I'm not in favor of burning at the stake for these Bible changers, but you would have thought some of them would have gotten the message. Of course, all this passed over her like water off a duck's back. She went on to tell us that Tyndale's was the foundation of all the other versions, the Coverdale, the Thomas Matthews, the Great Bible, the Geneva Bible and Bishops Bible—right up to our King James in 1611.

She told us how James I had gathered his scholars around him, starting in 1604, when he summoned the leading divines of the Church of England to consider matters in dispute between the High Church and the Puritans. Then, in 1607, she said, the work was begun by fifty-four scholars from Oxford and Cambridge, and they did the job. But typically, she passed right over this, and went shooting right on to the 1870 English translation and the 1901 American, and God knows what else —completely missing the point, of course, that the King James version had stood for two and a half centuries before people even considered tampering with it, and when they did, the new ones didn't amount to a hill of beans beside it.

Next, if you please, she started in on what she called the "shortcomings" of the King James version. The shortcomings, mind you. Many forms of expression, she said, and I believe I am quoting her accurately, had become archaic and were not understood by young people today. And then she proceeded to give us a list of these—and I wrote every one of them down. They were "thou," "thee," "thy," "thine," verb endings in "est," "edst," "eth," "it came to pass," "whosoever," "whatsoever," "insomuch," "per adventure," "must needs," "would fain" and "behoove." And then, if you please, she sat down.

I don't know why, but it was that "behoove" that got me, and I just blurted out that if there was anybody in the room who didn't know what "behoove" meant, it would behoove them to leave. At this, she looked at me as if she was more interested in me than in what I was saying. I like that in a woman sometimes, but there's a time and place for that sort of thing, and this wasn't it. I didn't say so, of course. I waited until everybody had their Bibles out, and then I began with the Ten Commandments. We had already planned to begin with them. I quoted her right out of my idiotic *Revised Standard* with its stupid "You shall not do this" and "You shall not do that." And then I picked up the good old King James and really, if I do say so, rang out those wonderful words "Thou shalt not covet" . . . I was going to read her the whole of that one, but she interrupted me. She said that the fact was that people didn't use the "thou" anymore, they used "you." Well, I told her, they didn't keep the Ten Commandments anymore, either. I told her there wasn't a single solitary thing wrong with the good old "thou." And then if you please she repeated that the young people today didn't like the word "thou." The young people! Can you picture it? I'm afraid I raised my voice at that, and you should never raise your voice when you are arguing with a woman. That's just descending to their level. But what I said made sense. I told her of all the people who didn't keep any of the Ten Commandments, the young people were the worst. I told her the only commandment they kept was not bowing down to graven images—and I wouldn't bet on that. Finally, I told her that maybe the young people could think of the old "the," "thou," "thy," and "thine" like the French "tu-toi-ing"—God knows they ought to be able to understand that, with all the sex they have.

Well, I admit, I certainly shouldn't have said that, because you should never mention sex in front of a woman. It's embarrassing to them, and they just don't understand it anyway. So then I did what we were supposed to do, I turned the floor over to Edgy Bull, who read from that awful New American Bible. Edgy's really a very bad reader, but he did his best. "You shall not covet," he read, "your neighbor's house. You shall not covet your neighbor's wife, nor his male or female slave, nor his ox, or ass, nor anything else that belongs to him."

We all jumped on that, of course. Never mind the young people, we told her—this was the American Bible and the American government was breaking that commandment every single day of its life. And obviously one of the reasons they were breaking it was that the language had been changed. "For God's sake, woman," I told her, "they've coveted everything I've got and the only reason they don't covet my ox and my ass is that I haven't got an ox and I haven't got an ass."

Well that ox and those *s*'s were murder on Edgy's hearing aid. He thought we were talking about sex. Anyway, when we finally got that cleared up, everyone started reading their Commandments out of their Bible, until we got to Tubby. Tubby couldn't find the Ten Commandments. Tubby in the Bible is a fish out of water. So Fog Horne went over to help him, and sure enough, Tubby didn't have any Ten Commandments. He only had the New Testament in that damn *Basic English Bible* of his. No wonder they did it in 850 words—they didn't finish the job. Through it all, we kept at her, hammer and tongs, about that damn "you" thing. Fish Frobisher stood like a rock. "Dust thou art," he thundered, "and to dust thou shalt return." And, right on cue, Witter came in with "You are dust, to dust you shall return" in his equally ridiculous *New English Bible.* Not all the nuts are on this side of the Atlantic.

In the middle of all this, the General brought up "verily." I never would have thought the General had it in him—remember, he didn't even have a Bible. But he stood there like a Lion of Judah himself—which is an expression he won't like—and kept saying, "It's 'verily, verily I say unto you' and not 'truly,

truly, I say to you.' " Well, all of us wanted to know where the devil he even knew that these damn new Bibles had "truly" instead of "verily," and it turned out that his new girlfriend had told him about it. The General really is surprising sometimes.

Reverend Anderson, of course, called "verily" an archaism. Archaism my foot. I suppose I'm archaic. I also remember Fish reading—he really reads beautifully, you know—"Whither thou goest, I will go," and then of course I had to come up with, out of my horrid *Revised Standard,* "Where you go, I will go." Where you go for God's sake. Who in the devil doesn't know what "whither" means? Well, we picked the wrong one that time, because Edgy thought we'd said Witter, but no matter. Incidentally, I thought Edgy held up his end just fine. He was a bearcat when he read that idiotic "my cup overflows" instead of "my cup runneth over," and "by the mouths of babes and innocents." Imagine, "by the mouths of babes and innocents," instead of the way God wrote it—"out of the mouths."

Fish did Paul to a T. Paul is good, you know—I've quoted him before. He's very sound on women. First Fish read, from the good old King James, "Though I speak with the tongue of men and angels, and have not charity, I am become as sounding a brass or a tinkling cymbal." Then I picked up my *Revised Standard* and started, "If I speak." If I speak, for heaven's sake, and ended up, "I am a noisy gong or a clanging cymbal." A noisy gong! What the devil's that? The dinner bell? Witter's *New English* was just as bad. The same "noisy gong and clanging cymbal," and Edgy's *American Bible* was even worse. "If I speak with human tongues and angels as well, "it said—honest to God, they missed the whole point of the Bible. The *Good News Bible* gave us "noisy gong and clanging *bell*"—on the theory, I suppose, that the bell was better news than a cymbal. As for

Tubby's *Basic,* it started out "If I made use of the tongues of men and angels . . ." Maybe they didn't have the word "speak" in their 850, but they had "sounding brass" and a *"loud tongued* bell." I wonder who chose those 850 words anyway.

As if this weren't enough, all those damn new Bibles went haywire over that word "charity." Imagine tinkering with that beautiful "And now abideth faith, hope and charity." The greatest of these, as Paul said, is charity. And it is charity, dammit, charity. It's the only good use of it in the whole awful history of that word. It doesn't have a damn thing to do with giving something to somebody else, or all these damn appeals I get in the mail. But I tell you every one of these new Bibles, after first fouling up that "and now abideth"—they didn't understand the *eth,* I suppose—anyway, after fouling that up, they said, "and now abides faith, hope and love." It's so absurd. *Love.* I tell you the Bible ought not to be allowed to use that word—it's been so totally corrupted by the young people today.

Anyway, speaking of love, the next thing we all zeroed in on was the Song of Songs. Can you imagine, in these new Bibles, they even changed that phrase "the way of a man with a maid." Changed it to "maiden." I remember Witter saying that maybe the young people didn't know what a maid is—after all, you can't get a decent one anymore. That broke the ice a little. But the whole Song of Songs thing was difficult to discuss with that woman there. After all, it's the most sensual passage in the whole Bible. But by this time we all had our backs up, and we'd made up our minds that if she wanted to do such a damfool thing as be a minister, then she would damn well have to take the consequences. Fish read it beautifully, but each time after he would read "Thy hair is as a flock of goats that appear from

Mount Gilead," I would have to read, "moving down the slopes of Gilead" or some drivel like that one Edgy would read, in that awful *Good News,* "Your hair dances like a flock of goats bounding." Imagine! Bounding. Poor Tubby. He got so excited about it but he was really stuck. No Song of Songs in his *Basic Bible* at all.

I still remember the way Fish read, "Thy lips are a thread of scarlet and thy speech is comely." That's one of the worst troubles with nowadays—the girls don't have comely speech anymore. And sure enough, when Edgy read from that *American Bible* they didn't have anything about speech. All they said was, "Your mouth is lovely." Your mouth is lovely! My Standard had it that way too. Mouth lovely! Sounds like an ad for a new toothpaste. I tell you it was enough to make you swear off Bibles, let alone on them.

Finally, we came to that moving passage in King James, "Thy two breasts are like two young roes that are twins, which feed among the lilies." Do you know what my *Standard* did to that? "Your two breasts are like two fawns, twins of a gazelle." Honestly, twins of a gazelle, that's what it said. Witter's *New English* was right on a par with that. "Twin fawns of a gazelle." Roes, dammit, it's roes! As if that weren't enough, the *American Standard* had "Your breasts are like twin fawns, the young of a gazelle, that browse among the lilies." Young, browse. It turns your stomach. And the *Good News Bible* said, "feeding among the lilies." Feeding. It's that same damn explicit thing they're always doing which ruined sex nowadays for everybody.

All in all, we'd gotten so engrossed in the Song of Songs that we'd almost forgotten that damn girl minister. It was really amazing. Here we had proved, in chapter and verse, just as we had set out to do, that every single change in the Bible was absurd. And yet she wouldn't admit a single solitary one of them. You just can't overestimate how stubborn people are nowadays. Here's your King James version, good enough for your fathers and your forefathers and their forefathers, and yet it's apparently not good enough, well, for these aftermothers, or whatever they are.

Just the same, when she finally got up to go, the parting was perfectly polite—after all, we're a gentleman's club, and she was a woman. But the minute she was out the door, I assure you, we could say what we pleased. And I tell you we had a knockdown dragout postmortem, not only on the Bible changes but on the whole rotten idea of women as ministers. We all agreed that after all the main time you want ministers around are in times of great personal stress—funerals, marriages, divorces, times like that. And the last thing you want to worry about is will some woman do the job right? For one thing women—at least the kind of women that get to be ministers and in other positions where you don't want them—are the very ones who never admit when they are wrong. And you certainly don't want them to advise you during a time of stress, particularly when they're going to be telling you what it is *you've* done wrong.

The General brought up an interesting point—about women in the Army. He said many of his best officers felt that the idea of having women in the lower ranks had some merit to it—it kept the men happy. And they could do very good work in places like supply depots. But the minute you put a woman over a man in the field, he said, you didn't have an army—you had one more damn marriage.

The General was on firm ground there. He's had a very

sloppy personal life, as I think I've mentioned. And frankly, if he marries that silly redhead, he'll rue the day, as Edgy Bull and some of the rest of us, who haven't been any too blessed at the altar, are all too well aware. Actually, if the truth be known, by the end of the evening, we had all gotten a little lugubrious, which reminded me of that wonderful passage in the King James, "Come unto me, all ye who travail and are heavy laden."

I went to look it up in the King James and do you know what? I couldn't believe my eyes. It said, "Come unto me, all ye who *labor* and are heavy laden."

It didn't seem possible, but somebody had even got to the King James.

Anyway, that ended that. And, speaking of ending, this brings to a close this book for my lady readers. My last chapter, as they can readily see from its title, is obviously not for them. I shall be sorry to lose them, as I was in my chapter about women, and I hope they will forgive me. I plead only that it is devilishly hard in these times to attempt to write a book for both men and women. In any case, I thank them for their charming presence so far, even if unseen. And I now bid them a fond adieu.

CHAPTER IX

A Frank Talk
About the Boudoir

AFTER the changes which I have mentioned in previous
chapters—I have decided, after a great deal of thought, to
have a special chapter on the subject of sex. It's not really that
important, of course, but that's just the point. In my lifetime
it's been elevated to a position out of all proportion to its
importance. As a matter of fact, I don't like even using the word
"sex"—indeed it seems only yesterday that when my father had
the usual man-to-man talk about the subject, he never once
used the word. I doubt that he ever used the word except
perhaps when there were men of his own age present.

But I remember that talk well—my father had it with me in
his den just before I was married for the first time. These things

are always difficult for fathers—and to be frank they are just as difficult to write about or at least ought to be for a decent writer of which nowadays I sometimes feel like saying me and who else. But no matter. In any case, the young people today can make all the fun they want of the old birds and bees, but dammit, man, your birds and bees talk with your father is probably the most important father-son talk you will ever have in your life—save for your talk about your choice of college, your choice of career and your choice of club.

My father handled it beautifully. He never looked at me, of course. That would have been embarrassing for both of us. He just kind of looked diagonally across me and cleared his throat —in those days people cleared their throats much more meaningfully than they do today—and he said that now that I was going to get married it was time we had a talk. He said that Cornelia was a fine girl and that he had known her family for a long time and she was perfectly suitable and he was very happy about it all. But he also said there was one thing I should know right at the beginning and that was not to expect too much out of the physical side of marriage. He said it was a very over-rated thing by a lot of men, particularly young men who didn't know the first thing about it, and that a lot of damned fool older men ruined their lives over it. But, when you came right down to it, when all was said and done, it was over and done with very quickly, at least from the man's point of view. From the woman's point of view, though—and here my father cleared his throat again—it apparently meant much more emotionally than it did physically, and frankly they were just damn difficult about it. For one thing, he said, they were terribly damn slow about getting ready for it—which was going to be a very difficult problem for me unless I knew about it in advance and made allowances for it. His father, he said, had been a very wonderful person but he had never really made clear to him about this damn slowness of women and frankly several times in his early days with my mother, the whole thing had been over and done with before my mother knew what was up.

My father smiled a little at this, and coughed. My father rarely made jokes on purpose but when he made one by mistake, he usually coughed. Anyway, his point was that I would have to learn to be patient. A decent girl, he told me, really didn't care very much about the physical thing and certainly didn't enjoy it, but if she were brought up properly, as certainly Cornelia was, she was also brought up not to refuse a man unless she was really sick. In which case I could tell, because she would say she had a headache. And I should certainly take the hint and leave her alone. But even at other times, and he made this very clear, I would really have to "love her up," as he put it, an awful lot before I did anything. Or otherwise—and here my father cleared his throat again—I would experience all manner of difficulties. The trouble was, he pointed out, that by that time I probably wouldn't enjoy it much either. All in all, he said, perhaps the best thing to do was sort of compromise. In other words, to "love her up" some—for the principle of the thing—but not to do it so much that I didn't get any enjoyment out of it. And in any case, not to worry too much about it. Because not only did worry ruin it, but also, if she was really the right sort of girl, as again he was sure Cornelia was—she wasn't going to worry too much about it either. She was going to realize it was just something a husband did which a wife had to put up with in return for being looked after and sharing all the important things about marriage, like having a home and children and friends and things like that.

My father also advised me that if I found the physical thing really very irritating, not to worry too much about that either, because by that time Cornelia would be finding it even more irritating and I could always find—here my father waved his hand—the other kind of women to do it with. Most men, he said, found that the physical side of things was much better when it was done with somebody who wasn't your wife. Because then you could—and here my father cleared his throat a final time—do a lot of things no decent man would ever even want to do with his wife.

I told you my father did it beautifully, but at the time I didn't really realize how beautifully. Today, however, after two marriages—to Cornelia, and awful Muffie—I now realize how wise my father was. Indeed today I don't think I would change a word in giving advice to a son of mine on the subject—or, for that matter, to one of you who's reading this. But what use would it be? I just thank God my father never lived to see what has happened to this subject in my lifetime. They used to put women on a pedestal—now, for Pete's sake, we've put *sex* there.

Talk about changes from Caesar's death to my birth, and you'd be hard put to come up with anything which can hold a candle to this sex thing. All right, you had some changes in your sex down through the ages—you had a lifting of purdah here, a legitimizing of prostitution there. But my point is you had nothing to disturb your basic fact that it was something you did but you didn't *talk* about it. Except, of course, when someone had a really good story and told it after dinner with the cigars—after the women had left the room.

Well now, in a sense, for this last chapter at least, the women have left and we can talk about sex the only way it should ever be talked about—in my opinion or in any other decent man's opinion—man to man. The point is, when you come right down to it, what have we today? Sex, sex, sex, that's what we have. It's coming out of our ears. We're awash in sex—or perhaps I should say we're unwashed with it. Anyway, it comes at you from everywhere. And it's right out in the open. We have sex in the streets, for heaven's sake. You drive along the street and every other sign is "Girls" or "Topless" or "Bottomless" or even "Totally Nude." By which, I presume, they mean literally in the altogether. Can you picture what this change is for me? I tell you, from the wedding night to the day of my divorce, I never saw Cornelia in the altogether, and if I ever even came close, I immediately averted my eyes, as any decent man would. It was the same thing with Muffie. Muffie was more careless about such things than Cornelia was—she never had the advantages of the upbringing Cornelia had—but still, even with Muffie, I at least made the *effort* not to look at her.

And here I am talking about just *looking*. Today, if you can believe these damn books and magazines and motion pictures and even television, people are not just looking—they're *doing* it. You hear women talking about their "love lives," as these moderns put it, just as if they were a man talking about his career. In my day no decent man ever talked about such a thing, let alone women, and if he did, he had the decency not to mention it in front of women. Honestly, when I think of all the sex these college kids have today, and all the girl students they have right there in their rooms with them, it makes my blood boil. If there had to be change like that in my lifetime, why in hell didn't it happen sooner? At least then I would have been able to enjoy it. When I think of all the trouble I used to go to just to arrange things so I could ride home after a dance with a girl in a rumble seat! But what's the use? I don't suppose my young readers today would know what a rumble seat is.

It really is terrible—far worse than Caesar could have had any idea of. I tell you you can't do anything today without having some sex thing smack you in the face. You can't even read a book, let alone go to a motion picture, without running the risk of either a nasty shock if you're alone, or, if you're with a female companion, acute embarrassment. I remember when Fish Frobisher and I and The Society to Put Things Back the Way They Were tackled the question of sex in the Club Library. We all worked like Trojans, but we had a terrible job. Of course even in the old days, the old-timers had library trouble. My Uncle Bagnalls told me about it. Evidently you've always had the wrong type of writer and the wrong type of book—your "penny dreadfuls," they were called then. And, in the magazines, you had your *Police Gazette* and your *National Geographic.* I don't like to couple those two, but frankly the editors of the *Geographic* used some very questionable judgment in pictures illustrating articles on Africa and Bali and Tahiti and places like that.

But my point is in those days they were the exceptions, not the rule, and they were relatively easy to control—the old-timers just put those books and the *Gazette* and certain issues of the *Geographic* in the locked room. I remember Uncle Bagnalls used to call it the locker room. But these days, I promise you, we are faced with a whole new ball game. We'd have had to lock up the whole damn Library. I'm not exaggerating. I tell you, The Society to Put Things Back the Way They Were had to get rid of virtually every so-called "modern" novel—except, of course, for a handful written by Club members. But very few Club members, you know, write novels. After all, these days

240

there are so many things crying out to be written about in non-fiction that you find precious few Club members with either the time or the inclination to fool around with fiction. Fiction, when you come right down to it, is primarily a women's thing anyway.

Which brings me to another point—and it's one more reason why the damn Government or somebody ought to do something about all this sex in fiction today. It's very simple. When you're a boy, when you're young, you have a very strong sex urge. But when you grow up and begin to think about more important things, it naturally begins to subside—unless you're a pervert or something. When you're a girl, on the other hand, if you were the right sort of girl, even when you were young, you were never really interested in it, and you naturally left it to the other kind of girl to be interested in it. But as I believe I have mentioned before in my chapter on Women, now what has happened—and this sex thing has played a big part in this —is that both kinds of girls have been ruined. Make no mistake about this. You've ruined the nice girl by making her think she ought to be interested in it, and you've ruined the other kind of girl by making her think she's respectable and so can get away with murder—you know, demand you marry her and all that sort of thing. It's a damn revolution is what it is. I hate revolutions anyway. I don't think I've ever been in favor of a single one. But a sex revolution is really the final straw. Because what you have today, whether you know it or not, is sexual Bolshevism.

People say it all began with Freud. Frankly, I don't know where the devil it began—I just wish it would stop. But I'll tell you one thing. It all happened, as I've said before, right in my lifetime. And it may well be the death of me. Remember, Freud's own death didn't occur until 1939, which happened to coincide, as I am sure many of you do know, with the year when I was already in my thirties. So, in a sense, we were actually contemporary.

I'll tell you another thing, and that is that in researching this book I checked this fellow Freud out and he was basically all right. He had a perfectly respectable engagement to his wife— four years—and they had a perfectly respectable marriage with six children and all the rest of it. He even belonged to a perfectly good Club. It was for doctors only, of course, but you can't hold that against him—after all he was a doctor. My theory is he went haywire when he started that damn self-analysis of his. These so-called analyses these psychiatry fellows are always endlessly doing on other people are bad enough, but you can imagine a full-grown man doing one on himself. And on top of it all, even after he had done the damn thing, which took three years, by the way, from then on he spent the last half hour of every day continuing it. That, by the way, is one of my main objections to this whole damfool field of psychiatry—they never finish. My father always said you can tell what a man's made of by whether or not, if you give him something to do, he finishes the job.

Anyway, as if all that self-analysis business wasn't enough, Freud next started in on that incredible dream nonsense. In my opinion, no self-respecting man ever paid the slightest attention to his dreams. All of us have them occasionally. I have them, even Fish Frobisher has them—he told me he has them. But the *reason* we have them is because it's something you ate. I, for example, can't eat bird after ten o'clock at night—not even squab. But this fellow Freud wasn't satisfied with dreaming at night. He had daydreams too. "I dreamed," he wrote, "for days at a time." Well all I can say to that is we have fellows like that at the Club. But at least they're asleep when they dream, and we try to keep them out of those chairs by the window. It gives the Club a bad name.

Then too, of course, there's all that "Oedipus complex" nonsense, about loving your mother and hating your father, and all the rest of it. Well, Freud was really off-base there. Look it up. All right, Oedipus did kill his father. But he didn't do it on purpose—he did it by mistake. In fact, when the Oracle of Delphi told him he was fated to kill his father and marry his mother, the whole idea was so utterly distasteful to him that he vowed there and then to leave Corinth and never return. Freud just never did his homework. Finally, that "id" thing. Id—my foot. Frankly, I haven't got the slightest idea what my id is. And I wouldn't know my ego from my libido if I fell over them. But what I do know is that a man my father knew went to a lecture with Freud and asked him, just before they got there, what he was going to lecture about. And do you know what Freud said? He said he didn't know—he was going to leave it to his subconscious. Just think for a moment what would happen to you if I told you I was going to leave my next paragraph in this book to my subconscious. You'd get pretty slim pickings, I assure you.

One time Freud really got his comeuppance, though. He was going to give a lecture to a society over there which included some women in its membership as well as men—always a mistake. But I'll say this for Freud. He not only worried about the suitability of his paper for a mixed audience, he actually sent it on to them ahead of time for approval. The society read it, and wrote him back please to give, in the first half of his lecture,

243

only "drawing room examples." After that, they said they would provide an interval for the ladies to leave—and then he could go on with the rest of it. Freud never did give the lecture —people like that are always prickly, you know—which I always thought was a pity. The fact is, if we allowed ladies at Fortnightly that's exactly the way we would have handled the situation.

Of course there were many others besides Freud who contributed to the sexual mess we're in today. That Havelock Ellis, for one. Now there was a man who should have known better. After all, he was English. But in his way, he was just as responsible as Freud for this thing. Look at some of his titles—every single one of which, I am happy to say, The Society to Put Things Back the Way They Were has taken care of. *The Erotic Rights of Women!* What in the name of St. Peter are the erotic rights of women? Eros wasn't a woman, for Pete's sake. Look it up. He was a man. He was a male god, as a matter of fact. But that was that damn Ellis' title just the same. He hadn't done his homework any more than Freud had. And that book of his was published in 1918. Remember, that was when I was just ten years old. No wonder I never had a chance for a decent sex life. It was ruined before it began.

Speaking of being ten years old, that Ellis was just as bad as Freud when it came to preoccupation with what they called "infantile sexuality." Well, they were right about the first part of it, at any rate. Infantile is exactly what it is. Ellis, you know, wrote a whole book called *The Sexual Life of a Child.* I tell you if there is one thing that makes my blood boil, it's people who talk about children having sex. I've forgotten whether it was Freud or Ellis who said that a new-born baby can have an erection. What nonsense! People who look at a thing like that, let alone study it or write about it, ought to be ashamed of themselves. And I tell you, they bear a heavy responsibility for what's happening today. Most children, as I'm sure I made clear in my chapter on children, are little monsters. If you don't discipline them, you get big monsters, that's what you get. And that's just about what we've got today—a whole generation of big monsters.

I am sorry for my English friends reading this, but I've got to put another Englishman right up there with Ellis. In fact he was, in some ways, worse. D. H. Lawrence was his name. No relation to the good Lawrence, of course, the Arabia fellow. This Lawrence wrote *Lady Chatterley's Lover,* which is just plain filth from cover to cover. The amazing thing is where a fellow like that found all that much sex. My Uncle Bagnalls lived through that same period, and he spent a lot of time in England, and he always had an eye for the ladies—but I promise you to the day he died he never had one of those kinds of experiences that Lawrence wrote about.

With *Lady Chatterley's Lover,* incidentally, we had something of a problem as The Society to Put Things Back the Way They Were. After all, what the fellow was writing about wasn't sex today—it was, in a sense, historical sex. And so it had value from that point of view. And then you had the problem that there were those critics who seemed to feel that Lawrence also had literary merit. Of course you can't go by critics. Some of them, I am told, have about as sloppy a personal life as Lawrence himself. But as I told Fishy, after I'd finished *Lady Chatterley,* either you do the job right or you don't do it at all. And the fact was that there wasn't the slightest doubt in our minds that the book could easily corrupt some of the younger members of the Club. And remember, this was a judgment made after reading every single word of it—in the privacy of my own room, of course. As a matter of fact, there was another of Lawrence's books that the critics praised widely. *Sons and Lovers,* is what it was called. But we didn't have to worry about that one, because somebody at the Club had stolen it. I understand it's mostly about women anyway.

As if Freud and Ellis and Lawrence weren't enough, then we had to have Kinsey. Thank God that book never got into the Club. Remember that wonderful cartoon of the woman sitting there reading *The Kinsey Report* and suddenly looking up at her husband and saying "Is there a *Mrs.* Kinsey?" But seriously, that Kinsey "report" turned out to be exactly what we didn't need at exactly the time when we didn't need it most. Of course I never read it, and nobody I know ever did either. But the point was they read about it—you couldn't avoid it. And, as I understand it, what it did say was that we all cohabitated not only like animals but *with* animals. Now really! Can you imagine Fish Frobisher in bed with a sheep?

But even Kinsey is nothing to what you find in books today. Even English *women* are writing them. Women, mind you, in the country which, at the time it ruled the world taught its women that, if they didn't like sex, they should just lie there, as the expression was, and "think of England." Now, I suppose, they just lie there and think of doing it again. I'm not exaggerating either. I found a book over there on my last trip in the library of the Reform Club. I picked it up because it was the first book I'd ever seen which had "sex" in the title, but which nonetheless had a perfectly decent title. It was called *Men: The Sensitive Sex.* Well, I was reading along in this book, minding my own business, and what do you think I came to? I came to a statement that certain MP's recently demanded that Parliament curtail its night

246

sittings because those sittings were "ruining their love lives."
Can you believe it! English MP's! Maybe it's time for the men to
lie there and think of why the sun has set on the British Empire.
And now they've got a woman for Prime Minister.

Actually, your corner newsstand in England is just as bad
today as your corner newsstand in this country. You find magazines for sale with pictures right on the cover that would em-
barrass a goat. Honestly, sometimes I feel, when I am going by
a newsstand, just as I felt when Cornelia was getting ready for
bed. But the fact is you look pretty foolish going by a newsstand with averted eyes. But it's all so tiresome and such nonsense. They think that by inundating us with sex that we'll roll
over and play dead. Well, I assure you, we won't. The only way
they'll win is over our dead bodies. After all, you can't change
the eternal verities—in sex or anything else.

From the moment we announced our Fortnightly on the
trouble with sex—well of course we didn't use that word, we
wouldn't have been that crude, we used the phrase "The Trouble with Women"—well, I want to tell you, we were deluged.
We had had to open it to the whole Club, of course—there was
so much pressure—and everybody and his brother wanted to
come. At first I gave them the benefit of the doubt—that they
wanted to come and help us do something about stopping this
awful modern sex menace. But when I realized a lot of them,
particularly, I am sorry to say, a lot of the younger ones, wanted
to come just because they wanted to—well, I put my foot down.
I made a hard and fast rule that nobody could come who wasn't
either fifty or older or who hadn't been married at least once.

The Professor was responsible for getting our speaker. And
I say this not for a moment trying to take the blame off my own

shoulders. The ultimate fault was mine. I should have known better than to allow the Professor to have any say in the matter. The Professor has about as much knowledge of what's what socially as an orangutan. Honestly, he's brought some of his own students to the Club, and they have no more business at a gentleman's Club than I've got in a charwomen's powder room. And yet there it was—I let him do the job. I really don't know why. I can only plead that what chance did I have? Do I look like someone who'd know how to find someone who's a sex expert? I don't even believe there *is* such a thing. I know nowadays we've made a fetish of specialization and you have all these damn experts on just about anything you can name. But sex experts, really! Next they'll have sneezing experts.

But no matter. It's water over the dam now. The fact is it was my fault even if it was the Professor's suggestion. Or perhaps I should say suggestion*s*. Because it turned out to be not one person but two people. A couple, if you please. And an unmarried one, of course—like so many of them nowadays. In fact neither one of them had ever been married—and yet they ran what they called a "sex clinic." Picture it. Not married and never married and yet running a sex clinic. Really, the gall of some people these days is—well, one of the most galling things about nowadays. They were Californians, incidentally. And that's where their clinic was. California has a lot of things like that out there apparently. It's because, as I understand it, of the sun. Too much sun, you know, addles your brain, although I imagine that's less of a problem out there than it would be elsewhere.

I couldn't believe that couple when they walked in that night. In the first place, and I am not making this up, they were dressed exactly alike, in God-awful unisex jump suits, or whatever they are. Just picture it—a jump suit for a Fortnightly dinner—but of course, again, it was our fault. You should never ask people like that except *after* dinner. In the second place, and I am not making this up either, the only way you could tell them apart was that the man looked more like a woman and the woman looked more like a man. She was really frightening, that woman. She had a voice that reminded me of the foghorn on the *Ile de France.* The man you just felt sorry for—you just thought he was one more mouse. But I tell you when he opened his mouth, he was just about as bad as she was. You couldn't tell him anything, I assure you. They were both something out of a book, and of course they were trying to sell one, which I shall not dignify by giving the title here.

Right when they came in, they ignored everybody else, even the Professor, who, after all, was responsible for them. Even after I'd introduced them, they ignored me and started right in on the General. People like that, with no social experience, are always impressed by titles and they obviously thought he was in charge. Well, I set them right on that score. I also took them right over to Fish Frobisher. They just looked at him and he just looked right back without saying a word. I'll tell you one thing. Fish can say more by not saying anything than those two could say in a lifetime. When Henry came over to take the drink orders, the woman, if you please, asked for a scotch and soda, while the man asked for grape juice. That gave you some idea of what we were up against. Henry never blanched, though— he just went downstairs to look for some. And while we were all waiting, the man said he'd given up drinking because while it was all right for women, with men sex and liquor didn't mix. How can you say anything to something like that?

At dinner for some reason they insisted on trying to talk to

Edgy Bull, which was stupid of them because Edgy really never gets his hearing aid adjusted until after dinner. And with the noise at dinner, it's just impossible for him. Not that it wouldn't have been impossible anyway—honestly they asked questions of total strangers no one in his right mind would ask old friends. For example, the very first thing they asked Edgy—and again I'm not making this up—was if he was bisexual. Edgy replied right away, which is always a bad sign. He said no, he hadn't had one since he was a child. He thought the man had asked him if he had a bicycle. Next, when they got that straightened out, the woman turned to poor Edgy and, out of a clear blue, asked him how many times a week he and his wife had intercourse. At this Edgy shook his head and said no, she didn't. That time it turned out he thought he'd been asked if his wife played the horses.

Well it served them right. But I assure you, nothing stopped them. Without so much as by your leave, they launched into a long song and dance about people who are heterosexual or homosexual or bisexual all having the same personality traits —that we are all, as they put it, androgynous. Whereupon just when we thought Edgy was back with us, Edgy said that there was an Andy Rogers in his class. He never did get that one straightened out, so we just had to leave him behind. They hadn't asked one word, mind you, about the Fortnightly, but they spent the entire soup course talking about some ridiculous experiment at their damned clinic where they had "traditional males," as they called them, and "traditional females" and also these androgyns, whatever they were, and then they conducted an experiment and proved that these androgyns made "better contacts" with strangers than traditional people. This, they said, proved that society should discourage "traditional sex roles" in favor of androgynous ones—that boys in school shouldn't be encouraged just to play with soldiers or girls with dolls, but that they should alternate. Think of it. Alternate. Fog Horne and I just looked at each other. Maybe, Witter said, if they played with big enough dolls, nobody would complain. You have to admire Witter, he always tries to break the ice.

It seemed hours before the main course came. And, speaking of that, these two—our guests, mind you—had the incredible gall to criticize the dinner. It was a perfectly good dinner too —chicken croquettes, $6.50 we were paying, $13.00 for the two of them. Naturally I wouldn't put up with that. To this the man said, looking at the woman, I might add—those kinds of people can never look you in the eye—that in honor of the occasion we should have served a sexier meal. Witter asked if he meant we should have had ginseng. Witter is very knowledgeable on things like that. But the man shook his head. No, he told us, ginseng wasn't on his list. At this Tubby got very excited. Tubby had no business in the conversation at all, but Tubby loves anything about sex—God knows it's gotten him into enough trouble in his life—and sure enough the combination of food and sex was too much for him. He wanted to see the list. So we all had to wait while the man got his briefcase out and ruffled through it and came up with the most idiotic list I ever saw. I asked Henry for a pencil and I wrote it down exactly as the damfool gave it to us:

anise	eel	oysters
carroway seeds	fennel	peppers
carrots	garlic	pimientos
caviar	leeks	radishes

celery	licorice	snails
chocolate	marrow	thyme
chutney	nutmeg	truffles
dill	olives	vanilla

What nonsense, really. Actually, for a few days afterwards, I did try it. I mean I used the list as a kind of basis for a diet—strictly as an experiment, of course. But I might have known it was nonsense. I didn't feel the least bit sexier than the day before I began. But that's neither here nor there. While we were having our dessert—which wasn't vanilla ice cream, by the way, it was strawberry—both Tubby and the General wanted to know what a sex clinic was. Tubby you'd expect, but I thought for the General to encourage these people was very poor form. But then the General is very unstable sexually, as I've told you. In any case the couple said there wasn't any actual sex at the clinic at all. You ought to have seen Tubby's face at that. They said that the first two days of their "course" or whatever it was, were spent in getting both "sexual partners"—that's what they called them. They never once used the words "husband and wife"—talking about their "dysfunctions," whatever they are. Imagine talking about things like that—and in front of total strangers. And yet they seriously believed in it. They said it was very important to get things out in the open.

That's the trouble with these birds nowadays. They think all you have to do is get everything out in the open, and then everything will be all right. Probably next they'll want it on television. Well, I'll tell you one thing. It won't be all right. Why do you think parts of your body are called your private parts? Because they're private, that's why, they're not public. Actually there is nothing about sex that should ever be talked about in public. And very seldom with anybody else. And particularly not with some girl you're trying to do it with. The only way sex is worth a damn—and I say this with a lifetime of experience behind me—is in secret and by surprise. The best sex of all, when you come right down to it, is to take the girl completely by surprise.

Where was I? Oh, those people. Well, Tubby and the General just went on asking them questions, so of course they went on answering. They apparently gave their "patients" what they called "sexercises." Really, that's what they called them. They said they were based on the technique of those Masters and Johnson people—of "sensate focus" and "non-demand pleasure." People like that think that by using big words other people will think they know something, when all they needed to do was ask someone with experience, like myself. Anyway, the long and short of it is we finally, willy-nilly, got through to the sex part and it turned out they used what they called "surrogate sex partners." Honestly, that's what they said—surrogate. I presumed it was some way of making prostitutes legal. But they were very sensitive about it. The man twice repeated that if anyone tried to treat his surrogate sex partner like a prostitute they would quickly set him straight. The partner was there, he said, to correct your dysfunction and that was all.

Again you ought to have seen Tubby's face. But the worst was still to come. Because, looking right at Tubby, the man said that the principal male problem his clinic had to cope with was premature ejaculation—that ninety percent of his male patients had it. I don't know how he could have known that was Tubby's problem—but it is. Tubby has told me so himself. Tubby is just like a rabbit when it comes to sex. In any case, the man, looking right at Tubby, said that the surrogate sex partner was taught to nip the thing in the bud by giving the fellow, right in his private parts, I understood the man to say, a good pinch. At this point Edgy turned white. It turned out he thought the man said that the girl would give him, down there, a good punch.

Well, we all had a good laugh at that, of course. But the next thing sobered us up quickly enough. Because, not content to leave well enough alone, the man next said that of course they also used *male* surrogate sex partners. At first I thought he was starting to talk about homosexuality, and I raised my hand— we weren't going to have any of that at Fortnightly, I assure you. But it turned out he wasn't talking about homosexuality. It was worse. He was talking about sending *women* patients to *male* surrogate sex partners. It was really beyond belief. Imagine, a decent wife and her husband going to a place like that and all right, her husband goes to his surrogate girl. Well and good. But then *she* goes to a *male* surrogate. I tell you, I don't think anyone said another word during the rest of the dinner. What was there to say? It was disgusting.

All that, mind you, *before* their damned speech. I still had no idea of whether they were both going to speak together or if it was going to be first one and then the other. So I had to ask them. It turned out that just the woman was going to speak— which was one piece of good news, anyway. And, no matter how bad the woman would be, I knew the man would be worse. By now, I had taken a really strong dislike to him. So when he told me he would handle the question period, I just nodded. But I gave the woman a perfectly decent introduction, although I kept it very brief.

Actually, it wasn't as bad at the beginning as you might have thought. It was just all about this idiotic self-love thing the young people nowadays are so hipped on. Obviously they have to be. I guess it's the only way they'll get any. But this woman told us, and again I am not exaggerating, that at the damn clinic they told people that they had to love every part of their bodies before they could be ready for someone else's love. "I stand in front of my mirror," she said, "and say 'I'm yummy.'" Now I know what you're thinking, but I swear on the Bible that's exactly what she said. "I'm yummy." I can swear it because Edgy didn't hear it. He thought she said funny, because he asked what was funny. Edgy hates to miss jokes.

This fool woman, if you can picture it, wanted us to stand in the altogether in front of a mirror and stare at every part of our bodies, from our head down. "Your hair," she said, "your forehead, your eyelids, your eyes, your cheekbones, your nose, your mouth, your neck"—she went on and on. And I tell you, by the time she got to her private parts, I was shaking my head at her. But I couldn't stop her. In the interests of decency, I'll pass over that part, but I'll tell you she spent fifteen minutes of our time, mind you, on her damn *feet*. "You have to be careful about your feet," she said, "because your feet are inclined to be very lazy sexually." Edgy didn't get that either. But when he asked me what she said, I refused to repeat it. I told him he was better off not knowing, that the damn woman had gone around the bend. And I didn't bother to keep my voice down, either.

But of course you can guess where all this idiotic self-love was leading. It was leading right straight to masturbation—that's where it was leading. And, sure enough, we got there. And again, none of us could believe it, but this damn woman was in *favor* of it. Masturbating, mind you, something every decent boy outgrows with puberty. Well, we all just looked at each other, and while we were doing that she said she wasn't just talking about boys and girls masturbating, she was talking about adults. We were so concentrated on the "adult"—imagine, full-grown men doing it—that we literally didn't hear her say the word "girls." Or perhaps it was just one of those things that is so awful when you first hear it that your mind just doesn't take it in. But then we did a real double take. The woman really did mean it—that *girls* did it. I honestly don't think that any of us in our whole lives had ever even considered such a thing. And this woman was in *favor* of that too! How anyone in their right mind could be in favor of it. I would have thought it was against the law. Witter knew I was very upset, because he leaned over and said, "If it makes boys blind, what to you suppose it does to girls? Deaf?" Witter was only trying to make a joke, but frankly we were all too upset for jokes.

But there was more to come, I assure you. The woman next started matter-of-factly, now—and again I am not exaggerating —on orgasms. Just stop and think for a moment what it was like for us. A woman talking orgasms in a gentleman's Club. And not just men having orgasms, that was bad enough, but then, if you please, she moved on to *women* having them—clitoral orgasms, vaginal orgasms, even multi-orgasms. You never heard such nonsense. Of course, it was just plain filth is what it was, and she must have realized what she was doing, because in the middle of it she suddenly said that women shouldn't pretend to have orgasms. I can't tell you what a relief it was to hear that—so far it was the only thing in her entire talk that I had agreed with. Obviously, it isn't right for any decent woman to allow herself to get so excited that she even thinks she's having such a thing. But just when we were, for the first time, agreeing with her, the damn woman went on to say that the reason women shouldn't pretend to have orgasms was that they shouldn't have to pretend—they *should* have them. By now we were pretty hardened, but I tell you when she said that, the whole thing was so totally beyond our comprehension that we were aghast. The more she described that kind of woman, the more I wanted to burst out and ask her how she would feel about her brother marrying one. But what was the use? *They* weren't even married.

The end of her speech was just incomprehensible. She said that the biggest problem facing women today was that men were losing their sexual drive before women do. Of course this was just arrant nonsense. Even that awful Muffie not only didn't mind in the slightest when I began to lose my virility— she welcomed it, as a matter of fact, as any decent woman would. But this woman had the gall to stand there and tell us that while boys are very virile when they're young, they "peak," as she put it—which I thought was a very unfortunate expression—earlier than women and therefore women, who are "conditioned" by false values in our society—that's exactly the way she put it—to marry men older than they are, are faced with the fact that when they're at their peak—I've forgotten what she called it for them—well, anyway, what she was trying to tell us was that men are over the hill when women haven't even reached the top of the hill.

And what was this awful woman's wrong solution to her wrong premise? It was, if you can picture it, for women to choose, as their "sexual partners"—that was obviously their phrase for everything from wives to mistresses—men at least ten years younger than they were. She then quoted a Marjorie Proops—whoever the devil she was, but the woman said she was English, if you can believe it, which I don't—who said that a thirty-year-old woman would do much better with a boy of eighteen or nineteen than with a man of thirty-five. A woman of thirty, she said, should never look at a man of thirty-five or older. When you're out "hunting"—imagine, hunting!—you should be looking for high school boys or college students.

As if those damn college kids didn't have enough sex with those girls right in their dorms, now they were also going to have predatory thirty-year-olds prowling around after them. Again I couldn't resist a bit of nostalgia, and thinking back to some of those lonely evenings I'd spent at college when I wasn't even able to pick up a girl on the streets. And now these kids were being handed everything with a silver spoon. But of course the whole idea of older women and younger men was not only preposterous, it was also disgusting. And besides, what about all the second marriages? After a man gets tired of his wife and naturally wants a younger one. What was her solution for that fellow? To join a monastery? Honestly, the idea of an older woman "going with," as they say nowadays, a young boy—it just goes against nature, that's what it does. I've known many men who have wives thirty years their junior, who get along just fine. And if life isn't exactly a bed of roses—you will pardon the expression—for the girl, so what? She at least knows it won't go on forever. And afterwards she'll have plenty of time to enjoy life—on his money. That's the way the good Lord intended our lives to be. After all, the important thing for a man is the woman's looks. And they just don't look as well when they get older. No decent, self-respecting woman ever gave a damn what a *man* looks like. I imagine we all look pretty much the same to them anyway—the way, for example, people of a different color look to us.

I missed the next-to-last part of her speech when I was thinking about all that, but I came back, unfortunately, in time for her peroration. "Before we have our question period," she said, "I'm going to ask you a question. Do you or do you not want to go forward and fight, shoulder to shoulder, with your sex partner in her battle for orgasmic fulfillment?" Then, thank God, she sat down.

Again we just looked at each other. Of course the very last damn thing we wanted to do was go forward anywhere, let alone shoulder to shoulder with her. But after a moment I pulled myself together and got up and introduced the man, who, I said, would handle the questions. I didn't have any questions, of course, and one look at Fish told me he didn't have any either. He had just sat through the whole thing like a Sphinx, but I know Fish so well, I know what he's thinking, even when he has no expression on his face. He looked at me as if he had smelled something and it didn't smell good. There was a long, embarrassing pause, and the General, of all people, up and asked the first question. He asked how many times the man thought the average man, in his opinion, was supposed to be able to do—well, things, as the General put it—in one night? The man never really answered it, either. He just launched into a long song and dance about two tribes in Africa, the Thonga and the Chagga who, he said, were supposed to average four performances a night but the Aranda of Australia averaged five times a night. Well, of course the minute you get into tribes and things like that the General forgot what he was asking about and wanted to know if they were Communists. And the man, it turned out, didn't know anything about that.

The General had broken the ice, and from that time on there were questions from all over the room—all of them on the same silly subject. Honestly, the man had sex statistics on the brain and it was obviously contagious because now the damn Club members had it. I made a few notes for what they were worth. For example, the man said that the Emperor Yang Ti, of the Sui Dynasty, had the most mistresses of anybody—he had 3,000—and apparently kept them all happy—that Don Juan held the record for the most love affairs, 2,365, and that Guy de Maupassant held the individual record of making love, in front of witnesses, to 20 women in an hour.

As a writer I must admit I did find that interesting—after all, de Maupassant was a writer too. But otherwise the whole thing was just asinine. You would have thought the man was talking about the Olympics. Furthermore, some of the "records" were very depressing. For example, first he told us about one man who had the most orgasms, 30.1 a week over a thirty-year period but just when I was trying to figure out what .1 of an orgasm was, he next went on to say that one woman had 100 orgasms in an hour. All of us knew about nymphomania, of course—but I tell you that statistic was a holy terror. And speaking of that, the man then told us not to go by that—that the average woman achieved orgasm in eight minutes but some did it as quickly as one minute and some took as long as thirty minutes. It was, he said, up to us.

Again, that endless "up to us." Everything these days is always up to us—never the other person. But the final straw was when some damn fool in the back of the room asked the man what was the record for holding an erection, and sure enough the fellow went back in his briefcase and came up with an answer. He said it was an Arab named Abul-Haylukh. He held an erection, the man said, for thirty days. Imagine, thirty days! And before they had all that damn oil, too.

Those questions would have gone on and on, but finally I called a halt. Our guests, I said, had another appointment. You have to say something, you know. Anyway they took forever at the door. Those socially inexperienced people always do. Finally I literally had to help them out. And then the Professor talked and talked—about nothing, of course. I could see through it right away—he was obviously trying to put off the inevitable—that he was the one who had to be held responsible for the Fortnightly descending to our all-time low. Finally, I told him just to shut up. You have to handle him that way once in a while—professors, you know, are terrible talkers. I took stern measures with the General and Tubby, too. I certainly was in no mood to hear anymore from them. After all, they had hardly covered themselves with glory either. But anyway, after that, Fish and Edgy and Fog Witter and I held what really amounted to our own postmortem, to see if we could salvage anything of value out of the damn evening.

I had already, of course, salvaged something from the point of view of my book. Certainly you'd be hard put to it to go back all the way to the death of Caesar and find anything up to my birth to compare with that couple talking like that in a gentleman's Club. But otherwise the whole thing had been awful except that now we knew there was no question about it—this sex thing was far more dangerous than any of us up to that evening had any idea of. After we'd calmed down, all of us agreed that where these modern sex people really go wrong is in their terrible over-emphasis of the whole thing. We agreed too that it was part and parcel of everybody, particularly the young people, having too much time nowadays. And all this everlasting talk about leisure. In the old days, for example, nobody ever heard of sex in the daytime—even on weekends. Remember, you worked Saturday mornings, and you went to church Sunday mornings. Sunday was no day for sex anyway —except, I suppose, among the atheists. And Saturday afternoon you either played your polo or your court tennis or, if you were too poor to have ponies and didn't have a tennis court, I suppose you took up golf or something.

That was another thing, too—these modern sex people have tried to make sex a sport. You can see how our minds moved logically from point to point. Well, I can assure you, we all put the kibosh on that. Sex just isn't up to being a sport, in any way, shape or manner. It takes too short a time, to begin with—and there is no suspense and no winning and losing and no rules, or anything else that makes a good sport. It's just not a sport, and yet these modern fellows would have us all go at it just as if it were one. Honestly, they talk about improving your sex life as if you were improving your tennis game. Most of this nonsense comes from California—like our guests did. They play a lot of tennis out there, you know, and I think really what happens is, with the hot sun, and all, they just get tennis and sex confused. One day they work on their backhand and the next, I presume, on their backside—that sort of thing. Witter made the best suggestion. Maybe we should all have a coach, he said —they could send in plays from the bench.

In the final analysis all of us agreed that our guests might be all right in their own little world, but they'd have mighty hard sledding when they got out into the real world. It was perfectly clear, for example, why they weren't married. If they ever did get married, they'd find out they'd have a lot more on their minds than just sex. And they'd better have, because as anyone who has been married knows, there's nothing worse for sex than being married.

Oh, one amusing thing did happen. Just after we agreed to reach the conclusion that we hadn't learned a single, solitary thing, Henry came in to take the final drink orders before the bar closed. And you know what? Not one of us, not even Fog Horne, wanted one. Then we looked at each other, and burst out laughing. Those damn guests evidently had made one point that had apparently gotten into our subconscious, about not drinking before bedtime—you know, that it was bad for sex. For men only, of course. Even in my days in college you had to try to get that second drink down your girl if you wanted the evening to amount to anything. It was too bad that liquor was bad for men and sex, but on the other hand it was certainly a blessing that it wasn't bad for women. The good Lord giveth, as I've always said, and the good Lord taketh away.

Usually, after we sing our song and adjourn, I go right to bed. But that night, for some reason, I didn't want to. Instead, I had a very strong urge to call Marjorie. Nothing to do with what we had been discussing at Fortnightly, of course—Marjorie is, after all, a nice girl. Just the same, I had this urge to ask her if she would have dinner with me.

So I did—and you know what? I enjoyed myself so much that I never once mentioned either my book or the trouble with women.